For Better or Worse

*Translation as a Tool for Change
in the South Pacific*

Edited by
Sabine Fenton

LONDON AND NEW YORK

First published 2003 by St. Jerome Publishing

Published 2014 by Routledge
2 Park Square, Milton Park, Abingdon, Oxon OX14 4RN
711 Third Avenue, New York, NY 10017, USA

Routledge is an imprint of the Taylor & Francis Group, an informa business

Copyright © 2003 Taylor & Francis

All rights reserved. No part of this book may be reprinted or reproduced or utilised in any form or by any electronic, mechanical, or other means, now known or hereafter invented, including photocopying and recording, or in any information storage or retrieval system, without permission in writing from the publishers.

Notices
Knowledge and best practice in this field are constantly changing. As new research and experience broaden our understanding, changes in research methods, professional practices, or medical treatment may become necessary.

Practitioners and researchers must always rely on their own experience and knowledge in evaluating and using any information, methods, compounds, or experiments described herein. In using such information or methods they should be mindful of their own safety and the safety of others, including parties for whom they have a professional responsibility.

To the fullest extent of the law, neither the Publisher nor the authors, contributors, or editors, assume any liability for any injury and/or damage to persons or property as a matter of products liability, negligence or otherwise, or from any use or operation of any methods, products, instructions, or ideas contained in the material herein.

ISBN 13: 978-1-900650-67-0 (pbk)

Typeset by
Delta Typesetters, Cairo, Egypt

British Library Cataloguing in Publication Data
A catalogue record of this book is available from the British Library

Library of Congress Cataloging-in-Publication Data
Translation as a tool for change in the south pacific / edited by Sabine Fenton.
p. cm.
Includes index.
ISBN 1-900650-67-3 (pbk. : alk. paper)
1. Translating and interpreting--Oceania. I. Fenton, Sabine.
P306.8.O37 T7 2003
418'.02'0995--dc21
                        2003012233

Front Cover

A reconstruction of the signing of the Treaty of Waitangi, 1840, shows Kawiti signing the Treaty, watched by witnesses Rev. Richard Taylor and Mr James Stuart Freeman (standing at right of table-end). At the second table Hone Heke (in cap) shakes hands with Governor William Hobson. The seated figure on Hobson's left (i.e. our right) is James Busby. The group of Maori in the left foreground are being challenged by one man (Marupo) with taiaha. Other figures include Joseph Nias, Willoughby Shortland, Rev. Henry Williams, William Colenso, Samuel Ironside, Felton Mathew, Charles Baker, Tamati Waka Nene, Patuone, Hakitara, Tareha and Whareahi.

From the Drawings & Prints Collection – Mitchell.
Creator: Leonard Cornwall Mitchell (1901-1971).
Published on the cover of the *New Zealand Journal of Agriculture*, January 1949.

Courtesy of the Alexander Turnbull Library, Wellington, N.Z.

For Daniel
who had to translate himself
several times in his young life

Contents

Introduction 1
SABINE FENTON

The Humpty Dumpty Principle at Work 11
The Role of Mistranslation in the British Settlement of Aotearoa
The Declaration of Independence and He Whakaputanga
o te Rangatiratanga o nga hapu o Nu Tireni
MARGARET MUTU

Survival by Translation 37
The Case of Te Tiriti o Waitangi
SABINE FENTON AND PAUL MOON

Translating the Ancestors 63
Grey's Polynesian Mythology
JOHN O'LEARY

Interpreting as a Tool for Empowerment 89
of the New Zealand Deaf Community
RACHEL LOCKER MCKEE

Translation in New Caledonia 133
Writing (in) the Language of the Other
The 'Red Virgin', the Missionary, and the Ethnographer
RAYLENE RAMSAY

Foreigner Talk to Exonorm 171
Translation and Literacy in Fiji
PAUL GERAGHTY

Decolonization by Missionaries of Government 207
The Tokelau Case
TONY ANGELO AND TIONI VULU

The Translation of Queen Sālote's Poetry 241
MELENAITE TAUMOEFOLAU

Notes on Contributors 273

Index 277

Introduction

Terra Incognita

In Translation Studies the Pacific region is terra incognita. While in other parts of the once colonized world postcolonial scholars have scrutinized the history and role of translation, exposing its close relationship with the colonizers, this has not yet happened in our region. The related disciplines of anthropology, ethnography, linguistics, and culture studies have already discovered the Pacific region as a rich and rewarding field of investigation. Translation Studies have yet to follow suit.

The contributors to this volume – translation specialists, scholars of Translation Studies, Literature, Law, Linguistics and Pacific Studies – open a window onto some of the South Pacific nations through translation. They are concerned with many aspects of the theory and practice of translation in colonial, postcolonial and contemporary contexts. While some writers in this volume of essays are beginning to disclose that in the Pacific, as in all other once colonized parts of the world, colonialism and translation went hand in hand, and to focus on the losses which have been so strongly emphasized in many comments on translation, others make a case for substantial gains through the power of translation, a notion that is still emerging in Translation Studies. All authors explore the vital role translation has played in defining, changing and redefining linguistic, cultural, ethnic and political identities in the nations of the Pacific. Examples of the role of translation in the change for better or for worse abound in the history of this region. These stories are being told here as a first attempt to bring this vast area to the attention of the Western academic world – the cultural audience of postcolonialism and into the mainstream of investigation in Translation Studies.

The Pacific Ocean, the largest geographical feature on Earth, is home to more than 20,000 islands and over 5 million indigenous islanders. They were the last people on Earth to be discovered by the Europeans, some as recently as 50 years ago. When the Pacific peoples encountered Europeans there were far-reaching consequences for both sides. "The collision of the two worlds changed both the Pacific and Europe" (Fischer 2002: xvi). While much of the world still today views the Pacific as a tropical paradise of small islands with white beaches and palm trees, the region, experiencing accelerated change, has been under pressure from political and social tensions. The latter half of the last century saw many islands emerge from the patronage of their colonial masters, demanding greater autonomy and indigenous rights. A 'New Pacific' is emerging from the struggles, "home to an innovative hybrid people wishing to incorporate the best of both worlds, the Pacific and the West" (*ibid.* 2002: xii).

Three distinct cultural areas make up the Pacific Islands. Melanesia comprises the islands of the Southwest Pacific below the equator, Micronesia lies to the East of the Philippines and North of the Equator, and Polynesia stretches out through the Eastern half of the South Pacific. Although this division into Melanesia, Micronesia and Polynesia is a rather crude categorization, attributed to the explorer Dumont Durville in 1828, it was adopted by early French and British anthropologists (Ward 1999: 188) and for the purpose of easy identification is used here. The contributors to this volume are concerned with three islands of Polynesia – New Zealand, Tokelau and Tonga – and two islands of Melanesia – New Caledonia and Fiji. The choice does not represent in any way a value judgement but is merely the expression of the contributors' research interests.

Some fifty years ago historians viewed the Pacific Islanders' encounter with the Europeans as a 'Fatal Impact' (Fischer 2002: xviii). "From this time onward the islands were pawns in the great game of international rivalries" (Oliver 1961: 97). Colonized by the British, French and Germans, the Pacific Islanders were mostly portrayed as naïve victims of foreign exploitation and domination. This view of the effects of colonization is also shared by many postcolonial writers on translation. They have scrutinized and exposed the role translation played in the processes of colonization and termed the close relationship between both the "shameful history of translation" (Bassnett and Trivedi 1999: 5). Today, however, many Pacific scholars recognize in their historic analyses the fact that the Pacific Islanders were not only victims but also played an active role in the cross-cultural events they were party to, helping to shape their own destinies. The writers of this volume of papers on translation in the Pacific are therefore putting forward a politics of double-inheritance on the one hand. Their essays provide evidence of the total transformation of the Pacific by the arrival of the Europeans. On the other hand, however, they also demonstrate the extent to which the changes were and still are today co-directed by the natives themselves. "More than any other issue, nationalist aspirations now define the politics of the South Pacific" (Robie 1989: 15). The positive role translation has played in redefining Pacific identities and guaranteeing their survival is thus also examined by some of the contributors. At a superficial level, the islands of the Pacific might exhibit aspects of a shared history. Yet each of them also has its own features. Tonga, for instance, is a monarchy, the only Kingdom in the Pacific. Thus the contributors to this volume have examined past and present complexities from the point of view of the individual nations they are discussing.

Each essay provides us with evidence of change through translation, the inevitable tool of cross-cultural encounter. Each essay is a study of translation as a tool for better or for worse in the Pacific.

The structure and organization of the volume is governed not by grouping essays around a topic, but rather by geographical considerations. Each island nation, represented by one or more essays, is briefly introduced at the outset, where key statistics are presented in order to give the reader an impression of its size and history in the Pacific.

Opening a Window

The book opens with four essays about Aotearoa/ New Zealand, by far the biggest island in the South Pacific. In the first essay, "The Humpty Dumpty Principle at work", *Margaret Mutu* takes us back to the roots of the modern nation of New Zealand. Mutu, who can trace her lineage and tribal affiliation back to the time when the Declaration of Independence and the Treaty of Waitangi were drafted in English and translated into Maori in 1835 and 1840, examines these two documents. She demonstrates how the translation strategies and practices of the translator Henry Williams led to serious mistranslations and consequently to a different understanding of the documents in the two languages, which were meant to carry the same meaning. Through her Maori Elders Mutu has access to the oral history of her people and from their accounts of past history, she refutes traditional historical accounts of the events leading up to the "Declaration of Independence". Her research indicates a much greater level of participation by Maori in shaping their own destiny than academic literature credits them with.

In the second essay "Survival by Translation: the Case of Te Tiriti o Waitangi", *Sabine Fenton* and *Paul Moon* confirm and extend Mutu's conclusions. They argue that the present strong Maori renaissance in New Zealand is empowered and sustained by the translation of the founding document of the New Zealand nation more than a century and a half ago. In the English treaty the Maori chiefs quite clearly cede their sovereignty to the Queen of England. In the Maori version, however, it is only the governance they relinquish, remaining in full possession and chieftainship of all their lands and resources. While these discrepancies did not prevent the total take-over of the country by Briton, they have been a source of Maori protest throughout the history of the nation, as the Maori clung to the promises of 'their' treaty – the treaty in their language. The authors suggest that Maori focus on the translation was responsible for survival at two different levels: firstly the survival of the original document, and secondly, Maori cultural and political survival in their own land. The translation incorporated a dual inheritance for all New Zealanders: at the outset it meant a tremendous gain for the colonizers and a fateful loss for the Maori, but today many past wrongs are being righted, and in the future loss and gain will have to be carefully balanced by every government of the country.

In the third essay about New Zealand *John O'Leary* introduces Sir George Grey, who has been described as "one of the most remarkable nineteenth century British colonial governors" (Jackson and McRobie1996: 122) and an outstanding figure in the field of translation in the Pacific. Although a soldier and civil servant, Grey had a keen interest in linguistic and cultural matters and accumulated an important collection of materials relating to Maori traditions and culture. His translations of these materials, in particular his *Polynesian Mythology,* were considered the most significant translations of the period, rivalling "one of the most successful translations of the nineteenth century, *The Rubaiyat of Omar Khayyam"* (Bassnett and Trivedi 1999: 6). But while Fitzgerald negated any artistic achievement in his Persian author's texts, Grey's translations demonstrate an unexpected depth of romantic sentiment, nobility and grandeur in the originals. Grey's translations received world attention and contributed to shaping the view of Polynesian mythology and of Polynesia within an entire European generation. In his essay O'Leary also sheds some light on Grey's intended audience, the European reader, who for the first time was being introduced to the voice of a Polynesian 'heathen and savage high-priest'.

The fourth essay by *Rachel McKee* places us firmly into our own time. Her essay is the only one on interpreting in this volume. In her paper McKee traces the history of sign language interpreting in New Zealand, beginning with an introduction to the culture and society of the Deaf. Historically viewed as socially disadvantaged and intellectually impaired because of their hearing and speech disabilities, deaf people were further disempowered by the fact that the language – sign language – which was most natural to them was banned in New Zealand. Oralism, speech and lip-reading was forced upon the Deaf, to their detriment. In the mid 1980s, however, a fundamental change took place. Based on new ideas and recommendations coming from the United States, the first interpreter training course was established. This had two all-important outcomes. Firstly it brought about the recognition of New Zealand's sign language as a true indigenous language and forced its development and secondly it gave a strong and powerful voice to the hitherto silent Deaf community. McKee demonstrates the extent to which interpreting has become a tool for change for improving the situation of the Deaf in New Zealand. At the same time, however, warns us that if in fact access to services and independence have not been achieved for the individual Deaf people, we may be getting a false impression of empowerment as a result of these changes.

From Aotearoa/New Zealand *Raylene Ramsay* takes us to Kanaky/ New Caledonia. Her paper takes as a starting point the centrality of translation to the emergence of a distinct New Caledonian history and literature. Analyzing the works of three translators from three different eras and in three different contexts, Ramsay evokes Homi Bhabha's notions of *hybridity* and *third space*. In postcolonial discourse *hybridity* occupies a central place. In Bhabha's discussion it is celebrated as a privileged position of intelligence due to the advantages of in-betweenness and the ability therefore to negotiate the difference (Bhabha 1994), the difference between colonizer and colonized, the 'French' and the 'natives'. The concept of *third space* serves as a mode of articulating the effects translation had and the new possibilities it engendered. "For me the importance of hybridity is not to be able to trace original moments from which the third emerges, rather hybridity to me is the 'third Space', which enables other positions to emerge" (Rutherford 1990: 211).

Louise Michel translated legends and folk tales which are among the earliest published translations from Kanak languages into French. Deported for her revolutionary activities in Paris, she continued to spread her ideals of freedom and justice among the colonized indigenous population in which she saw unrealized power, grace and nobility. Her translations are imbued with the empathy she felt for the natives and particularly the women. Her stories speak of women healers but also of warrior women like herself and even of a female Faust. Ramsay suggests that, with her translations, Michel created a third space which can be described as early feminism or early anthropology.

In the second part of her essay, Ramsay discusses Maurice Leenhardt, missionary and anthropologist, who, a generation later carried out biblical translations and translations of Ajië texts into French. In doing so he formed a third space which prefigures Bhabha's postcolonial concept of hybridity and challenges his notion of untranslatability. For Ramsay, the third space Leenhardt creates is a site of cultural dialogue, incompleteness and change in which the hybrid identity of the translator undergoes a certain degree of reverse acculturation. While Leenhardt's premise of an evolving 'primitive' Kanak has been open to criticism by postcolonial ethnography, his translational strategies, once questioned by both sides, would find favour today with contemporary translation theorists.

Ramsay's third case study investigates the concept and state of hybridity in the Kanak contemporary context by analyzing the work of, and contributions to translation by two collaborating scholars, Bensa and Rivierre, one an ethnographer, the other a linguist. They record and translate narratives of alliances which maintain the balance between the various clans and languages, and they create sites within their own culture which Ramsay suggests could be labelled third spaces of historical competition for Kanak land and authority.

In conclusion Ramsay poses the question of the value of the three very different third spaces created by the translators in her case studies. Her answer is a promise of a complex future and a new culture beyond biculturalism, in which hybrid spaces and writing in the language of the Other – translation – will play an increasing part.

Fiji, our next island nation, shares with New Caledonia the astonishing linguistic diversity typical of Melanesia. *Paul Geraghty*'s essay "Foreigner Talk to Exonorm: Translation and Literacy in Fiji" provides valuable information on the history and development of the Fijian language. His essay is a poignant example of both the good and the bad effects of translation. The arrival of the missionaries in the early nineteenth century brought Fijians a written language, but the native language itself underwent such fundamental changes through translation that the original spoken form was denigrated and its speakers were greatly disadvantaged, as they still are today. The translation and distribution of the Bible, the missionaries foremost concern, created a lingua franca, Old High Fijian, within a multilingual nation. However, it was a language created by foreigners lacking in language skills and influenced by their 'Europeanness', it was an 'Exonorm'. But since it was the language of the Scriptures and the 'Masters', Fijians accepted it as superior to their own native Fijian. This 'Exonorm' was reinforced over the years and became the norm for Europeans in authority. All written translations were in Old High Fijian, including the Deed of Cession. While there are some similarities with the translation of the Treaty of Waitangi, for instance the claim that the translation was the original when this was not the case, the signing of the Deed of Cession has not become the defining moment in Fijian history in the way that the signing of the Treaty of Waitangi has become for all New Zealanders. Fiji was never a reluctant colony, and even after independence in 1970 Fijians retained their affection for their former colonizers. The Fijian language was slow to regain some of its previous prestige but this was finally achieved when the 1977 constitution accorded English, Fijian and Hindustani equal status in the State. Geraghty concludes his article with some concerned comments on the future of this tripartite language policy and its effect on Fijian society, where there is no tradition of education and training of translators.

The question of language and translation is also the focus of the article by *Tony Angelo* and *Tioni Vulu*. When in 1976 the United Nations Decolonization Committee visited the tiny South Pacific nation of Tokelau, it initiated a process of decolonization. Until 1993, annual reports to the New Zealand Government by the Committee reflected the slow pace of change in Tokelau. However, in the last decade an accelerated pace has been noticeable as more Tokelauans become involved in creating their nation's destiny.

The authors trace the path of Tokelau, three small atolls which are equal to one another and which have no designated capital, from being administered by a colonial power outside Tokelau to achieving a modern form of self government through translation. They draw their evidence from government documents published since 1980, which exhibit the enormous difficulties the translators had to tackle: these included the introduction of alien ideas of law and government into a traditional Tokelau society via existing and newly-created Tokelau vocabulary and the management of the linguistic and cultural clash that resulted in resistance to the social acceptance of the new ideas. In these documents, the missionaries, (not of the Church, but of government) and their translators demonstrate that cultural change is much slower than linguistic change. These missionaries were less successful than the religious missionaries who introduced Christianity over a few years and replaced the local deity by the Christian God. By contrast, the traditional government system was not replaced. The new and the old today exist in parallel, creating a hybrid mix that the Tokelauans themselves are having to resolve.

In the final essay *Melenaite Taumoefolau* translates and comments two poems by the Tongan Queen Salote. She uses aspects of the Tongan language and culture as the starting point to explain the difficulties in translating the Tongan Queen's poetry into English. In the strictly hierarchical Tongan society everyone knows their place, in public as in family life. When these positions and their inherent meanings, especially those of the highest ranks in the land, are alluded to by metaphors and symbols, the uninitiated reader without cultural knowledge lacks the key to unlock the deeper meaning of the poetry. Tongan culture is so deeply embedded in Queen Salote's poetry, that he translator has to act as a mediator between the cultures of the source and target languages, a role the translator fulfils here by way of an accompanying commentary to the translations. Structural differences between Tongan and English are not less challenging and Taumoefolau's commentary gives an insight into her translational decisions when dealing with features such as the complexities of the Tongan pronoun system.

In her translations Taumoefolau addresses not only readers of other languages and cultures but also the many Tongans living outside Tonga today who have already lost much or all of their mother tongue, as well as any cultural knowledge of their home land. For them Taumoefolau's translations mean a regaining and preservation of their cultural heritage.

Future Perspectives

How are we to conclude this offer of insights into the way translation has brought about change for better or worse, as evidenced in all but one of these essays on nations in the South Pacific? Each author has demonstrated in great detail the diversity of issues raised when translations are investigated as sites for intercultural contact. Clearly it would be contrary to the purpose of this collection to bring all strands together under one convenient label.

Rather it is the aim of this volume to encourage further research. We believe there is scope for much more in-depth investigation into the encounters between the South Pacific Nations and the Europeans, using translation as a burning glass through which to pinpoint, define and explain the dynamics of this encounter. The nations of the South Pacific, of which we have only considered a small number in this volume, are a rich and rewarding site for further revealing the features that unite these essays, namely the role of translations in effecting change which might be for better, which might be for worse.

References

Bassnett, Susan and Harish Trivedi (1999) *Post-Colonial Translation*, London and New York: Routledge.
Bhabha, Homi (1994) *The Location of Culture*. London and New York: Routledge
Fischer, Steven Roger (2002) *A History of the Pacific Islands*, Houndmills U.K.: Palgrave.
Jackson, Keith and Alan Robie (1996) *Historical Dictionary of New Zealand*, Auckland: Longman.
McGeveran Jr. *et al.* (2002) (eds) *The World Almanac and Book of Facts 2002*, New York: World Almanac Books.
Oliver, Douglas L. (1961) *The Pacific Islands*, Honolulu: University of Hawaii Press.
Robie, David (1989) *Blood on their Banner*, London: Zed Books.
Ward, Alan (1999) *An Unsettled History*, Wellington: Bridget Willliams Books.
Rutherford, J. (1990) 'The Third Space: Interview with Homi Bhabha' in J. Rutherford *Identity, Community, Culture, Difference*, London: Lawrence and Wishart, 207-221.

Aotearoa New Zealand*

Background: The British colony of New Zealand became an independent dominion in 1907. In recent years the government has sought to address longstanding native Maori grievances.
Land Area: 268 680 sq km
Capital : Wellington
Population: 3 908 037; 79.1% European, 9.7% Maori, 3.8% Pacific Islanders
Languages: English (official), Maori (official)

---

* The statistical information for all countries was taken from the world Factbook : www.cia.gov/cia/publications/factbook/geos/nc.html/, accessed 15-12-2002.

The Humpty Dumpty Principle at Work

The Role of Mistranslation in the British Settlement of *Aotearoa*
The Declaration of Independence and
He Whakaputanga o te Rangatiratanga o nga hapu o Nu Tireni

MARGARET MUTU
The University of Auckland

> Abstract. *From 1840 to this day Māori have protested that English immigrants to New Zealand were acting far in excess of the rights they had been afforded. Those rights derived from acknowledgement made by the King of England in 1836 of the paramount authority of Māori chiefs in New Zealand as set out in He Whakaputanga o te Rangatiratanga o nga Hapu o Nu Tireni (the Māori version of the Declaration of Independence) and the subsequent signing of Te Tiriti o Waitangi, a Māori language treaty made between Māori and the Queen of England. The rights conveyed included allowing the Queen of England to take responsibility for maintaining peace and good order amongst English immigrants while they lived under the paramount authority of Māori chiefs as the rulers of their own country. Examination of the original nineteenth- century documents setting out these rights and conditions reveals that mistranslation has played a significant role in allowing the suppression of the protests of Māori by English settlers. While the Māori versions of official documents uphold the Māori understandings, the English versions do not. The English versions convey the erroneous notion that Māori were unsophisticated, child-like and desperately seeking English protection. Written histories of New Zealand almost all either disregard or refute the Māori language versions of these documents and Māori understandings of the nature of the Declaration and the Treaty. Oral traditions of many Māori tribal groups around the country, on the other hand, have maintained these understandings. As a result Māori continue to assert their sovereignty over New Zealand despite the severe disadvantages they now live under both numerically and in terms of all officially measured socio-economic indicators.*

In his 1989 paper 'Humpty Dumpty and the Treaty of Waitangi' Bruce Biggs noted that in drawing up *Te Tiriti o Waitangi*, the Māori language version of the Treaty of Waitangi, Henry Williams used the Humpty

Dumpty principle, assigning a range of meanings to various Māori words he used. It was Humpty Dumpty who said to Alice "When I use a word it means just what I chose it to mean, neither more nor less".[1] As such many of the meanings Henry Williams assigned to Māori words in *Te Tiriti* were not meanings known to Māori. In the traditions of the Far North of *Aotearoa*/New Zealand, one of the reasons many *rangatira* [leaders, nobles, chiefs] signed *Te Tiriti* was because of its apparent confirmation of *He Whakaputanga o te Rangatiratanga o nga Hapu o Nu Tireni*, that is, the Māori version of The Declaration of Independence, which they had signed several years earlier. That Declaration had recognized the existence and *mana* [power, authority, dignity derived from the gods] of a group of *tino rangatira*, paramount leaders, which it called *Te Whakaminenga o nga Hapu o Nu Tireni*, the Confederation of the tribal groupings of New Zealand. The Māori of that document was also written by Henry Williams.

Like the land deeds written in Māori during this period and up until the 1850s, Māori considered that this document fairly reflected the verbal agreements they had reached after long discussion. This paper considers what a Māori understanding of the events leading up to the signing of the Māori Declaration of Independence might have been along with what their understanding of the document itself might have been as it was read out to them by Henry Williams.[2] I will call that document *He Whakaputanga*. I then comment on the quality of the language of that document before examining the official English translation, which I will call The Declaration. In 1835, Māori would not have understood the English of The Declaration. I note the frequent use of the Humpty Dumpty principle employed in translating The Declaration into *He Whakaputanga* and in doing

---

[1] Gasson, Roy (ed.) 1978: 168 *The Illustrated Lewis Carroll*, London: Jupiter Books.
[2] I would like to acknowledge and thank the many *Taitokerau* (Northland) *kuia* and kaumatua (female and male respected elders) who assisted me in coming to an understanding of what *He Whakaputanga* and its various aspects might have meant to our ancestors who signed it. All are descendants of the original signatories. They included McCully Matiu, Māori Marsden, Taki Marsden, Hūhana Reihana, Reremoana Rēnata, Eruera Taurua, Mohi Manukau, Mānuera Tohu and Nuki Aldrich. Sir Hugh Kāwharu also advised me on the *whenua rangatira* at Ōrākei. I would also like to acknowledge the help, advice and discussion of my colleagues at the University of Auckland; Richard Benton, Jane McRae, Deanne Wilson, Hineira Woodard, Rapata Wiri, Tane Mokena and in particular our Māori library staff, Robert Sullivan, Richard Barnett and Jenny Bryan. However any errors are mine alone.

so, comment on the choice of Māori equivalents for key terms used in The Declaration. I then consider the nature, extent and effect of those mistranslations, drawing on my earlier work on the Māori language land deeds, and noting the consistency of the message conveyed in the Māori language by the Europeans that many *rangatira* in *Te Taitokerau* (the most northern region of *Aotearoa*/New Zealand) trusted.

1. Historical Background

Over the past 1000 years or so, Māori migrated from various parts of Polynesia to a country they called *Aotearoa*. When Europeans arrived some 700 years later they called the country New Zealand, a name that Māori came to associate with English participation in the country. In the early 1830s the entire country was still firmly in the control and under the authority of the myriad of Māori tribal groupings, or *hapū* that made up its population. It was the *hapū*, under the leadership of their *rangatira* [leaders, chiefs], who controlled the lands, seas, resources and people within the territories over which they held absolute and paramount authority. There were very few European immigrants resident at that time and almost all of them were English and lived in the northern parts of the country, *Te Taitokerau*, particularly around the *Pēwhairangi,* the Bay of Islands. The language of communication and trade was Māori, as were all customs and culture. While some English immigrants, particularly traders, married into local *hapū* and assimilated themselves into Māori society, others, particularly the missionaries, remained somewhat apart. The missionaries' sole purpose for being in the country was to impose their English religious beliefs on as many Māori as they could. In order to achieve that to their satisfaction they also needed to impose English culture and values on Māori. While Māori welcomed some aspects of English culture, such as literacy and English technology, they firmly rejected other aspects, such as the English notion of their superiority over other races.

The literature is replete with the accounts of various European observers on the events leading up to the signing of the Māori language *He Whakaputanga*. Most say that the British resident, Busby, who drafted the English language Declaration, was acting on instructions from his London-based superiors to utilize chiefly authority "to encourage a more settled form of orderly rule and law so that the chiefs might eventually accept responsibility for controlling European behaviour" (Orange 1987: 14). He was apparently also acting on a perceived threat from a Frenchman who claimed he was going to "establish a sovereign and independent state on some land he possessed, or thought he possessed, on the banks of the Hokianga river".[3] Busby had received a letter from him to that effect on 9 October 1835 (*ibid.*). *He Whakaputanga* was signed just 3 weeks later on 28 October. Busby had stressed to Māori that "he would be a facilitator of European-Maori contacts" (*ibid.*: 16) and, the literature claims, he attempted to create an independent Māori government (*ibid.*: 18).

John Ross, however, claims that the drafting of The Declaration with such uncharacteristic haste had more to do with the rivalry between the British Resident Busby, and the Additional British Resident at Hokianga, McDonnell (Ross 1980: 86-9). Whatever the case might have been, it was the British who claimed the initiative for the setting up of *Te Whakaminenga o nga Hapu o Nu Tireni*, the Confederation of the *Hapu* of New Zealand.

Although the British Colonial office acknowledged The Declaration of Independence[4] most histories are summarily dismissive of it.[5] However, recent Māori scholarship is mindful of its continuing relevance for Māori[6] and draws on the extensive oral tradition that exists setting out Māori accounts of what took place. For example, Lindsay Cox in his book *Kotahitanga* (1993: 43) points out that there is Māori oral tradition, which gives an alternative interpretation to the beginnings of the Confederation. Submissions presented to the Parliamentary Select Committee on Māori fisheries indicated that it was a Māori initiative rather than Busby's. That tradition records that *Te Whakaminenga* first met in 1816. It indicates a much greater level of Māori participation in events leading up to the signing of *He Whakaputanga* than is indicated elsewhere in academic literature. In fact it would appear that the impetus for the actions came from *Te Whakaminenga*. It is an interpretation, Cox says, which "explains the apparent paradox, which Busby's unusually hasty actions have left for historians, and also his inability to maintain the momentum of the movement – it was not his and it continued without him" (*ibid.*).

The sheer practicalities of the situation lend much more weight to Cox's analysis than to the British claims. *He Whakaputanga* was signed by 34 *rangatira* at Waitangi on 28 October. The fact that they met there on that day and formalized an agreement means, in Māori terms, that the nature

---

[3] John Ross 1980: 83.
[4] *Facsimiles of the Treaty of Waitangi*.
[5] See, for example, Orange 1987, Chapter two.
[6] In particular, Walker 1990, Cox 1993, Durie 1998 and Mutu and Matiu 2003.

of the agreement had already been thoroughly debated and worked through well beforehand, and probably over several years. Such an agreement could never be made *de novo* in just one *hui* [gathering]. The oral tradition states that the *hapū* [groups of related families] had become increasingly concerned at the lawlessness of the *Pākehā* [non-Māori of European descent] living amongst them (*ibid*.: 40) and had come together over a period of many years in an effort to find a solution. In some of the northern traditions, the impetus came from leaders including Hongi Hika and Waikato who had travelled to England on a trading mission. While they were there they not only met with the King of England, they also assisted Professor Lee at Cambridge University in writing the first scholarly grammar of the Māori language.[7] It was Hongi, the traditions say, who returned to *Aotearoa* with suggestions of how the *hapū* could deal with the increasing lawlessness of the *Pākehā*. That included the *hapū* coming together for that and many other purposes, including Māori international trade, a trade that flourished for many years. *Te Whakaminenga* had been operational for many years before the signing of *He Whakaputanga*. By that time Māori were making increasing demands for the Pākehā to control their own people.[8] For this they looked to those Europeans they considered to be the most capable and responsible to take the lead in this respect, and chose the missionaries and the British Resident for what were to them, obvious reasons.

On the part of the British Resident he had been appointed by the King of England. Since the King of England was the chief of all English chiefs, he must therefore be of great *mana*. Hongi and Waikato could confirm that that was the case from their meeting with the King and observance of his subjects' attitude towards him. To hold such *mana* he must be able to ensure that his people lived under the *tikanga* or laws passed down from their ancestors, laws Hongi and Waikato had seen in action in England. Such a person, in Māori eyes, must also be of the highest honour and integrity, and be the appropriate person with whom the *rangatira* could forge a personal and aristocratic alliance. Hongi Hika and Waikato had already reported that they had done that and that alliance could then be confirmed by the King sending his representative to live among the *hapū*. He had already done that in the person of the British Resident.[9] Further-

---

[7] A Grammar and Vocabulary of the New Zealand Language. 1820.
[8] Cox 1993: 40.
[9] Salmond (1991: 6) points out that this is consistent with Māori practices of the times whereby "it was not uncommon in Māori kinship politics to seal an alliance by sending (*tuku*) a chiefly person from their own territory to that of another group..."

more, in doing so the King acknowledged the *mana* of the *rangatira* as equivalent to his.

Snippets of this tradition are present in *Pākehā* histories. Claudia Orange (1987: 10) notes that Hongi Hika "was favoured with an audience with George IV [and]...carried back the idea that he had come to some agreement with the King". Although she dismisses the importance of the meeting she concedes that "in northern Maori tradition it was understood as a special bond". She comments (*ibid.*: 13) that the arrival of the British Resident "might well have been seen ... as indicating British recognition of the Maori people as their equals ... There was more than a suggestion of ambassadorial representation to an independent country".

On the part of the missionaries, they had demonstrated by their actions on the ground that they were very caring, honest and reliable people whose responsibility for spiritual matters gave them special status. Despite the often disparaging remarks about the missionaries in *Pākehā* literature my *kaumātua* and *kuia* have told me repeatedly that they were 'good people'. It was not they, but rather their descendants who violated the solemn agreements and understandings the missionaries had with the various *hapū* by, for example, selling land allocated to the missionaries for church purposes only. This is the reason the question posed in the title of my paper (Mutu 1992) 'Cultural Misunderstanding or Deliberate Mistranslation?' was left unanswered. For the main aim of that paper was to assess as conclusively as possible what a Māori understanding of the documents would have been rather than to pass judgement on the translator. Likewise in this paper my main concern is the Māori understanding of The Declaration of Independence as conveyed to them in *He Whakaputanga*. However, here, I will comment on some of the effects of the mistranslations between the Māori and English versions of the documents.

2. The Declaration

By way of background to The Declaration itself: *He w[h]akaputanga o te Rangatiratanga o Nu Tireni* was first drafted in English by Busby (although this is not obvious from the Māori document) and then translated into Māori by Henry Williams. It was first signed by 34 *rangatira* on 28 October 1835 at Waitangi and subsequently signed by 18 other *rangatira*, including my ancestor, *Te Morenga*, up until 1839. The last *rangatira* to sign it was *Te Wherowhero* on behalf of *Ngati Mahuta* on 22 July 1839.

The most southern *rangatira* to sign was *Hapuku* from Māhia peninsula.[10] All the *rangatira*, except for *Te Wherowhero* and *Hapuku* were from *Te Taitokerau*.

The official original Māori document (which is in fact the translation) has four clauses in which

> Clause 1 declares the ultimate authority of the paramount chiefs over their own lands and the existence of the *Te Whakaminenga o nga Hapu o Nu Tireni* (the Confederation of the tribal groupings of New Zealand).
>
> Clause 2 defines kingship to be the *mana* of the paramount chiefs of *Te Whakaminenga*. It declares that that resided in the paramount chiefs present at the meeting and declared that the paramount chiefs would never give any law-making power to anyone else for the lands over which they held authority.
>
> Clause 3 announced that the paramount chiefs would meet every autumn at Waitangi to set down laws, and invited the strangers of the south[11] to join *Te Whakaminenga*.
>
> Clause 4 announced that the paramount chiefs would send 'an equivalent' (translation) of their Declaration to the King of England who had acknowledged their flag, and asked the King to aid and assist them in discharging their responsibilities of protecting and looking after those of his subjects living here, by leaving them a mentor to assist as they learnt the new ways of his people.

While there have been a number of commentaries on the *Te Tiriti o Waitangi* and the Māori language used in it, very little has been said about its predecessor, *He Whakaputanga,* and even less about the Māori language used in that document. Ruth Ross (1972: 141-2) makes passing mention of it in her paper on the Treaty of Waitangi as does Ranginui Walker in his 1990 *Ka whawhai tonu matou; Struggle without End.* Yet *He Whakaputanga* is still a very important part of the oral traditions of *Te Taitokerau* at least. Nuki Aldridge, a descendant of Hongi Hika, has made

---

[10] Nuki Aldridge, personal communication.
[11] That is, the southern iwi. In 1835, there were very few links between the northern tribes and other tribes and as such they were strangers to each other. Once marriages took place to seal alliances, those tribes were no longer termed tauiwi (Nuki Aldridge, personal communication).

a detailed study of the language of *He Whakaputanga* and discussed it with me at length.

I have reproduced *He Whakaputanga* in full, Appendix 1, along with my translation (in italics) and the translation provided by the British Resident to the British Under Secretary of State (in Arial font). There I have highlighted several phrases in bold face where the translation can be assessed as less then accurate. I will comment on several of these in discussing the differences between my translation and that of Henry Williams.

3. The Language of *He Whakaputanga*

The Māori language used is not dissimilar in its style to the land deeds which were being written in the same period. Each was attempting to convey concepts expressed in complex quasi-legal English language in a language that had no facility for such a style. Notwithstanding that the language of English legal documents is inherently awkward, translating such a document into Māori would have been virtually impossible in 1835 no matter how good the translator might have been. For there were no words in Māori to convey concepts such as sovereignty, independence and collective capacity.[12]

The language of *He Whakaputanga* is somewhat awkward and not as well crafted as the later *Te Tiriti o Waitangi*. For example, Williams uses '*mea*' or derivatives of it ten times in *He Whakaputanga*.[13] '*Mea*' often functions as a substitute word, a word used as a filler when a speaker is looking for an appropriate term. Williams uses it to translate 'declare, exercise, appoint, agree, say' of which only 'say' can be fairly translated as '*mea*'. This is a case of assigning new (and differing) meanings from the source language (English) to a word in the target language (Māori). This is the translation strategy that Biggs defined as the Humpty Dumpty principle.[14]

Although the use of first person plural pronouns (we, our) implies the document was written by the *rangatira*, it is clear from the language used

---

[12] Biggs (1989: 303-5) gives a helpful summary of the practical problems involved in translating between two unrelated languages.
[13] He uses it five times in the longer *Tiriti o Waitangi* to convey 'thing, say, do' which are fair translations, and 'invite, appoint' which are not.
[14] Biggs (1989: 304).

that they are not the authors. Like the land deeds,[15] it lacks the finesse one would expect in the formal speech of a *rangatira*, being devoid of tribal and ancestral references, *whakataukī* or proverbial sayings and the use of metaphor and allusion. The sentences are also unusual. Although they are grammatically correct, they are very long.[16] Māori was characterised at that time by Robert Maunsell as "delight[ing] in short sentences".[17] Yet despite these characteristics, the document is still comprehensible and its intention clear.

4. Williams' Translation

Officially, the English version is the translation of the Māori, and the Māori document is the official original. In reality, however, it is the opposite. Yet the (English) version sent by Busby to the Under Secretary of State has a note appended stating that it is "a correct copy of the Declaration of Chiefs, according to the translation of Missionaries who have resided ten years and upwards in the country".[18] In considering the translation problems it is more helpful to consider the translation as it was actually carried out, with the source language English and the target language Māori.

The message conveyed by the English document is fundamentally different from that conveyed in Māori. It records the chiefs

- declaring the country to be an independent state under the name of the United Tribes of New Zealand,
- declaring sovereignty to lie in the chiefs as a collective body (rather than in their individual capacities) and forbidding any other legislative authority or function of government to exist in their territories,
- agreeing to meet in congress at Waitangi in the autumn of each year to set down laws and inviting the southern tribes to join their body of United Tribes,
- agreeing to send a copy of their Declaration to the King of England thanking him for acknowledging their flag and asking him to be a parent for them in their infant state.

---

[15] Mutu 1992: 80.
[16] Also noted for the land deeds (Mutu 1992: 81).
[17] Maunsell, R. 1842: 121 *Grammar of the New Zealand Language,* Auckland: J.Moore.
[18] Facsimiles of the Treaty of Waitangi.

In order to discuss the sources of that difference I will consider the most problematic phrases and clauses that I have highlighted in my transcription and translation of *He Whakaputanga* in Appendix 1. In doing so I am mindful of the difficulties all translators who attempt fair and accurate translations face as their translations are then translated back into the source language. The well-known Japanese to English examples are 'angry raisins' for 'grapes of wrath' and 'licence to commit lustful pleasures' from 'liberty and the pursuit of happiness'.[19]

At line 1.3 in Appendix 1, Williams translates 'Independence of our country' as '*Rangatiratanga o to matou whenua*'. My back translation of the Māori is 'paramount authority over our land'. In the Māori it is clear that the *rangatira* are dealing only with those lands over which they individually held authority as the heads of their respective *hapū* and not over something broader as implied in the word 'country' used in the context 'Independence of our country'. In terms of their own *tikanga* or laws, the *rangatira* could not say anything else. Furthermore, one of the clear messages implicit in *He Whakaputanga* is that each chief of each *hapū* fully acknowledges and respects the *mana* of every other chief in respect of his own lands. My *Collins English Dictionary* says that 'independence' is a state of autonomy, or being free from the control of others. While that was certainly the case for each of the *rangatira* within their own respective territories, and can also be inferred from the term '*rangatiratanga*', that word is not an accurate translation of the term 'independence'.

An important consequence of Williams' use of '*rangatiratanga*' to translate 'Independence' occurs in his translation of the Treaty of Waitangi. There he uses '*rangatiratanga*' to translate 'full, exclusive and undisturbed possession', a term carefully scripted to avoid the notion of independence, since Māori had supposedly ceded that to the Queen of England. This is a clear and more serious case of the application of the Humpty Dumpty principle.

At line 1.4 Williams translates 'Independent State' as '*whenua rangatira*'. Discussion of the term '*whenua rangatira*' with many native speaking *kaumātua* and *kuia* indicates that, like the terms *mana* and *tapu*, there is no single word or phrase in English that would suffice as a translation. However, none of the possible range of equivalences bears any semblance to the term 'independent state'. So Humpty Dumpty is operating

---

[19] Biggs (1989: 303) quoting Kluckhohn, Clyde, *Mirror for Man* (1950: 144).

again. For most their '*whenua rangatira*', which translates literally as 'chiefly land', is all the land to which they have absolute right as *mana whenua*, land which is uncontested, land which might well have been set aside to commemorate a particularly fine event or occasion. William Williams' 1844 dictionary gives 'to be quiet, to be peaceful' as a second meaning of *rangatira*. The example he gives there is "*Ka whenua rangatira tenei*. The land is quiet". This meaning changes in the 1871 edition to 'in a state of peace'. In the 1975 edition it is *whenua rangatira* that has the meaning 'state of peace' and the second meaning for *rangatira* is no longer listed. Speakers all indicated that the notion 'state of peace' is inherent in the meaning of '*whenua rangatira*' but is by no means the only possible translation.

At line 2.1 Henry Williams translates "all sovereign power and authority within the territories of the United Tribes of New Zealand" as "*ko te kingitanga ko te mana i te whenua o te whakaminenga o Nu Tireni*". I have translated that back as "the kingly authority is the ultimate power, authority and control of the land of the Confederation of New Zealand". In other words Williams has defined this new term 'kingitanga' as the *mana whenua* of *Te Whakaminenga*. Examination of how '*kingitanga*' was used in the *Te Paipera Tapu* (the *Bible* in Māori) would tell us what Henry Williams meant this word to mean but tells us little about how Māori in 1835 would have understood it. The word '*kingitanga*' is derived from the word '*kīngi*' a word borrowed from the English 'king'. In 1835 those Māori, such as Hongi Hika and Waikato, who had spent time in England and met the King, might have had some notion of what a king was, but to comprehend all the implications of the term and its relationship to the very complex English notion of sovereignty is not a straight forward matter, even for English scholars. There is little chance that the overwhelming majority of *rangatira* who signed *He Whakaputanga* had an even remotely accurate understanding of what Williams was trying to convey in the term '*kingitanga*'. Biggs differentiates this translation strategy from the Humpty Dumpty principle. Here the translator is borrowing from the source language in order to express a term for which there is no word in the target language. He explains "It should be obvious that when individuals meet a new word, in their own language or another, it has (for them) no meaning until they connect it with some aspect of their own experience, and in one sense…it is not a word at all" (Biggs 1989: 305). In other words there would have been little or no meaning that Māori could associate with the word.

The term '*mana*' on the other hand, is a word the *rangatira* would have been very clear about, and particularly '*mana i te whenua*'. It is sometimes argued that '*mana*' is the closest translation equivalent to 'sovereignty'. While it may be the closest it is by no means an accurate translation. The meanings in both words derive from fundamentally different sources; '*mana*' is power, authority and control derived from the gods and has strong spiritual inherent meaning.[20] The meaning of 'sovereignty' on the other hand derives from secular origins. Given that in Williams' sentence he defines *kingitanga* as *te mana i te whenua*, this is the meaning those listening would have assigned to the new word *kingitanga*.

Other authors[21] have pointed out that while Williams used *mana* (and *kingitanga*) in *He Whakaputanga* for 'sovereignty' he used a completely different term, '*kāwanatanga*' in *Te Tiriti*.[22] The term '*kāwanatanga*' does occur in *He Whakaputanga*. There it is used to translate 'function of government'. However, like '*kingitanga*', it derives from a word borrowed from English; '*kāwana*' from 'governor'. But unlike *kingitanga,* which Williams does define in Māori, *kāwanatanga* remains undefined in both *He Whakaputanga* and *Te Tiriti*. Biggs (1989: 305) points out that there is no way Māori could have understood much of what Williams meant by the term '*kāwanatanga*'. This then is the Humpty Dumpty principle in its ultimate form: for only Williams knew what he really meant by the term. Like Alice and the Jabberwocky poem, Māori questioned Williams on the meaning of *Te Tiriti* and he answered them. However no record has survived of the actual (Māori language) questions put to Williams by Māori as they debated the Treaty on 5 February 1840, or the answers he gave, also in Māori. It is clear nevertheless, that Williams did not convey any notion close to the sovereignty that the English Treaty said they were giving to the Queen. For that would have to have involved the use of the word *mana*, which would effectively have put a stop to the *rangatira* signing *Te Tiriti*.

At line 2.2, Williams translates "entirely and exclusively in the hereditary chiefs and heads of tribes in their collective capacity" as "*kei nga Tino Rangatira anake i to matou huihuinga*". I have translated that back as "only with the paramount chiefs at our meeting". The problem with

---

[20] Marsden 1975: 118.
[21] R. Ross (1972:141), Walker (1990: 98).
[22] See Biggs (1989: 305) for a discussion of its use there.

Williams' translation here is that it conveys no notion of the collective capacity of the *rangatira*. The English implies that the collective can overrule individual paramount chiefs, something which even the European observers of the time knew could not be done. Any such attempt would be seen as an attack on the *mana* of that paramount chief and his *hapü* and would not be tolerated.

One of the most frequently quoted parts from The Declaration is part of the fourth clause in which the *rangatira* supposedly entreated the King to be "a parent of their infant state". It no doubt suited British intentions to portray Mäori as childlike. Claudia Orange (1987: 31) notes the "distorted impression of an enfeebled Maori race and a secured British ascendency". For Mäori, British ascendancy at the time simply was not the case. Apart from being numerically far superior to Europeans in the 1830s and 40s, the country was theirs and the Europeans their guests whom they looked after and protected. It makes no sense then, that they should ask the King to treat them as infants in their own land. Williams' translation does not in fact convey that message. At lines 4.6 and 4.7 "*koia ka mea ai matou ki te Kingi kia waiho hei matua ki a matou i to matou Tamarikitanga*" translates literally as "hence we say to the King that he should leave a mentor for us in our 'childhood' (i.e. as we are learning their ways)." While '*matua*' is usually translated 'father, parent' it is also commonly used, most particularly as a term of address, for a guide or advisor who plays a special role. For example, *kaumätua* in a *hui*, in thanking the *kaikarakia* (person who has led the prayers), will address him as '*matua*' even though he may be of the generation below the *kaumätua* rather than the one above him, if the meaning of 'parent' is taken. '*Matua*' here is a term of respect. The appropriate translation of it in He Whakaputanga is 'mentor'. '*Tamarikitanga*' is 'childhood' but is being used metaphorically here to indicate 'as we are learning the ways (of the King's people)'.

At line 4.8 "that he will become its Protector from all attempts upon its independence" is translated as '*kei wakakahoretia to matou Rangatiratanga*'. This translates back as "lest our paramount authority be denied" and mentions nothing about a protector. Of course, the use of the word 'protector' follows on from the notion of the 'parent/infant' relationship.

In pointing out the distorted nature of the Päkehä attitude that Mäori were somehow childlike and feeble, Orange (*ibid.*) does point out "in fact, some years after 1840, New Zealand would have been British in name but continued to be largely Mäori. Had the Mäori people been presented as more capable, however, British intervention could scarcely have been justified".

5. Conclusion

In 1836, correspondence between one of the King of England's spokesmen in London and the King's representative in New South Wales noted that the King has received and read the Declaration of Independence and would afford to the chiefs his support and protection.[23] With their *mana* and *rangatiratanga* duly recognized and acknowledged, *hapū* and their *rangatira* went on to sign the Treaty of Waitangi between themselves and the Queen of England in 1840. The Treaty agreed that the Queen of England would assume a role of *kāwanatanga* in New Zealand in order to ensure that no harm came to Māori and lawless Pākehā, but at the same time the Queen agreed to and would support the paramount authority (*tino rangatiratanga*) of the *rangatira* and the *hapū* over their lands, homes and everything they valued. Furthermore, the Queen of England agreed that, as part of her *kāwanatanga* role, she would protect Māori and afford to them all the rights of British citizens. The articles of the Treaty were called *ture*, laws, and hence set down the underlying laws on which the nation of New Zealand was to be built.

It is claimed that the Treaty of Waitangi countered The Declaration.[24] However as Ranginui Walker (1990: 99) points out "the British colonists assumed they held sovereignty while the Māori acted as if they never surrendered it". For *Te Taitokerau* at least, the reason for that is clear. In the first article of *Te Tiriti* (and the Treaty) The Declaration is acknowledged by the naming of *Te Whakaminenga*, the Chiefs of the Confederation of the United Tribes of New Zealand. Furthermore there was nothing in *Te Tiriti*, which denied the mana of the paramount chiefs, and nothing, which nullified *He Whakaputanga*. All it did was relieve them of responsibility for the lawless *Pākehā*, as they had passed that responsibility over to the Queen of England. It was, after all, something they had been demanding for some time. The Queen would do that through a mechanism *Pākehā* called *kāwanatanga*. *Te Tiriti* then guaranteed that everything over which they held *mana* would remain as such but that they would also be able to fully access the benefits brought by the Europeans. That the English

---

[23] Facsimiles of the Treaty of Waitangi.
[24] Durie 1998: 3.

'translation' of the Treaty conveyed a totally different message whereby the paramount chiefs ceded their *mana* (called sovereignty in the English document) to the Queen of England was a notion inconceivable to those *rangatira* and one they and their descendants have refused to accept to this day.

Likewise in their dealings with their lands, the deeds in Māori show clearly that the *rangatira* were not surrendering their *mana whenua*, but rather temporary use rights only to that land.[25] In my 1992 paper I made a detailed analysis of the large number of inaccuracies in the English translations of the Māori language pre-Treaty land deeds in Muriwhenua. Through this I was able to demonstrate how simple it was to mistranslate in order to claim before the Colonial Land Commissions that Māori had sold their lands, when in fact they had not. The impossibility of conveying the English notion of 'selling land' in a language that did not contain the concept of land as property, that is, as an alienable commodity, has been noted in the literature on other countries colonized by the English. For example, Cheyfitz (1991: 8) makes this point in respect of North American Indians. Robinson (1997: 88) in considering works on the role of translation in the colonization of North America, India and the Philippines by Europeans concludes that "translation has indeed been a tool of colonial dominance" and that "it is likely that the patterns of 'mistranslation' that Rafael (1993) discovers amongst the Tagalogs have their counterparts in every colonized culture around the world" (*ibid.*: 95). There is no doubt that mistranslation also played a major role in the English settlement of New Zealand.

Despite the huge impact of English settlement on Māori, the fact that Māori lands had never been sold was successfully passed down to the descendants of the *rangatira* who signed the deeds. They continuously maintained that their *mana whenua* remained and that the lands were still theirs, regardless of the imposition of the English title system. However it was not until 1997 and the *Muriwhenua Land Report* that the Crown finally recognized that Māori had not, in fact, 'sold' their lands.

The devastation to Māori, which occurred as a direct result of the mistranslations lulling them into a false sense of security, has been horrific. Māori have protested since 1840 that the agreement they entered into with the Queen of England had been disregarded and broken by Eng-

---

[25] Mutu 1992.

lish settlers. They have constantly berated *Päkehä* for trampling on the *mana* of Mäori. The lawlessness of the *Päkehä* escalated after the Treaty was signed, rather than diminishing. The greed of English in acquiring Mäori land in breach of the Treaty left many *hapü* landless, and in a state of poverty and deprivation that exists to this day.

Mäori protests were all ignored until 1975 and the establishment of the Waitangi Tribunal. The Tribunal was established by an act of parliament as a commission of inquiry to investigate claims by Mäori of breaches of the principles of the Treaty of Waitangi.[26] More than one thousand claims have been registered of which the Tribunal has reported on 125. It considers huge volumes of evidence provided by both claimants and the Crown. Their reports demonstrate in the most graphic terms that numerous breaches of the Treaty have occurred over the past 163 years, and that the affects of those breaches on Mäori have been extreme and are on-going.

Yet Mäori continue to assert their *mana* and *rangatiratanga* as the true owners of this country right down to this day. More research into how Mäori viewed and recorded events occurring around them will help us all to gain a better understanding of Mäori aspirations. Up until at least the beginning of the twentieth century those views would most probably have been conveyed in Mäori. Until thorough studies are carried out into the oral traditions which have survived in many *hapü*, and the extensive documentation that has been left behind by Mäori authors including manuscripts, letters and newspapers, we will continue to be only minimally informed about the Mäori knowledge of New Zealand accumulated and developed over more than a millennium. That includes the history and traditions of this country, which all New Zealand citizens at least have a right to know and understand.

---

[26] *Treaty of Waitangi Act* 1975.

References

Biggs, Bruce (1989) 'Humpty Dumpty and the Treaty of Waitangi', in I.H. Kawharu (ed) *Waitangi: Maori and Pakeha Perspectives of the Treaty of Waitangi*, Auckland: Oxford University Press.
Cheyfitz, Eric (1991) *The Poetics of Imperialism: Translation and Colonization from The Tempest to Tarzan*, New York: Oxford University Press.
Cox, Lindsay (1993) *Kotahitanga: The Search for Māori Political Unity*, Auckland: Oxford University Press.
Durie, Mason (1998) *Te Mana, Te Kāwanatanga: The Politics of Māori Self-Determination*, Auckland: Oxford University Press.
Facsimiles of the Declaration of Independence and the Treaty of Waitangi. 1877 (reprint Government Printer: 1976).
Gasson, Roy (ed) (1978) *The Illustrated Lewis Carroll*, London: Jupiter Books.
Hanks, Patrick (ed) (1985) *Collins Dictionary of the English Language*, London: Collins.
Lee, Samuel (1820) *A Grammar and Vocabulary of the Language of New Zealand*, Cambridge: Church Missionary Society.
Marsden, Maori (1975) 'God, Man and Universe: A Maori View', in Michael King (ed) *Te Ao Hurihuri: Aspects of Maoritanga*, Auckland: Reed.
Mutu, Margaret (1992) 'Cultural Misunderstanding or Deliberate Mistranslation? Deeds in Maori of Pre-Treaty Land Transactions in Muriwhenua and their English Translations', in *Te Reo: Journal of the Linguistic Society of New Zealand*, Vol 35: 57-103.
------ and McCully Matiu (2003) *Te Whānau Moana: Ngā kaupapa me ngā tikanga – Customs and Protocols*, Auckland: Reed.
Orange, Claudia (1987) *The Treaty of Waitangi*, Wellington: Allen and Unwin.
Rafael, Vicente L. (1993) *Contracting Colonialism: Translation and Christian Conversion in Tagalog Society Under Early Spanish Rule*, Durham, NC: Duke University Press.
Robinson, Douglas (1997) *Translation and Empire: Postcolonial Theories Explained*, Manchester, UK: St Jerome.
Ross, John O. (1980) 'Busby and the Declaration of Independence', in the *New Zealand Journal of History*, Vol.14: 83-89.
Ross, R.M. (1972) 'Te Tiriti o Waitangi: Texts and Translations', in the *New Zealand Journal of History*, Vol 6: 129-157.
Salmond, Anne (1991) 'Submission for Waitangi Tribunal, Muriwhenua Land Claim', Waitangi Tribunal Division WAI45 Doc# D17.
Waitangi Tribunal (1997) *Muriwhenua Land Report*, Wellington: GP Publications.
Walker, Ranginui (1990) *Ka whawhai tonu matou: Struggle without End*, Auckland: Penguin.

Williams, H.W. (1975) *A Dictionary of the Maori Language*, 7th edition, Wellington: Government Printer.
Williams, W. (1844) *A Dictionary of the New Zealand Language and a Concise Grammar*, Paihia.
------ (1871) *A Dictionary of the New Zealand Language*, 3rd ed. London: Williams and Norg.

APPENDIX 1
He wakaputanga o te Rangatiratanga o Nu Tireni
(The official original text as translated by
Rev. Henry Williams)
A declaration of the Paramount Authority in respect of New Zealand
(M. Mutu translation)
Declaration of the Independence of New Zealand
(as drafted by James Busby, British Resident)

1.1   Ko matou ko nga Tino Rangatira o nga iwi o Nu Tireni i raro mai o Hauraki
      We, the paramount chiefs of the tribes of New Zealand north of Hauraki
      We, the hereditary chiefs and heads of the tribes of the Northern parts,

1.2   kua oti nei te huihui i Waitangi i Tokerau 28 o Okatapa 1835
      met at Waitangi in the North on 28 October 1835
      being assembled at Waitangi, in the Bay of Islands, on this 28th day of October 1835,

1.3   ka wakaputa i te **Rangatiratanga o to matou wenua**
      *and declared the **paramount authority over our land***
      declare the **Independence of our country,**

1.4   a ka meatia ka wakaputaia e matou he **Wenua Rangatira**
      *and it is said we declare **a state of peacefulness/the land is uncontested/the land is at peace/some land dedicated for this occasion***
      which is hereby declared to be an **Independent State,**

1.5   kia huaina Ko te wakaminenga o nga hapu o Nu Tireni.
      which is to be called The Gathering/Confederation of the Tribal Groups of New Zealand.
      under the designation of The United Tribes of New Zealand.

2.1   **Ko te Kingitanga ko te mana i te wenua o te wakaminenga o Nu Tireni**
      The kingly authority is the ultimate power, authority and control of the land of the Confederation of New Zealand
      All sovereign power and authority within the territories of the United Tribes of New Zealand

2.2   ka meatia nei **kei nga Tino Rangatira anake i to matou huihuinga**
      *and is said here to lie **only with the paramount chiefs at our meeting***

is hereby declared to reside **entirely and exclusively in the hereditary chiefs and heads of tribes in their collective capacity,**

2.3 a ka mea hoki e kore e tukua e matou te wakarite ture ki **te tahi hunga ke atu,**
*and we also say that we will never give over law-making power to **any other persons***
who also declare that they will not permit **any** legislative **authority separate from themselves in their collective capacity** to exist,

2.4 me te tahi Kawanatanga hoki kia meatia i te wenua o te wakaminenga o Nu Tireni
or any other governing body to be spoken of in respect the land of the Confederation.
nor any function of government to be exercised within the said territories,

2.5 ko nga tangata anake e meatia nei e matou e wakaritea ana ki teritenga o o matou ture
The only people who we have said are authorised to set down our laws
unless by persons appointed by them, acting under the authority of laws

2.6 **e meatia nei e matou i to matou huihuinga.**
we have been speaking of at our meeting.
regularly enacted by them in Congress assembled.

3.1 Ko matou ko nga Tino Rangatira ka mea nei
We the paramount chiefs say here
The hereditary chiefs and heads of tribes agree

3.2 kia huihui ki te runanga ki Waitangi a te Ngahuru i tenei tau i tenei tau
that we will meet at the council at Waitangi in the autumn of each year
to meet in Congress at Waitangi in the autumn of each year,

3.3 ki te wakarite ture kia tika ai te wakawakanga kia mau pu te rongo
to set down laws so that judgement will be correct, that peace will prevail,
for the purpose of framing laws for the dispensation of justice, the preservation of peace

3.4 kia mutu te he kia tika te hokohoko
that wrong-doing will end, that trading will be conducted properly and correctly,
and good order, and the regulation of trade;

3.5 a **ka mea hoki ki nga tauiwi o runga kia wakarerea te wawai**
*and **we also say to the foreigners of the south to abandon fighting***

and **they cordially invite the Southern tribes to lay aside their private animosities**

3.6   kia mahara ai ki te wakaoranga o **to matou wenua**
      *so that they can give thought to saving **our land***
      and to consult the safety and welfare of **our common country,**

3.7   a kia uru ratou ki te wakaminenga o Nu Tireni.
      and so that they can join the Confederation of New Zealand.
      by joining the Confederation of the United tribes.

4.1   Ka mea matou kia tuhituhia he pukapuka
      We said that a document/letter is to written
      We also agree to send

4.2   ki te ritenga o tenei o to matou wakaputanga nei
      concerning the compilation of this Declaration of ours
      a copy of this Declaration

4.3   ki te Kingi o Ingarani hei kawe atu i to matou aroha
      to the King of England to convey our warm acknowledgement
      to His Majesty the King of England, to thank him for

4.4   nana hoki i wakaae ki te kara mo matou.
      that he has agreed with the flag for us.
      his acknowledgement of their flag;

4.5   A no te mea ka atawai matou, ka tiaki i nga pakeha e noho nei i uta
      And because we look after and protect the Europeans living ashore here
      and in return for the friendship and protection they have shown, and are prepared to show, to such of his subjects as have settled in their country,

4.6   e rere mai ana ki te hokohoko, koia ka mea ai matou ki te Kingi
      who come here to trade, so therefore do we say to the King
      or resorted to its shores for the purpose of trade, they entreat

4.7   kia waiho hei **matua ki a matou i to matou Tamarikitanga**
      *that he leave **a mentor for us in our "childhood" [i.e. as we are learning their ways],***
      that he will continue **to be a parent of their infant State,**

4.8   kei wakakahoretia to matou Rangatiratanga.
      lest our paramount authority be denied.
      and **that he will become its Protector from all attempts upon its independence.**

4.9 Kua wakaetia katoatia e matou i tenei ra i te 28 o Oketopa 1835
We have all agreed on this day, the 28th of October 1835
Agreed to unanimously on this 28th day of October, 1835,

4.10 ki te aroaro o te Reireneti o te Kingi o Ingarani.
in the presence of the King of England's Resident.
in the presence of His Britannic Majesty's Resident.

Paerata	Auroa	HareHongi
Hemi Kepa Tupe	Ware Poaka	Waikato
Titore	Moka	Warerahi
Rewa	Wai	Reweti Atuahaere
Awa	Wiremu Teti Taunui	Te nana
Pi	Kaua	Tareha
Kawiti	Pumuka	Kekeao
Te Kamara	Pomare	Wiwia
Te Tao	Marupo	Kopiu
Warau	Ngere	Moetara
Hiamoe	Pukututu	
Te Peka	Eruera Pare te kaituhituhi	Hone Wiremu Heke
English Witnesses	Henry Williams	James Clendon
	George Clarke	Gilbert Mair

Ko matou ko nga Rangatira ahakoa kihai i tae ki te huihuinga nei
We the chiefs, even though we did not reach this meeting
---no translation---

no to nuinga o te kaipuke no te aha ranei – ka wakaae katoa
because there were so many ships or for whatsoever reason, all agree
---no translation---

ki te waka mutunga Rangatiratanga o Nu Tireni
to the ?final paramount authority of New Zealand
---no translation---

a ka uru ki roto ki te whakaminenga.
and enter into the Confederation
---no translation---

Nene
Huhu   } English writing
Toua
                    Panakareao
1836
13 January   Kiwi Kiwi

9 February	Tirerau	
29 March	Hamiora Pita - Matangi	No te Popoto
	Tawai -	No te Mahurehure
	Mete	No Ngati Moe
	Patuone	No te Ngati Rangi
1837		
25 June	Parore	No te Ngati Apa
"	Kahu	No Ngati Tautahi
12 July	Te Morenga	No Te Rarawa
1838	Mahia	No Te Hapouri
Jany 16	Taonui	No te Popoto
Septr 24	Papahia	No te Rarawa
25	Hapuku	No te Watu apiti (Hawkes Bay)
1839 July 22	Ko te Werowero	Na ko Ngati Mahuta - ko Kakawai he kai tuhituhi

Glossary

N.B. A bar (macron) over a vowel indicates that it is a long vowel. (Vowel length is phonemic in Mäori.)

Aotearoa	Mäori name for the North Island of New Zealand
hapü	group of related families
He Whakaputanga	abbreviation of He Whakaputanga o te Rangatiratanga o nga hapu o Nu Tireni, the Mäori translation of The Declaration of Independence
hui	gathering, meeting
iwi	group of hapü tribal groupings
kaikarakia	person who leads prayers
kaumätua	respected elders, decision-makers for hapü and iwi, sometimes includes kuia
kuia	respected older woman/women, decision-makers (along with kaumätua) within hapü and iwi
mana	power, authority, ownership, status, influence, dignity, respect derived from the gods
mana whenua	power, authority, ownership derived from the gods in respect of land
Mäori	ordinary, the original people of Aotearoa
Päkehä	non-Mäori of European descent

rangatira	chief, leader, one who has the ability to keep the people together
rangatiratanga	chieftainship, paramount authority, including the general notion of sovereignty, rights of self-determination, self-government, the authority and power of hapü and iwi to make decisions and to own and control resources
tapu	acredness, restricted, spiritual power or protective force
Te Taitokerau	the most northern region of Aotearoa which takes in the Auckland region to the north of the Waitematä and Manukau harbours, and all of Northland
Te Tiriti	abbreviation for Te Tiriti o Waitangi, the Mäori language version of The Treaty of Waitangi
Te Whakaminenga	abbreviation of Te Whakaminenga o nga Hapu o Nu Tireni, The Confederation of the Hapu of New Zealand
tikanga	customary, correct way of doing things, protocols
tino rangatira	paramount chief
whakataukï	proverbial saying

Survival by Translation
The Case of *Te Tiriti o Waitangi*

SABINE FENTON
The University of Auckland

PAUL MOON
Auckland University of Technology

>   Abstract. *The Treaty of Waitangi was signed in 1840 by a representative of the British Crown, and a translation of it into Maori by over 500 Maori chiefs. The Treaty is considered the founding document of the New Zealand Nation. However, over the years serious misunderstandings have emerged as to what had actually been signed. While in the English version Maori had ceded their sovereignty to the British Crown, no such fundamental cession was agreed to in the Maori version.*
>
>   *In this article the Treaty of Waitangi and its translation are investigated in their role as a double-edged tool: first in the hands of a colonizing power conquering a nation, and secondly in the service of the colonized redressing past wrongs. The article begins by outlining briefly the historical background and the context in which the translation occurred, followed by an analysis of the main areas of misunderstanding in the two texts. The article then demonstrates how throughout history the translation not only ensured the survival of the Treaty of Waitangi itself but also that it became the corner-stone of Maori resistance and the guarantor of their economic and cultural survival. The present day societal impact of the Maori resistance based on the translation is explored and some future trends are suggested.*

When in the 1980s, translation studies turned to anthropology, ethnography and colonial history, postcolonial translation studies emerged as a new field of investigation. The realization that translation throughout the centuries had been an indispensable tool in the conquest and occupation used by the colonizing powers led to the examination not only of texts but also of the politics of empire. The study of translation and empire has revealed how imperial powers have operated when they turned conquered nations into docile subjects. Douglas Robinson identifies three major roles played by translation in postcolonial studies:

1. translation as a channel of colonization
2. translation as a lightning rod for cultural inequalities continuing after the collapse of colonialism
3. translation as a channel of decolonization
(Robinson 1997: 31)

These roles of translation are representative of and influence separate stages of a conquered nation's history, "from a colonial *past* taken as harmful; through a complex and conflicted *present* in which nothing seems easy or clear-cut; to a decolonized *future* taken as beneficial" (*ibid.*).

This article specifically examines the role of translation as a channel of both colonization and decolonization in the context of the New Zealand nation. Some scholars of postcolonial theory have questioned whether white settler colonies like Australia, Canada, New Zealand and even the United States should be considered 'postcolonial'. This article takes the position that New Zealand was colonized by the British Empire and that the document that gave the British Crown the mantle of legitimacy and its translation constitute indeed a postcolonial issue.

The document was the Treaty of Waitangi. The translation of it from English into Maori,[1] the language of the indigenous people of Aotearoa[2] New Zealand, is the translation that had an enormous effect on all New Zealanders. The Treaty of Waitangi, New Zealand's founding document, has survived 160 years and this survival has depended a great deal on the translation. The history of the Treaty of Waitangi exemplifies the way Walter Benjamin (1923) has taught us to think about translation. Reversing the accepted direction of thought from original to translation he has shown that the survival and continued life of the original text depends on its translation. And he goes even further in his revolutionizing thought when he posits that in the translation "the life of the original attains ... its ever renewed and most abundant flowering" (*ibid.* 1923: 72). The idea that the translation marks the original's stage of continued life, modifies or supplements it finds further elaboration by Jacques Derrida (1985).

---

[1] See appendix 1 for the English version, appendix 2 for the Maori version and appendix 3 for a back-translation of it into English.
[2] Aotearoa is the Maori name for New Zealand. Originally it applied only to the North Island, but since the early twentieth century ethnologists have been using the name for the whole of New Zealand. The name is also being used by those who want to foreground or include Maoridom in the name of the country.

Translation injects new blood and life into a text and guarantees its survival. Although both Benjamin and Derrida had purely literary texts in mind, we want to show that their ideas are also applicable to our case study of the Treaty of Waitangi and its translation into Maori. We will endeavour to show firstly how the Treaty was kept alive and grew and matured over the years through a focus on its translation. Secondly we will demonstrate that as much as the translation was the tool used by the British colonizers to establish their power base, it also became in the course of history a site of resistance, the focus of hope of the colonized Maori population, and finally a channel of decolonization. For as the Treaty's very survival was guaranteed by its translation, so was the Maori people's cultural and political survival and continued life.

While the history and the lives of Maori and Pakeha[3] have become irrevocably linked since the Treaty was signed in 1840, the translation of the Treaty of Waitangi was pivotal to the fact that there were now two societies in New Zealand, each developing differently. There also remains to this day a separate and contradictory conception of what the Treaty meant and means to each group. What is certain is that the Treaty contained the seeds of continuing conflict over land, power, and authority as each party interpreted the Treaty document in their own language differently. It soon became clear that the two documents did not say the same thing. In the ensuing constitutional development of New Zealand, the Treaty soon began to fade from the Pakeha view. In 1846 Earl Grey from the Colonial Office in London referred to the Treaty dismissively as the 'so-called Treaty'[4] in his instructions to Governor Grey. In 1877 Chief Justice Prendergast declared the Treaty a 'legal nullity' which "blew the Treaty into a judicial limbo for the better part of a century" (Kawharu 1995: x). To the British, seizure of power over and within New Zealand made the Treaty irrelevant in a very short time.

But many Maori never lost sight of 'their' Treaty, the Treaty in their language. From the very beginning, the Treaty had as much a spiritual as a worldly dimension for them. It united them in their faith in Queen Victoria and the promises she made to them in the Treaty, and in the Queen as the Head of the Church that many had only recently been converted to. The more the Treaty became unnecessary for the British in their assumption of power, the more those Maori clung to their version and its promises.

---

[3] Pakeha refers to New Zealanders of European origin.
[4] Earl Grey, cited in Marais, p. 278.

Since the day when the Treaty was first signed on 6 February 1840, monumental changes in all aspects of life have occurred in New Zealand for both Maori and Pakeha, all emanating either directly or indirectly from the translation. Whether they have been for better or for worse is still hotly debated today. Two narratives have evolved, two stories need to be told.

In the following we will briefly outline first the historical background and the context in which the translation occurred, then look at the translation itself, and finally examine some of the important changes that have occurred because of the translation.

1. The Historical Context

In the early nineteenth century initial Pakeha interest in New Zealand did not come from the British Colonial Office but rather from traders seeking whales, flax, and timber. The traders were a small group, accepted by the Maori, valued for giving them access to technology and arms. By the 1830s, however, a rapid increase in the number of Pakeha immigrants began to adversely affect the indigenous population. Their economic and social ways of life were disrupted. Confrontations over land seizures and other disputes were now no longer settled in traditional Maori ways but by the use of firearms. Epidemics, alcohol abuse and violence contributed to a Maori depopulation and a difficult life for the new settlers.

The traders were followed by the first missionaries to New Zealand under the auspices of the Church Missionary Society (CMS). It had established its first foothold in New Zealand in 1814. Samuel Marsden, the chaplain of the convict colony of New South Wales of Australia, established the first Mission in the Bay of Islands in the North Island of New Zealand. From the very beginning he did not only spread the Gospel but also instilled the belief in the Maori that the British Crown had a special, paternal interest in the welfare of them. Missionary activities continually worked at promoting and nurturing this protective relationship. With a growing assimilation of the Maori population and many Pakeha settlers out of control, the Church was ready to take advantage of this situation promoting its vision for New Zealand. This vision was that of a Maori New Zealand with a limited involvement of the British Crown mainly to stem the growing lawlessness of the British subjects. However, in spite of continual pressure, the Colonial Office was reluctant to make such a commitment.

British attitude was grounded on the one hand in an appraisal that

"New Zealand offered little scope for investment and a very limited market" (Sinclair 1991: 55), and on the other hand by the Government's wish not to extend its Empire. Wars and unrest in many parts of the Empire were stretching overworked officials in the Colonial Office to their limits as they tried to cope with the demands for help by the motherland from around the world. In these circumstances, New Zealand affairs had been given the label of 'minimum intervention' (*ibid*.). A further element causing a reluctance to formally intervene was the strong humanitarian conscience of the time and British sensitivity towards foreign powers. It led to a preference by the Colonial Office to see British interests advanced by missionaries and private enterprise.

This challenge was taken up by the New Zealand Company. Like many other colonizing companies, it was founded to buy land in the colony and sell it at a high price to potential settlers. By 1839, the Company claimed to have purchased and secured thousands of acres of land in New Zealand, ready for settlement. However, a general atmosphere of lawlessness, alcohol abuse, violence and crime still pervaded the European community and severely affected the Maori population. But since Britain had no hold over New Zealand nothing could be done to reign in the unruly British subjects. When the New Zealand Company's land purchases reached an extent beyond what was ethical or even credible, the British Government finally stepped in and gave instructions for the annexation of New Zealand. Captain William Hobson was charged with treating with the Maori, and securing sovereignty for the British Crown in exchange for British citizenship and protection from foreign powers. This was to come about peacefully through a treaty and with the 'free and intelligent' (Orange 1987: 14) consent of the Maori chiefs. Hobson, who had no legal training, drafted the treaty document with the help of the British Resident in the Bay of Islands and Chief Clerk James Busby. The document was then translated overnight into Maori by the Head of the Church Missionary Society operations in New Zealand, the Reverend Henry Williams and his son. Hobson and Williams were united in the cause of achieving British sovereignty over New Zealand. Both had received instructions from their superiors. Under the humanitarian influence in England, Lord Normanby's instructions to Hobson were that the Maori "must not be permitted to enter into any contracts in which they might be the ignorant and unintentional authors of injuries to themselves".[5] The Bishop

---

[5] Normanby to Hobson, 14, 15 August, 1839, CO 209/4, 251-82.

of Australia had urged Williams to "induce them to make the desired surrender of sovereignty to Her Majesty" (Rogers 1973: 24). On 6 February 1840, Hobson signed the English version of the Treaty of Waitangi and the assembled Maori chiefs signed the translation into Maori – Te Tiriti o Waitangi – in the Bay of Islands.

The fact that the Treaty of Waitangi exists in English and in Maori was seen as a generous concession by the British to the indigenous population. Conceived in a spirit of goodwill towards the natives, the translation, however, turned out to become the legacy of a divided nation and a corner-stone of race relations in New Zealand.

2. The Text and its Translation

A close examination of the two Treaty texts shows that there was a significant divergence of meaning on some of the most important points. Crucial terms were not translated into the "closest, natural equivalents" (Nida 1982:13) of Maori but were Maori words and concepts employed or transliterated to convey the meanings that the missionaries had given them in the translation of the Bible but which were understood differently by the Maori in other contexts. When Bruce Biggs compared both texts in order to establish whether the translation was "in any reasonable sense equivalent to the Treaty", he came to the following conclusion:

> The answer has to be 'no', not just because its language is stylistically and grammatically awkward, but because the words chosen to translate crucial terms in the Treaty are not equivalent, either because they mean something else, or because the Maori words are more general and less precisely defined than the English. (Biggs in Kawharu 1989: 310)

In the following comparison[6] of the Treaty and its translation we will focus on the key elements which over the years have created the 'Treaty Issues' and polarized some aspects of race relations in New Zealand: the concepts of sovereignty, property, and ownership. The English Preamble sets out the objectives: the Queen's desire to protect the Maori people from the excesses of British settlement, to "obtain sovereign authority",

---

[6] For a close examination of the Treaty and its translation into Maori see Fenton and Moon 2002.

and to establish a "settled form of Civil Government" to maintain order and peace. In Article One, the chiefs of the Confederation and all independent chiefs "cede to the Queen of England, absolutely and without reservation, all the rights and powers of Sovereignty".

The key concepts in the Preamble and in Article One of 'sovereign authority', 'civil government', and 'powers of sovereignty' were all translated by the same term of *kawanatanga,* a "transliteration of 'government' and 'government' means something less than sovereignty" (Sharp 2001: 37). There did exist another term which some analysts believe would have conveyed the meaning of the complex concept and made the intention of the Treaty absolutely clear: "The word *mana,* the only equivalent to the concept of sovereignty" (Walker 1972: 4). The term was current and in frequent use in 1840.

In return for the cession the Queen gave certain guarantees. The English version promises:

> ... the full, exclusive, and undisturbed possession of their Lands and Estates, Forests, Fisheries, and other properties which they may collectively or individually possess so long as it is their wish and desire to retain the same in their possession.

The translation into Maori, however, not only omitted the condition of collective and individual ownership but also failed to mention forests and fisheries under the guarantee of possession but rather talked of *taonga,* undefined 'treasures' or all that is important to Maori. *Taonga* includes lands, forests and fisheries but it is not restricted to these things. It has a much wider meaning. It refers to both material and cultural possessions or attributes of the Maori. It includes for example the Maori language.

Further confusion arose from the translation of the words "guarantee the full exclusive and undisturbed possession" of land as *te tino rangatiratanga* [chieftainship]. The concept includes authority and the right to exercise control and comes close to the concept of sovereignty. According to the Waitangi Tribunal,[7] *rangatiratanga* could mean 'the highest chieftainship' or even 'the sovereignty of their lands' (Waitangi Tribunal 1983: 59).

Neither the term *kawanatanga* for 'sovereignty' in the Preamble and in Article One, nor the translation of *te tino rangatiratanga* for

---

[7] The Waitangi Tribunal was set up by the government in 1975 to make recommendations on claims relating to the principles of the Treaty of Waitangi.

'guarantees the full possession' of Article Two indicated in any way to the Maori that the document they were asked to sign implied the annexation of New Zealand by Britain.

The Second Article also talks of the selling and buying of land. It states that:

> The Chiefs of the United Tribes and the individual Chiefs yield to her Majesty the exclusive right of Pre-emption over such lands as the proprietors thereof may be disposed to alienate ...

Nowhere in the translation is the Crown's exclusive right to handle all land transactions mentioned. The term of pre-emption was translated as *hokonga*, a term commonly known by Maori but it described only the acts of buying, selling and bartering without any referral to the Crown's exclusive right of pre-emption. Moreover, the exclusivity of the Crown's right to purchase Maori land was Hobson's corruption of the British policy in which the Crown would only have the first option to purchase Maori land.

While there are a number of other important mistranslations and omissions, it is primarily the above mentioned concepts and the Maori understanding of them that have caused Maori, for over 160 years, to cling to their Tiriti and claim back what the original text stated they had lost. These efforts contributed to the continued life of the Treaty of Waitangi.

Over 500 Maori chiefs signed the Tiriti o Waitangi and after they had either signed or put their mark on the document, William Hobson, the representative of the British Crown shook the hand of each chief and said, "'*He iwi tahi tatou*' – 'We are now one people'" (Orange 1987: 55). There was a tragic irony in this statement as the very document that was meant to unite Maori and Pakeha proved to become the most significant symbol of what separated them. What the British had failed to understand was that by their own translation of the Treaty into Maori, they did indeed get the chiefs' signatures, but they had also created an instrument with which to resist their take-over. Had the translation conveyed correctly the meaning of sovereignty and used the word *mana*, "no Maori would have signed or would have had the right to sign" (Ranginui Walker in Sharp 2001: 39). But signed it was and the translation became thus not only a tool of imperialism for the British legitimizing their take-over but also a site of resistance and survival for many Maori. Loss and gain were bound up together in the Maori Tiriti o Waitangi.

3. Enforcing the Mandate

Once the Treaty was signed and safely in their hands, officials in New Zealand began to enforce the mandate they believed it had given them: the alienation of Maori land for the Crown and British settlement and the process of civilization of the Maori. As the automatic assumption of governmental powers by the Crown over Maori began to take place, the Treaty faded from view in the constitutional development of New Zealand. It was later only given passing mention. By the 1870s the imposition of British government over Maori was virtually complete, with the last serious resistance broken by victory over Maori in the land wars.[8]

From the 1970s onwards, however, the Treaty was brought back into the consciousness of many New Zealanders as the meaning of the Treaty of Waitangi, in both English and Maori began to be re-examined. It began to be exposed to argument and theorizing by a number of university scholars (Ross 1972, Orange 1984, Kawharu (ed.) 1989, Sharp 1990) as well as the Waitangi Tribunal. Their investigations embraced issues of international law, Maori sovereignty, the constitutional basis of the country and numerous other areas. For the purpose of this study it is not necessary to repeat the expanses of material – most of which has evolved in comparatively recent times. In the following only a few authors shall speak for a great number of scholars. Jane Kelsey (1984) in her comprehensive study of British legal imperialism as it affected New Zealand documents a devastating development for Maori. Over a century and a half a multitude of laws were passed stripping the Maori of their land, their economic base, suppressing their language and culture. With judicial contempt for the promises of the Treaty of Waitangi, Maori were excluded from the governmental system that was a Pakeha institution. A policy of speedy assimilation was deemed to be the best protection of the Maori people.

In the early years after 1840 when the Treaty was signed, Maori had prospered.

> In 1857 the Bay of Plenty, Taupo, and Rotorua natives being about 8000 people – had upwards of 3000 acres of land in wheat, 3000 acres in potatoes, nearly 2000 acres in maize, and upwards of 1000 acres of kumara (sweet potato). They owned nearly 1000 horses,

---

[8] The Land Wars confirmed British and settler military superiority over Maori. They also symbolised the 'Triumph of British rule in the colony' (Cox 1993: 89).

200 head of cattle, 5000 pigs, 4 water-powerd mills, and 96 ploughs, as well as 43 coasting vessels averaging nearly 20 tons each, and upwards of 900 canoes. (Firth 1959: 446)

Their good fortune, however, dwindled with their diminishing land ownership. In 1840, 66 million acres of land were Maori owned, 50 years later this had fallen to an estimated 34 million. While in 1911, Maori still owned 11 million acres, by 1975 this was reduced to an estimated mere 3 million acres (Sharp and McHugh 2001: iii – iv). The population fared no better. 50 years after the Treaty was signed, it had fallen by more than 50%, and at the end of the century, it was widely believed that the Maori were a dying race.

The predicted demise of the Maori, however, did not eventuate. As the diseases introduced by Europeans ravaged their numbers and the pressures of assimilation grew, Maori were able to retain and sustain much of their cultural heritage. In part, the memory of the Treaty supported their resilience in adverse circumstances and fed their fight for survival. In all their struggles since 1840 – for the return of their land, their language and culture, the right to determine and control all things Maori – the translation of the Treaty of Waitangi into Maori was the corner-stone of their protest and resistance. "From the 1860s, the Maori protest movement increasingly cited the Treaty of Waitangi as the basis of their claims" (Ward 1999: 19).

4. The Treaty as a Focus of Resistance

It was clear from the outset that there was a considerable difference in the understanding of the Treaty between Pakeha and Maori. Robert Fitzroy, Hobsons' successor as Governor, was aware that Maori understanding of the Treaty was at variance with the British version. But he essentially ignored this fundamental constitutional dilemma because of his belief that circumstances had overtaken the 'problem', and through his dismissal of the Maori interpretations of the Treaty as being mere 'minor objections'.

> That the natives did not view all its [the Treaty's] provisions in exactly the same light as our authorities is undoubted; but whatever minor objections may be raised, the fact is now unquestionable that the loyalty, the fidelity and co-operation of the natives in New Zealand, has hitherto depended mainly on their reliance on the

honour of Great Britain in adhering scrupulously to the Treaty of Waitangi...[9]

The 'minor objections', however, that Fitzroy referred to have become over the years one of New Zealand's major problem which the country is still trying to resolve today. While for Pakeha the importance of the Treaty waxed and waned, for many Maori its role and status has never changed. It is now and has always been one of the sacred treasures of Maoridom.

One of the methods of deducing the meaning of the Treaty as it was presented to Maori in 1840 is through examining later actions undertaken by Maori. Many of these actions indicate a strong awareness of the Treaty among Maori communities at a time when the agreement had all but become extinguished in the minds of most Europeans. In addition, there is a specific understanding of the Treaty, revealed through certain initiatives that support the contention that the cession of Maori governance in the Treaty was expected from the Maori viewpoint to be confined to the Crown governing Europeans living in the colony.

The following survey of the legacy of the Treaty is deliberately impressionistic rather then comprehensive. The overall theme born out by the review supports the conclusion that the translation of the Treaty of Waitangi served as a focal point in uniting many Maori into a union of purposes. The Maori protest movement, based on the Maori translation, has kept the Treaty alive for both Pakeha and Maori.

In the nineteenth century two major initiatives exemplified the Maori struggle to regain the autonomy that according to the Maori translation they had never renounced. One of these was the King Movement, in which the idea of installing a king as a focus for Maori aspirations found wide acceptance. It was a tangible and enduring manifestation of the spirit of *kotahitanga,* or unity, between the 1850s and 1870s. It sought to free Maori from the tightening grip of European political control and had emerged and consolidated as a response to the demands that had been imposed on them as the culture of the settlers bit deeper and deeper into traditional Maori life. The leaders devised an organization opposed to the assimilationist policies of the British and capable of practising self-government. Their ambitions were derived from their conviction that the Treaty had promised that British rule would only apply to the settlers. They believed that the Treaty's guarantee of *rangatiratanga* or

---

[9] Robert Fitzroy, cited in D.V. Williams, p. 73.

chieftainship confirmed their autonomy and allowing a relationship of equality with the settler government. When fighting broke out over land in the 1860s, government attitudes towards the movement hardened and the need to review, meaning to curtail further, Maori rights was deemed necessary. In 1869 the Minister of Native Affairs, Christopher William Richmond, wrote a memorandum to his Cabinet Colleagues trying to convince them to adopt his hardened attitude towards Maori land ownership and the Maori King:

> We ought not to be yielding. I have been mediating the return of confiscated land question and cannot see my way in it, whilst I do see immense advantages in holding to the land as the one great means of inducing immigration now or shortly hereafter . . . I hope you will take my view on this . . . and harden your hearts a little to Sir W. Martin (Chief Justice and strong supporter of the Treaty of Waitangi) and Tawhiao (Maori King). It is for their good. (Quoted in Ward 1973: 227)

The other Maori initiative that addressed the Treaty from a distinct Maori perspective in the nineteenth century was the Kohimarama Conference of 1860, reconvened in 1879, 1880, and 1881. While in the 1870s "the Treaty receded from the settler consciousness" (Orange 1987: 195), they had by now surpassed the Maori population, these conferences or 'Maori Parliaments' as they came to be known sought to foster interest in the Treaty among Maori and explore its meanings. The focus on the Treaty was meant to keep it in "'living remembrance' for the sake of those at the conference and their descendants" (*ibid.*: 192/93). All conferences voted to support the Treaty, the *Tiriti o Waitangi,* as it was translated into the Maori language. This fact is only explicable when it is considered that from the Maori understanding, the Treaty was the only tangible promise they believed offered them a prospect for self-government, something that had been savagely eroded since the signing of the Treaty in 1840. Comments made at the 1879 Parliament demonstrate the extent to which Maori believed in their rights:

> The Queen stipulated in the Treaty that we should retain the *mana* (chieftainship) of our lands ..
>
> Eruena Paerimu
>
> The words of the Queen were that the *mana* of the chiefs would be left in their possession . . .
>
> Te Hemara

> The Queen in the Treaty of Waitangi promised that the Maoris should retain their *mana*. The word is correct . . .
>
> Waata Tipa
>
> We ought to have authority over all our lands . . .
>
> Hori Tauroa[10]

1882 saw the demise of the Maori Parliaments due to a lack of effective power and government opposition. Although they did not come to any concrete resolutions, the Maori Parliaments nevertheless laid the groundwork for organised political activity in later years.

Protest activities were not limited to New Zealand. As no redress of their grievances was coming forth from the authorities at home, Maori leaders considered going to the source and taking their appeal to England and the British Monarch herself who had promised their protection in the Treaty *(Tiriti)*. The encouragement they received from English sympathizers, in particular from the Aborigines Protection Society, seemed to validate this undertaking. In the 1880s, two missions took their protest and appeal based on the Tiriti to London only to return bitterly disappointed and disillusioned. Both delegations were refused an audience with the Queen even though the Maori King Tawhiao was part of the second mission. Colonial officials informed them that their appeal had not followed proper procedures and that the British Government was no longer in a position to interfere in New Zealand's internal matters since the Colony had achieved self-governance in 1852 and had adopted a constitution. Any appeal would have to be directed to the authorities in New Zealand. Fêted by their sympathizers, yet empty-handed, they returned home. But hope persisted and over the years further delegations went to England but no tangible results came from these appeals. When the fourth King Te Rata with three supporters presented an appeal in 1913, they were no more successful than their predecessors. However, they did manage to be granted an audience with King George V and Queen Mary but only on the condition that they would not speak about their grievances (King 1977/ 1982: 74-75). The futile attempts to bring Maori grievances to the attention of the British Crown had, however, not been in vain. The well-publicized missions brought some benefit to Maori at home: they fixed the *Tiriti* even more strongly in their consciousness as the basis for their grievances and kept reminding the Pakeha that Treaty issues were

---

[10] Cited in Waitangi Tribunal, *Report on the Manukau Claim, Wai –8*.

not swept away by the constitution of 1852. The Maori *Tiriti o Waitaingi*, the translation of the Treaty of Waitangi, remained the touchstone of the continuing struggle.

The path the protest took in the twentieth century and which finally gave the Maori their greatest success and satisfaction so far led them to work from within the Pakeha system through the administrative and legislative channels of government. The question of sovereignty had moved to the background and the advancement of the Maori people on all levels became the driving force. The Ratana movement took up the challenge and was supported by a great number of Maori followers. Ratana, a powerful faith healer, formed a political party in the early 1920s on a platform of addressing current social problems but without loosing sight of past injustices. The first Ratana member entered Parliament in 1932. From 1934 onwards, the four seats dedicated to Maori were all held by Ratana members. Each one of them pledged to promote the struggle to regain their rights as promised by the *Tiriti*.

A major advancement of their cause came through alliance of Ratana with the Labour Party, formed in the 1930s. It was to last almost half a century. They were brought together by the similar philosophies of working for the ordinary man, Maori and Pakeha, and a commitment to implement the Maori Treaty. Courting the Maori vote, Labour had promised to set up a Royal Commission to investigate land claims and a Maori Council to grant them a degree of autonomy. When Labour did become the government in 1935, Ratana members worked inside the party to keep labour to their promises. However, it took 40 more years and organized Maori activity until this was achieved. During this time increased Maori urbanization and education led to sharpened activities by groups and organizations. They were "led by the educated children of the Maori elite, in organizations such as the Maori Graduates Association" (Ward 1999: 22). Their actions were informed by the struggles that other indigenous groups around the world were leading against their dominant governments and cultures. The crowning success of all Maori efforts came finally, when the government passed in 1975 the Treaty of Waitangi Act giving way to the setting up of the Waitangi Tribunal. "The Act stated that 'any Maori' or group of affected, or likely to be so, by any act or omission of the Crown in breach of the principles of the Treaty could lodge a claim with a new body – 'the Waitangi Tribunal'".[11] For the first ten years the Tribunal

---

[11] New Zealand Herald, 9 October 2000, p. A15.

only dealt with a small number of claims, mostly related to environmental issues, since it could legally address only issues, which arose since the passage of the Act in 1975. But this changed when a 1985 amendment extended the Tribunal's jurisdiction back to 1840, the year the Treaty and *Te Tiriti* were signed.

5. A Double-edged Success

With the extension of claims dating back to 1840, the Waitangi Tribunal as a framework for righting past wrongs became the most powerful tool for change in the history of Maori-Pakeha co-existence. However, there soon was an outcry by the opposition warning that the retrospective legislation and decisions would incite Maori activism even further, open the floodgates to claims and produce a Pakeha backlash. "Many New Zealanders are anxious about the prominence given to the Treaty, and the Waitangi claims process. They fear that the unity of the nation under parliament and the common law is being weakened" (*ibid.*: i). All these fears have come true to various degrees and are today part of the dynamics of everyday life in New Zealand that the nation as a whole has to work through, come to terms with in its continued search to find a modus vivendi. They center around the following themes:

5.1 Maori Land Claims

Claims have been lodged with the Waitangi Tribunal in growing numbers. "By 1995, the number of registered claims had increased to 480 and by August 1999 it was 869".[12] In 1995 the government had set the date of the year 2000 by which it had hoped all claims would be settled and allocated a budget for it of NZ$ 1 billion. But this has proved too optimistic a goal. Alan Wood, the contract historian to the Waitangi Tribunal extends the time line by a decade: "The year 2010 seems like a reasonable target date".[13] By then, NZ$ 2 billion will have been paid out to Treaty claimants, double the original fiscal cap.

5.2 The Maori Voice

It is strong and heard inside and outside of Parliament. In a speech to a

---

[12] New Zealand Herald, 9 October 2000, p. A15.
[13] New Zealand Herald, 6-7 February 1999, p. A15.

psychologists' conference in August 2000 the Associate Maori Affairs Minister, Tariana Turia, stated that the Maori tribes had suffered a 'holocaust' under colonization and that Maori violence was a phenomenon of "post-colonial traumatic stress disorder". The national debate that ensued is still continuing. A focal point of Maori protest remains: Waitangi Day, 6 February, New Zealand's official public holiday commemorating the signing of the Treaty. After bitterly divisive commemorations in 1996, the Government moved the ceremony to the capital of Wellington, and returned to Waitangi only four years later. In 1988, the then Leader of the Opposition and today's Prime Minister of New Zealand, Helen Clark, having attended the Waitangi ceremony, was snubbed and reduced to tears by a veteran Maori rights campaigner.

5.3 Maori Land Occupations

They are continuing as a means of protest. High profile occupations attract high profile media coverage. In 1999 there were six occupations. The Maori leader most associated with land occupation, Tama Iti, stated publicly: "We have an agenda, and land occupation plays a big part of it. We want people to know our concerns".[14]

5.4 Maori Sovereignty

The discussion of sovereignty is not a post-Waitangi Tribunal phenomenon. References to the fact that *tino rangatiratanga* had never been relinquished had been shaping the debate over Maori-Crown relations since the middle of the nineteenth century. However, nothing in New Zealand's history could compare with the 'bombshell' of the publication of Donna Awatere's 'Maori Sovereignty' in 1982[15] that tore the sovereignty debate wide open. "Nothing could cushion New Zealanders against the bombshell that detonated in 1982, the reverberations of which continue to the present" (Fleras and Spoonley 1999: 45). Awatere's thesis is radical and uncompromising. In a nutshell: Maori sovereignty was never surrendered with the *Tiriti* and the days of white supremacy are numbered. This dis-

---

[14] New Zealand Herald, 6-7 February 1999, p. A17.
[15] 'Maori Sovereignty', first published in a series of three articles in the feminist journal *Broadsheet*, in book form in 1984, Auckland: Auckland Women's Liberation.

course not only clearly pitted Maori against Pakeha but also propelled the Treaty and its translation decidedly into the foreground again.

5.6 The Pakeha Backlash

The predicted backlash came as expected. Awatere's well-publicized writings touched a raw nerve and created resentment. "Pakeha reaction spanned the spectrum from outrage to astonishment to bewilderment" (*ibid.*: 46). Many, who only knew the English version, were stunned to learn that *tino rangatiratanga* in the Maori version had never been extinguished and that these rights could be invoked and that Maori were ready to claim their rights. "The explosion of renewed Maori protest in the 1970s and 1980s reflected the instability of a situation that had been building up for over a century" (Ward 1999: i). Between 1975 and 1985 as New Zealand was shaken by the Maori sovereignty and land claims debate, dissent was channelled through the Waitangi Tribunal. But instead of recognizing this process as a way of defusing the debate, the Pakeha backlash focused on the Tribunal as an easy target. It was a costly process and the 'booming Treaty Industry' was decried in the New Zealand Herald, the country's leading newspaper. The question many people were asking, was "does processing Waitangi claims need a small army of lawyers, historians and consultants, at a cost of tens of millions a year?"[16] Terms like 'Treaty-mania', 'grievance industry', and 'culture of complaints' were banded around. An article entitled 'Treaty Industry is a Recipe for Anarchy' stated that "Middle New Zealand is saying the drawn-out Treaty claim process has gone too far and the Treaty should be abolished for the common good and racial harmony".[17]

The predictions of what the future holds are divided, but giving up on the Treaty seems highly unlikely for now. "Until New Zealand becomes a happier place for Maori as well as others, we are probably destined to rake over the past on Waitangi Day in any case".[18] This is the day when New Zealand commemorates its dual inheritance. While the Pakeha honour on this day the English version of the Treaty of Waitangi, in which

---

[16] New Zealand Herald, 14-15 November 1998, p. A15.
[17] The Evening Post, 25 November 1998, p. 5.
[18] New Zealand Herald, 6-7 February 1999. p. A20.

Maori sovereignty went to the British Crown, Maori are clinging to *Te Tiriti o Waitangi*, the translation into their language, which carries their ancestors' signatures, and which still sees them as the rightful owners of their land and their resources.

6. Conclusion

When Henry Williams with the help of his eighteen-year-old son translated the Treaty of Waitangi into Maori he could not have imagined the controversy it would cause. His underlying aim was to produce a translation that looked advantageous and felt safe to the Maori so that they would accept it and sign it. Williams' actions cannot be construed by us today to fit the well-worn cliché of traditore traduttore. They rather confirm the view that "translations are not made in a vacuum. Translators function in a given culture at a given time. The way they understand themselves and their culture is one of the factors that may influence the way in which they translate" (Lefevere 1992: 14). Williams was a product of his time, his religion, and the prevailing ideology. He firmly believed that Maori interests would be served best under British rule as he believed that Maori souls would be saved by believing in a Christian God. But he was also a practical man. He was no longer an Englishman living abroad but a missionary and a settler who had to make provisions for a very large family. "In sum, Henry Williams translated the Treaty of Waitangi for his day, not for posterity" (Head 2001: 108). Once the chiefs had signed the *Tiriti*, every facet of Maori life became subordinate to the Pakeha. The Treaty in the Maori language, however, became the counterbalance, the stumbling block for the Pakeha in their endeavour to gain total control. The translation became the uniting factor of the Maori protest movement and gradually the focus of considerable political activity. The substantial changes in character the Treaty text had undergone during the translation from English to Maori did not, in the end, consist only of infamous loss suffered in translation, but also guaranteed the Maori their cultural and economic survival and thus represents a considerable gain. "The long history of Maori protest contains some dominant themes. On the one hand, Maori have vehemently rejected assimilation to the point where they would become simply 'brown-skinned Pakeha' or one more minority in a multi-cultural New Zealand. Instead they assert their status as the first occupants of New Zealand, with particular rights under the Treaty" (Ward 1999: 22/23).

The history of the Treaty of Waitangi is a story of continuous, powerful confrontation of the source text with its translation. The translation invigorating the original text with recognition and importance, the new text gaining in significance as a result of competing with the original in the expression of the same thoughts. The translation made it possible that this conquered nation was able to advance through at least two of the stages mentioned above: from a colonial past, which the Maori experienced as harmful and disempowering to a "complex and conflicted present in which nothing seems easy or clear-cut" (Robinson 1997: 31). Whether their path will take them to the third stage, a decolonized future beneficial to them remains to be seen. In the present era of Treaty settlements, many Maori are hoping for a new relationship with the Crown, ". . . a new genuinely post-colonial relationship. It is a relationship that is based on the acceptance that Maori are a sovereign people because they were the original occupants, never having relinquished their independence by explicit agreement" (Maaka 1998: 204).

The Treaty of Waitangi still exists and has survived to this day because of its translation. Both texts have become two living works that have grown through the re-interpretations of their principles, and developed in their confrontation with each other. They represent a dual inheritance for New Zealand as a modern nation. How Maori and Pakeha have each taken up this legacy was summed up by a judge in the following way:

> Any reading of our history brings home how different the attitudes of the Treaty partners have been for much of our past 1840 history: on the one hand, relative neglect and ignoring of the Treaty because it was not viewed as of any constitutional significance or political or social relevance, and on the other, continuing reliance on Treaty promises and continuing expressions of great loyalty to and trust in the Crown. (NZ Law Report 1987: 672)

There is a general consensus that Treaty issues and Treaty politics will continue to dominate New Zealand's politics in ways scarcely conceivable a generation ago, ample proof of how the translation will keep the original text alive.

References

Awatere, Donna (1984) *Maori Sovereignty*, Auckland: Broadsheet.
Benjamin, Walter (1923) 'The Task of the Translator', in Hannah Arendt (ed) (1968), Harry Zohn (trans) *Illuminations*, New York: Schocken Books, 69-82.
Coates, Ken S. and Paul G. McHugh (1989) *Living Relationships: the Treaty of Waitangi in the New Millenium*, Wellington: Victoria University Press.
Cox, Lindsay (1993) *Kotahitanga: The Search for Maori Political Unity*, Auckland: Oxford University Press.
Derrida, Jacques (1985) 'Des Tours de Babel' in Joseph F. Graham *Difference in Translation*, Ithaca and London: Cornell University Press, 165-207.
Fenton, Sabine and Paul Moon (2002) 'The Translation of the Treaty of Waitangi: A Case of Disempowerment', in Maria Tymoczko and Edwin Gentzler (eds), *Translation and Power*, Amherst and Boston: University of Massachusetts Press, 25-45.
Firth, Raymond (1959) *Economics of the New Zealand Maori*, Wellington: Government Printer.
Fleras, Augie and Paul Spoonley (1999) *Recalling Aotearoa*, Auckland: Oxford University Press.
Head, Lindsay (2001) 'The Pursuit of Modernity in Maori Society', in Sharp and McHugh, *Histories, Power and Loss: Uses of the Past- A New Zealand Commentary*, 108, Wellington: Bridget Williams Books.
Kawharu, Ian Hugh (ed) (1989) *Waitangi. Maori and Pakeha Perspectives of the Treaty of Waitangi*, Auckland: Oxford University Press.
Kelsey, Jane (1984) 'Legal Imperialism and the Colonisation of Aotearoa', in Spoonley, MacPherson *et al.*, *Tauiwi, Racism & Ethnicity in New Zealand*, Palmerston North: Dunmore Press, 20-43.
King, Michael (1977) *Te Puea: A Biography*, Auckland: Hodder and Stoughton.
Lefevere, André (ed) (1992) *Translation/History/Culture*, London & New York: Routledge.
Maaka, Roger (1998) 'A Relationship, Not a Problem' in Coates and McHugh, *Living Relationships: The Treaty of Waitangi in the New Millenium*, Wellington: Victoria University Press, 201-206.
Marais, Johannes Stephanus (1927) *The Colonization of New Zealand*, Oxford: Oxford University Press.
Moon, Paul and Sabine Fenton (2002) 'Bound into a Fateful Union: Henry Williams' Translation of the Treaty of Waitangi into Maori in February 1840', *The Journal of the Polynesian Society* 111 (1): 51-65.
Nida, Eugene and Charles Taber (1982) T*he Theory and Practice of Translation*, Leiden: E. J. Brill.

NZ Law Report (1987: 672), Wellington: Butterworth & Co.
Orange, Claudia (1987) *The Treaty of Waitangi*, Wellington: Allen & Unwin.
------ (1984) *The Treaty of Waitangi. A Study of its Making, Interpretation and Role in New Zealand History.* PhD Thesis, Auckland University.
Owen, R.E. (1960) *Facsimiles of the Declaration of Independence and the Treaty of Waitangi,* Wellington: Government Printer.
Robinson, Douglas (1997) *Translation and Empire: Postcolonial Theories Explained*, Manchester: St. Jerome.
Rogers, W (1973) *Te Wirimu. A Biography of Henry Williams,* Christchurch: Pegasus Press.
Ross, Ruth (1972) 'Te Tiriti o Waitangi. Texts and Translations', *New Zealand Journal of History,* 6, pp 129-54.
Sharp, Andrew (1990) *Justice and the Maori,* Auckland: Oxford University Press.
------ (2001) 'Recent Juridical and Constitutional Histories of Maori', in Sharp and P. McHugh (eds) *Histories, Power and Loss,* Wellington: Bridget Williams Books.
------ and Paul McHugh (eds) (2001) *Histories, Power and Loss,* Wellington: Bridget Williams Books.
Sinclair, Keith (1991) *A History of New Zealand,* London: Penguin Books.
Spoonley, Paul, Cluny Macpherson, David Pearson and C. Sedgwick (eds) (1984) *Tauiwi. Racism and Ethnicity in New Zealand*, Palmerston North: Dunmore Press.
Tymoczko, Maria and Edwin Gentzler (eds) (2002) *Translation and Power,* Amherst and Boston: University of Massachusetts Press.
Waitangi Tribunal (1983) *Report Findings and Recommendations of the Waitangi Tribunal by Aila Taylor For and On Behalf of the Te Atiawa Tribe in Relation to Fishing Grounds in the Waitara District.* Wellington.
Walker, Ranginui (1972) 'The Treaty of Waitangi' in *Extension Seminar Papers,* Wellington: Victoria University Press.
Ward, Alan (1973) *A Show of Justice: Racial Amalgamation in 19th Century New Zealand,* Toronto: University of Toronto Press.
------ (1999) *An Unsettled History. Treaty Claims in New Zealand Today,* Wellington: Bridget Williams Books.

APPENDICES

Appendix 1: The Treaty of Waitangi (English text)

Her Majesty Victoria, Queen of the United Kingdom of Great Britain and Ireland, regarding with Her Royal Favor the Native Chiefs and Tribes of New Zealand and anxious to protect their just Rights and Property and to secure to them the enjoyment of Peace and Good Order has deemed it necessary in consequence of the great number of Her Majesty's Subjects who have already settled in New Zealand and the rapid extension of Emigration both from Europe and Australia which is still in progress to constitute and appoint a functionary properly authorised to threat with the Aborigines of New Zealand for the recognition of Her Majesty's sovereign authority over the whole or any part of those islands – Her Majesty therefore being desirous to establish a settled form of Civil Government with a view to avert the evil consequences which must result from the absence of the necessary Laws and Institutions alike to the native population and to Her subjects has been graciously pleased to empower and to authorise me William Hobson a Captain in Her Majesty's Royal Navy consul and Lieutenant-Governor of such parts of New Zealand as may be, or hereafter shall be, ceded to Her Majesty, to invite the confederated and independent Chiefs of New Zealand to concur in the following Articles and Conditions.

Article the First

The Chiefs of the Confederation of the United Tribes of New Zealand and the separate and independent Chiefs who have not become members of the Confederation cede to Her Majesty the Queen of England absolutely and without reservation all the rights and powers of Sovereignty which the said Confederation or Individual Chiefs respectively exercise or possess, or may be supposed to exercise or to possess over their respective Territories as the sole sovereigns thereof.

Article the Second

Her Majesty the Queen of England confirms and guarantees to the Chiefs and Tribes of New Zealand and to the respective families and individuals thereof, the full, exclusive, and undisturbed possession of their Lands,

Estates, Forests, Fisheries, and other properties which they collectively or individually possess, so long as it is their wish and desire to retain the same in their possession, but the Chiefs of the United Tribes and the individual Chiefs yield to Her Majesty the exclusive right of Preemption over such lands as the proprietors thereof may be disposed to alienate, at such prices as may be agreed upon between the respective Proprietors and persons appointed by her Majesty to treat with them in that behalf.

Article the Third

In consideration thereof, her Majesty and the Queen of England extend to the Natives of New Zealand Her Royal protection, and imparts to them all the Rights and Privileges of British subjects.

[Signed] W. Hobson
Lieutenant-Governor
(in Orange 1987: 258)

Appendix 2: Te Tiriti o Waitangi (Translation into Maori)

Ko Wikitoria, te Kuini o Ingarani, i tana mahara atawai ki nga Rangatira me nga Hapu O Nu Tirani, I tana hiahia koki kia tohungia ki a ratou o ratou rangatiratanga, me toratou wenua, a kia mau tonu hoki te Rongo ki a ratou me te ata noho hoki, kua wakaaro ia he mea tika kia tukua mai tetahi Rangatira hei kai wakarite ki nga tangata maori o Nu Tirani, Kia wakaaetia e nga Rangatira maori te Kawanatanga o te Kuini, ki nga wahi katoa o te wenua nei me ngaa motu. Na te mea hoki he tokomaha ke nga tangata o tona iwi kua noho ki tenei wenua, a e haere mai nei.
Na, ko te Kuini e hiahia ana kia wakaritea te Kawanatanga, kia kaua ai nga kino e puta mai ki te tangata maori ki te pakeha e noho ture kore ana.
Na, kua pai te Kuini kia tukua a hau, a Wiremu Hopihona, he Kapitana i te Roiara Nawa, hei Kawana mo nga wahi katoa o Nu Tirani, e tukua aianei amua atu ki te Kuini; e mea atu ana ia ki nga Rangatira atu, enei ture ka korerotia nei.

Ko te Tuatahi

Ko nga Rangatira o te Wakaminenga, me nga Rangatira katoa hoki, kihai i uru ki taua Wakaminenga, ka tuku rawa atu ki te Kuini o Ingarani ake tonu atu te Kawanatanga katoa o o ratou wenua.

Ko te Tuarua

Ko te Kuini o Ingarani ka wakarite ka wakaae ki nga Rangatira, ki nga Hapu, ki nga tangata katoa o Nu Tirani, te tino Rangatiratanga o o ratou wenua o ratou kainga me o ratou taonga katoa. Otiia ko nga Rangatira o te Wakaminenga, me nga Rangatira katoa atu, ka tuku ki te Kuini te hokonga o era wahi wenua e pai ai te tangata nona te wenua, ki te ritenga o te utu e wakaritea ai e ratou ko te kai hoko e meatia nei e te Kuini hei kai hoko mona.

Ko te Tuatoru

Hei wakaritenga mai hoki tenei mo te wakaaetanga ki te Kawanatanga o te Kuini. Ka tiakina e te Kuini o Ingarani nga tangata maori katoa o Nu Tirani. Ka tukua ki a ratou nga tikanga katoa rite tahi ki ana mea ki nga tangata of Ingarani.

> [Signed] William Hobson,
> Lieutenant-Governor
> (in Orange 1987: 257)

Appendix 3: A Back-Translation into English of Te Tiriti o Waitangi

Victoria, the Queen of England, in her gracious remembrance of the Chiefs and Tribes of New Zealand, and through her desire to preserve to them their chieftainship and their land, and to preserve peace and quietness to them, has thought it right to send them a gentleman to be her representative to the natives of New Zealand. Let the native Chiefs in all parts of the land and in the islands consent to the Queen's Government. Now, because there are numbers of the people living in this land, and more will be coming, the Queen wishes to appoint a Government, that there may be no cause for strife between the Natives and the Pakeha, who are now without law: It has therefore pleased the Queen to appoint me, WILLIAM HOBSON, A Captain in the Royal Navy, Governor of all parts of New Zealand which shall be ceded not and at a future period to the Queen. She offers to the Chiefs of the Assembly of the Tribes of New Zealand and to the other Chiefs, the following laws:-

I. The Chiefs of (i.e. constituting) the Assembly, and all the Chiefs who are absent from the Assembly, shall cede to the Queen of England for ever the government of all their lands.

II. The Queen of England acknowledges and guarantees to the Chiefs, the Tribes, and all the people of New Zealand, the entire supremacy of their lands, of their settlements, and of all their personal property. But the Chiefs of the Assembly, and all other Chiefs make over tot he Queen the purchasing of such lands, which the man who possesses the land is willing to sell, according to prices agreed upon by him, and the purchaser appointed by the Queen to purchase for her.

III. In return for their acknowledging the Government of the Queen, the queen of England will protect all the natives of New Zealand, and will allow them the same rights as the people of England.

(Signed)William Hobson
Consul, and Lieutenant-Governor
(in Orange 1987: 261-262)

Translating the Ancestors
Grey's *Polynesian Mythology*

JOHN O'LEARY
Australian National University

> Abstract. *Sir George Grey (1812-1898) is an important figure in the history of translation in the Pacific. His work as a translator, however, has been relatively little studied, despite the fact that his English-language version of Maori myths and legends, Polynesian Mythology (1855) exerted, and still exerts, a determining influence on how this Pacific mythology was and is perceived. In this article, Grey's intellectual and philological interests are described, his translation practices are discussed, and his book is analyzed in terms of other, earlier accounts of indigenous mythologies; also described are the book's intended audience, and Grey's treatment of his Maori-language source text, Nga Mahi a Nga Tupuna [The Deeds of the Ancestors] (1854). Special attention is paid to Grey's translation of the Hinemoa legend, which for complex historical and cultural reasons was extremely popular with Grey's mid-nineteenth-century European readers.*

> For the first time, I believe, a European reader will find it in his power to place himself in the position of one who listens to a heathen and savage high-priest explaining to him, in his own words, and in his own energetic manner, the traditions in which he earnestly believes, and unfolding the religious opinions upon which the faith and hopes of his race rest.
> Grey, Preface to *Polynesian Mythology* (1855: xi)

In the field of translation in the Pacific, the figure of Sir George Grey looms large. So important is he, in fact, that his omission in a study of this subject would create a serious gap, and greatly limit our understanding of the nature and role of translation, historically speaking, in this part of the world. Much work remains to be done in this area; this chapter is no more than a preliminary attempt to outline Grey's activities in this field, and suggest why they are of such interest.

Grey produced two translations, or versions, of Maori material, his *Polynesian Mythology* of 1855, and the *Proverbial and Popular Sayings of the Ancestors of the New Zealand Race,* published in 1857. While the latter work has its own distinct interest, it is Grey's *Polynesian Mythology* which will be the focus of this essay, for in terms of its influence it is the more important of the two texts, and is indeed arguably one of the most significant translations of the period, rivaling such famous Victorian cross-cultural productions as Edward FitzGerald's *Rubaiyat of Omar Khayyam* (1859). Through his *Polynesian Mythology*, Grey brought to the attention of an admiring world a hitherto almost unknown mythology. In New Zealand a reader judged Grey's book to be 'exceedingly interesting' (*New Zealand Quarterly Review* 1857: 60), while on the other side of the world, in Dublin, a reviewer stated that he had read Grey's book "with unabated interest from beginning to end" (*Dublin University Magazine* 1855: 26). Scholars, too, were fascinated by *Polynesian Mythology*. Carl Schirren in Germany, for example, a noted expert in the field, judged that the book contained the 'key' to the whole of Polynesian mythology (Schirren 1856:3 note 1).[1] The Royal Geographical Society of Vienna, for its part, responded to Grey's work by awarding him an Honorary Membership, while in Paris *Polynesian Mythology* was translated into French by Dr. René Primaverre Lesson for the Anthropological Society of Paris.

Contemporary writers, seeing in *Polynesian Mythology* a storehouse of novel material, hurried to mine its riches, finding in its myths and legends a nobility and grandeur – and in one legend in particular, that of Hinemoa, a depth of romantic sentiment – that was entirely unexpected. An example is Grey's friend Alfred Domett, who made extensive use of Grey's book in his epic poem *Ranolf and Amohia* (1872), one of the longest (if not the best) literary works ever produced in New Zealand.

When a second edition of the book was published in 1885, partly in response to popular demand, interest only increased, and since that time Grey's book has been repeatedly reprinted. New Zealand writers, especially, have been greatly influenced by the myths and legends contained in *Polynesian Mythology*. The young William Satchell, author of that classic study of Maori-European relations *The Greenstone Door* (1914), wrote to Grey asking his indulgence for having used the Hinemoa story in some of his own poems (Satchell, letter to Grey, undated). Rather later James K. Baxter drew on *Polynesian Mythology* in several different poems, most

---

[1] I am indebted to Nelson Wattie for the translation into English of Carl Schirren's comment.

noticeably in his beautiful lyric 'East Coast Journey', where the description of Hinenuitepo, the goddess of death ("with teeth of obsidian and hair like kelp") is clearly based on Grey's (Baxter 1980: 273). As Allen Curnow noted, "there is something strangely compulsive about the fascination which Grey's mythology – early and easily accessible in English – exerted upon successive generations of New Zealand writers, poets in particular" (Curnow and Oppenheim 1960: 71).

In the broader historical and cultural context, too, Grey's book stands out. Few other bodies of mythology were given to the world so suddenly and so completely as was Maori mythology by Grey – a partial exception is formed by the Native American legends and songs collected and translated by the explorer and US Government interpreter Henry Rowe Schoolcraft, who was active in the Great Lakes area of America from the mid-1820s.[2] The myths and legends of most of the rest of the New World were made available to European readers only at a much later date – Australians, for instance, had to wait till the end of the nineteenth century for the first collection of Aboriginal legends, and even then these legends appeared in an infantilized and highly edited form.[3] The contrast with the situation of Maori mythology is striking, and the difference was made, at least in part, by Grey, whose energy and commitment to the task of recording and then translating Maori myths and legends was singular, if not simple or unproblematic.

Significant as Grey's translation is, it has however received comparatively little detailed scholarly attention. Grey's political career, which saw him serve both as Governor and Premier of New Zealand, has been extensively chronicled, with at least four major biographies (Milne 1899; Collier

---

[2] Henry Rowe Schoolcraft (1793-1864) published numerous studies of Native American life and culture in the early and middle decades of the nineteenth century, in which he incorporated many English-language versions of Native American (mainly Chippewa and Ottawa) songs and legends. Particularly notable in this respect is his massive compilation *Historical and Statistical Information respecting the History, Condition and Progress of the Indian Tribes of the United States* (1851-7), which contained the first significant collection of Native American lyrics. Schoolcraft is little known now outside anthropological circles, but a poetic work that made extensive use of his writings, Henry Wadsworth Longfellow's *Song of Hiawatha* (1855), is famous to this day.

[3] See Katherine Langloh-Parker's *Australian Legendary Tales* (1896). While Langloh-Parker's interest in aboriginal culture was genuine, her knowledge of it was limited, and her book, while something of a milestone in the Australian cultural context, cannot be regarded as serious ethnography.

1909; Rutherford 1961; Bohan 1998) devoted to it. Grey's collecting and editing of his Maori material has also been discussed, by students of Maori culture and Maori scholars, and some significant conclusions drawn (I will allude to some of these below). Comment on *Polynesian Mythology* itself, however, has been sparser. Some has come from Grey's biographers: Rutherford (1961: 277), for example, devoted a careful but not very enlightening paragraph to the translation, while Edmund Bohan, in his recent biography of Grey, briefly discusses the reaction of Carl Schirren to Grey's work, but does not attempt a critical assessment of the book (Bohan 1998: 144).

Students of Maori culture, on their side, have made the occasional judgment on Grey's work. John Macmillan Brown, James K. Baxter's father, for example, deemed Grey's *Polynesian Mythology* "anything but satisfactory to the student of ethnology and folklore" (Brown 1907: 219), but did not elaborate on this comment. Anthony Alpers briefly discussed Grey's book and its immediate Maori source text, *Nga Mahi a Nga Tupuna*, in an appendix to his own collection of Maori myths and legends (Alpers 1964: 231-43); in a subsequent publication he attempted to place Maori mythology in its wider, Polynesian context, in the process characterizing Grey's version of the famous Hinemoa legend as one of New Zealand's "earliest pieces of tourist trash" and deploring its effect of "cheapening the Maori in a popular tourist location" (Alpers 1987: xvii). While interesting, even provocative, these comments do not constitute an extended critical discussion of *Polynesian Mythology*.

Some of the most valuable judgments of Grey's work have come from professional Maori scholars. In his introduction to a 1988 reprinting of Grey's book, for instance, Sydney Moko Mead condemned the translation as inaccurate and incomplete (McRae 1998: 13). Jane McRae has made highly useful (though necessarily abbreviated) comments on the book in her essay on Maori literature in the *Oxford History of New Zealand Literature in English* (*ibid.*: 13-14). Margaret Orbell (1995: 17-19), for her part, has written illuminatingly about the historical and cultural background surrounding the recording of Maori mythology in the mid-nineteenth century, while Ngahuia Awekotuku has rewritten the Hinemoa myth in an intriguing attempt to reverse what she sees as Grey's colonizing romanticism (Awekotuku 2001). The attention of Maori scholars, however, has generally focused on the Maori-language texts (especially *Nga Mahi a Nga Tupuna*) that underlie *Polynesian Mythology* and on the Maori informants, such as Te Rangikaheke (T.Curnow 1985; A.Thornton 1992), whom Grey made use of; there has been relatively little extended comment on the English-language work itself. A notable exception to the general dearth of detailed critical discussion of Grey's translation has been provided by Allan Meek (Meek 1990), who attempts to describe what he sees as the colonial and patriarchal psychology underlying the book.

This comparative neglect, while in some ways understandable, has had the effect of limiting our understanding of the nature and importance of Grey's work. It is of more than passing interest, therefore, to examine Grey's translation in detail, and to try to arrive at some conclusions about what it reveals about the mid-nineteenth-century European-Maori cultural encounter.

1. The Man behind the *Mythology:* Grey as Philologist and Intellectual

A good place to start is with the author, Grey himself. A successful soldier and civil servant, Grey had interests that extended far beyond military and government matters. Already, before his arrival in New Zealand, he had produced a vocabulary of Aboriginal languages, *A Vocabulary of the Dialects of South Western Australia* (1840). Almost as soon as he had landed in New Zealand in 1845 he had begun collecting Maori songs, myths and proverbs, an effort that bore fruit in *Ko nga moteatea, me nga hakirara o nga Maori* (1853) (translated as *Poems, Traditions and Chaunts of the Maories*), *Ko nga mahinga a nga tupuna Maori* (1854) (translated as *Mythology and Traditions of the New Zealanders*, and referred to here by its later title, *Nga Mahi a Nga Tupuna*), *Polynesian Mythology, and Ancient Traditional History of the New Zealand Race* (1855), and *Ko nga whakapepeha me nga whakaahuareka a nga tipuna o Aotea-roa* (which appeared in 1857 with English translations and explanations of its subject matter under the sub-title *Proverbial and Popular Sayings of the Ancestors of the New Zealand Race*). In addition, Grey produced a second collection of songs, *Ko nga waiata Maori* [Maori Songs]; this was printed in 1857 but not published till 1950 (Wattie 1998: 220, 382). On becoming Governor of the Cape Colony in 1854, Grey expanded his interests to include African languages and cultures, and even went to the lengths of employing a professional philologist, Wilhelm Bleek, to help him in his collecting and cataloguing (Stocking 1987: 86-7).

Grey's interests were not confined to living, indigenous tongues in newly acquired imperial territories; he also collected books and manuscripts from past ages, notably early editions of Classical writers, medieval manuscripts, incunabula, and Shakespeare Folios (Kerr 2000: 91-95). The result was a huge library that was, if not unparalleled, then certainly unusual for a government official. This library has since been split into two parts, one section held in the National Library of South Africa in Cape Town, the other in the Auckland Public Library in New Zealand. It remains a major resource, and a revealing index of Grey's intellect.

Grey's collecting activities, it is important to understand, were driven by much more than the practical curiosity of a Governor who wished to understand and converse with the peoples he ruled (R.Thornton 1983). Though he wrote no treatise on the matter, it is clear from the books he read, the intellectual circles he frequented when in London, and the occasional comment he made, that he believed that language represented the essence of what makes people human and could serve as a key to unlocking the history of the human race. Early in his life, for example, in a letter to Richard Owen, he had written that he hoped his study of ancient languages "might some day prove useful in any enquiry into the origin and dissemination of the different races of men" (Grey, letter to Richard Owen, 22 July 1837). Later, in a speech he gave to the newly-formed New Zealand Society, he concluded, ambitiously, that a study of Maori "laws, traditional customs and languages" would help "clear up and illustrate the history of the entire human race, of all time, considered as an harmonious whole" (Grey 1851: 15).

In this belief in the importance of language Grey followed nineteenth-century thinkers such as J.C. Prichard and Friedrich Max Müller. Study mankind's languages, their argument ran, and the human race's origins and essential nature would become clear. In particular, it was thought necessary to study the most remote and 'primitive' languages, for these were, in Müller's phrase, "the most ancient monuments of the human race" (Stocking 1987: 59) and as such were invaluable clues about its origins. Hence Müller's investigations of Vedic religious works (then thought to be the most ancient texts in the world), and hence, too, Grey's interest in the Maori language, for Maori at this period were generally seen as being 'ancient' and 'pure' by virtue of their long isolation from the main centres (as Europeans saw it) of civilization. When it came to studying ancient languages, moreover, one body of traditions – mythology – was deemed especially important, because mythological accounts generally preceded all others and were thought to enshrine the very oldest strata of language.

Müller, indeed, went even further, suggesting that language had actually *generated* myth (*ibid.*: 60).

For Grey, in other words, the collection, editing and publication of indigenous material, especially that relating to mythology, was no casual act. On the contrary, it had the potential to reveal important clues about man's essential nature and origin. Translating this material into English was, if not a necessary step (it was more important to have a record of this material in its original language, after all) nevertheless an important one, for it made this material available to the whole world rather than to a handful of specialists.

Translation, however, as translation theorists are right to remind us, is not a simple, transparent act. It is, rather, as Mary Snell-Hornby (1995: 47) puts it "a form of action across cultures – a cross-cultural event". *Polynesian Mythology* is undoubtedly such a 'cross-cultural event', and a very important one. Given the fact that it is indeed a translation, it is useful, before looking at Grey's book in detail, to consider translation practice in the mid-nineteenth century and, in particular, how Grey himself translated.

2. Twixt Metaphrase and Imitation: Grey as Translator

Grey had considerable experience of translations, particularly translations of religious and literary material. His library, as an 1888 catalogue shows, contained a variety of translated texts: examples in Pacific languages include *Pilgrim's Progress* in Fijian and *Robinson Crusoe* in Maori. In part, this experience had a practical origin. As Governor of remote, newly-acquired colonies, he had to understand the needs and grievances of indigenous peoples who, thanks to the missionary policy of not teaching converts English, generally expressed themselves in their own languages. Learning the local language or languages was part of Grey's job, and from there the step of writing down and then translating some of the more striking oral traditions he heard was not a large one. Sometimes, indeed, a knowledge of local oral tradition proved a necessity, since chiefs and orators might make frequent allusion to bodies of myth and legend in the course of their speeches, as was the case with Maori (Grey 1855: vi-vii).

Grey's experience of translation was not, however, just practical. From an early age he had been in the habit of translating European literature into English. He seems to have thought of himself as something of an expert, for in an 1832 English translation of Friedrich Schiller's historical tragedy *Fiesko; or the Conspiracy of Genoa*, for example, he wrote acerbic marginal notes such as 'a good deal added here', 'bad', and 'badly translated', occasionally supplying his own, improved translation of Schiller's German (Grey 1832: 12-16).[4]

Expert as Grey was (or thought he was) when it came to translation, he was still a man of his time, and it would be wrong to picture him treating his Maori source texts, when it came to producing *Polynesian Mythology*, with the hushed reverence of a Biblical scholar examining the Scriptures. Grey was no careful literalist, translating word by word and line by line with scrupulous regard for the original; when he thought fit, he had no qualms about abbreviating, editing and bowdlerizing his material. In this 'creative' approach to translation Grey was typical of his period, and was in fact following good Classical precedent. Both Horace and Quintillian, for example, had condemned pedantic, literal translations; nearer to Grey's own day, Alexander Pope in his *Iliad* (1715-20) and *Odyssey* (1725-26) had produced a very eighteenth-century Homer that was greatly admired, even though, arguably, it distorted the character of the ancient Greek epics. Grey, even so, was a great deal *more* respectful of his source texts than some of his contemporaries. FitzGerald, for instance, the translator of Omar Khayyam, was cheerfully contemptuous of "these Persians" and their verse in a way Grey never was of Maori and Maori material. Grey in fact much admired Maori poetry, judging it to be full of "the grace of fancy" and characterizing it as possessing both "a stern grandeur" and "a romantic glow" (Grey 1851: 12).

When it came to translating, Grey generally took the middle path recommended by Dryden in his 'Preface to Ovid's *Epistles*' (1680), avoiding the extremes of unreadable literalism ('metaphrase') and loose approximation ('imitation') (Snell-Hornby 1995: 11). Grey's aim appears to have been to help his reader become the equal of what the nineteenth-century German translation theorist Schleiermacher termed 'the better reader' (the more intelligent or acute reader) of the original text (Bassnett-McGuire 1980: 71).

Grey's Preface is revealing when it comes to the specifics of translation work involved in *Polynesian Mythology*. He states, for example, that his translation is, broadly, 'close and faithful' to its Maori source texts

---

[4] I am indebted to Donald Kerr of the Auckland Public Library for this information.

(Grey 1855: xi). Even given the more relaxed attitudes toward translation that prevailed in the mid-nineteenth century, this claim is not really true, as I will show; what is interesting is that Grey felt compelled to make it. Evidently he was keen to persuade his readers that what they were reading was pure, original and ancient. This desire to present his work as authentic is characteristic of Grey, and indeed of nearly all nineteenth-century European writing about Maori (the missionary Richard Taylor and the early ethnographer and novelist John White both made such claims).[5] We today would be much more cautious about making such a claim, in part because we are so much more aware than the Victorians of the determining influences of culture on texts, especially translated texts.[6]

3. Mythologies before the *Mythology*: Literary and Historical Background

Before looking in detail at Grey's book, it is useful also to consider briefly the literary background from which it emerged, and the readership to which it was addressed. Though it was groundbreaking, and recognized as such, *Polynesian Mythology* did not arise from a vacuum. Since the seventeenth century at least antiquaries and historians had been collecting and publishing the beliefs and legends of European peasantry, often in order to identify superstitious elements which could then be suppressed (Stocking 1987: 53-6). In the late eighteenth and early nineteenth centuries, with the rise of Romantic philosophies that emphasized the importance of the naïve and the primitive, this interest had taken a more positive turn. In the 1780s, for instance, Robert Burns had recorded in Lowland Scots verse the folk tales and superstitions of his native Ayrshire, while in the 1820s Thomas Croker had recorded the myths and legends of the Gaelic-speaking population of Ireland. Croker's book, *Fairy Legends and Traditions of the South of Ireland* (1828) was in Grey's library; its presence suggests that Grey had a particular interest in folklore and mythology, and it may well have given him the idea of making his own collection and translation.

Such scholarly interest was not confined to the mythology and traditions of Europe. Since the sixteenth century missionaries and travellers had been describing indigenous, non-European peoples, and in these early

---

[5] See Taylor 1855: vi, and the Preface to White's ethnographic novel *Te Rou* (1874) (White 1874: v).
[6] See Bassnett-McGuire(1980: 3-4); Snell-Hornby (1995: 22, 24).

accounts reference had sometimes been made to these peoples' beliefs and traditions. In 1724, for example, there had appeared a French study of Huron beliefs and customs; later in the century, the beliefs and traditions of, variously, Tahitians and !Kung (Bushmen) had been sketched, if not fully described.[7] Closer to Grey's own time, the American Henry Rowe Schoolcraft had been collecting and translating Native American myths and traditions from the 1820s (see above), some of which he translated (or had translated for him) and which he published in book form. In Australia, at about the same time, a few sporadic attempts had been made to collect and translate Aboriginal songs and legends (notably by Eliza Hamilton Dunlop in New South Wales). In the Pacific, meanwhile, some record had been made of Polynesian beliefs and traditions by missionaries such as William Ellis (Edmond 1997: 104-112). Many of these publications are in Grey's library, underlining his interest in this literature.

Of the various Pacific mythologies available to mid-nineteenth century readers, it was the Maori, in fact, that was among the best known, thanks to the writings of a succession of missionaries and travellers. The painter Augustus Earle, for instance, had alluded to the story of Maui drawing the land out of the sea in his *Narrative of Nine Months' Residence in New Zealand* (1832: 266). William Yate, a missionary, had mentioned several more of the Maui stories in his *Account of New Zealand* (1835: 142-4). Fuller descriptions of Maori myths and legends, by Joshua Polack (1840) and James Hamlin (1842), had followed in the 1840s (Hamlin's account, which appeared in an obscure Tasmanian journal, was especially detailed). In the 1850s, finally, there had been published Richard Taylor's vast, unreliable but fascinating *Te Ika a Maui* (1855) and Edward Shortland's calm, careful *Traditions and Superstitions of the New Zealanders* (1854, 1856). Both books gave detailed descriptions of Maori myths and legends; they act as valuable complements to, and sometimes commentaries on, Grey's work (Shortland in particular is very useful in this respect).[8] Both books are in Grey's library, but their publication dates

---

[7] See Josèphe Lafitau's *Mœurs des Sauvages Amériquains* (1724), Bougainville's *Voyage Around the World* (1772) and Barrow's *Travels in the Interior of Southern Africa* (1801). For a fuller discussion of these and other early European accounts of indigenous, non-European peoples, see Pratt 1986 and Pratt 1992.

[8] Shortland in fact included material from *Polynesian Mythology* in the 1856 edition of his book. He greatly valued Grey's work, judging it to contain "interesting and valuable matter", but was aware that some of the material in it had been modified to suit European tastes.

mean that they are unlikely to have influenced *Polynesian Mythology*.

There was, then, by 1855 a small but solid body of writing in existence relating to the myths and legends of indigenous New World peoples, notably those of Maori, some of which would have been known to Grey's reading public. Interesting and occasionally impressive as these accounts are, however, they are, in the end, just that: accounts. Even the best of them seldom match Grey's translations in dramatic power, being typically abbreviated reports of mythic action rather than direct, vivid descriptions of it. A case in point is the account of Maui's death. In Taylor's version the story is told swiftly, in a few discreet lines:

> His last work was to do away with death. He noticed that the sun and moon were not to be killed, because they bathed in the living fountain, the Wai ora Tane; he determined, therefore, to do the same and to enter the womb of Hine-nui-te-po, that is Hades, where the living water – the life-giving stream – was situated. Hine-nui-te-po draws all into her womb, but permits none to return. Maui determined to try, trusting to his great powers; but before he made the attempt, he strictly charged his friends, the birds, not to laugh. He then allowed his great mother night to draw him into her womb. His head and shoulders had already entered, when that forgetful bird, the Piwaka-waka, began to laugh. Night closed her portals, Maui was cut in two and died...(Taylor 1855: 30-1)

In Grey's book, by contrast, the demi-god's death, the reasons behind it, the plans Maui made and the way he dies are given in considerable, dramatic detail:

> Then Maui asked him [his father], "What do you mean, what things are there that I can be vanquished by?" And his father answered him, "By your great ancestress, by Hine-nui-te-po, who, if you look, you may see flashing, and as it were, opening and shutting there, where the horizon meets the sky". And Maui replied, "Lay aside such idle thoughts, and let us both fearlessly seek whether men are to die or live for ever". And his father said, "My child, there has been an ill omen for us; when I was baptizing you, I omitted a portion of the fitting prayers, and that I know will be the cause of your perishing".
>
> Then Maui asked his father, "What is my ancestress Hine-nui-te-po like?" and he answered, "What you see yonder shining so brightly red are her eyes, and her teeth are as sharp and hard as

pieces of volcanic glass; her body is like that of a man, and as for the pupils of her eyes, they are jasper; and her hair is like the tangles of long sea weed, and her mouth is like that of a barracouta". Then his son answered him, "Do you think her strength is as great as that of Tama-nui-te-Ra, who consumes man, and the earth, and the very waters, by the fierceness of his heat? Was not the world formerly saved alive by the speed with which he travelled? If he had then, in the days of his full strength and power, gone as slowly as he does now, not a remnant of mankind would have been left living upon the earth, nor indeed, would anything else have survived. But I laid hold of Tama-nui-te-Ra, and now he goes slowly, for I smote him again and again, so that now he is feeble, and long in travelling his course, and he now gives but very little heat, having been weakened by the blows of my enchanted weapon; I then, too, split him open in many places, and from the wounds so made, many rays now issue forth, and spread in all directions. So, also, I found the sea much larger than the earth, but by the power of the last born of your children, part of the earth was drawn up again, and dry land came forth". And his father answered him, "That is all very true, O, my last born, and the strength of my old age; well, then, be bold, go and visit your great ancestress who flashes so fiercely there, where the edge of the horizon meets the sky".

Hardly was this conversation concluded with his father, when the young hero went forth to look for companions to accompany him upon this enterprise: and so there came to him for companions, the small robin, and the large robin, and the thrush, and the yellow-hammer, and every kind of little bird, and the water-wagtail, and these all assembled together, and they all started with Maui in the evening, and arrived at the dwelling of Hine-nui-te-po, and found her fast asleep.

Then Maui addressed them all, and said, "My little friends, now if you see me creep into this old chieftainess, do not laugh at what you see. Nay, nay, do not I pray you, but when I have got altogether inside her, and just as I am coming out of her mouth, then you may shout with laughter if you please". And his little friends, who were frightened at what they saw, replied, "Oh sir, you will certainly be killed". And he answered them, "If you burst out laughing at me as soon as I get inside her, you will wake her up, and she will certainly kill me at once, but if you do not laugh until I am quite inside her, and am on the point of coming out of her mouth, I shall live, and Hine-nui-te-po will die". And his little friends answered, "Go on then, brave sir, but pray take good care of yourself".

> Then the young hero started off, and twisted the strings of his weapon tight around his wrist, and went into the house, and stripped off his clothes, and the skin on his hips looked mottled and beautiful as that of a mackerel, from the tattoo marks, cut on it with the chisel of Uetonga, and he entered the old chieftainess.
>
> The little birds now screwed up their tiny cheeks, trying to suppress their laughter; at last, the little Tiwakawaka could no longer keep it in, and laughed out loud, with its merry cheerful note; this woke the old woman up, she opened her eyes, started up, and killed Maui...(Grey 1855: 54-7)

As Grey put it in his Preface, in *Polynesian Mythology* the European reader heard (or seemed to hear) for the first time "a heathen and savage high-priest explaining to him, in his own words, and in his own energetic manner, the traditions in which he earnestly believes, and unfolding the religious opinions upon which the faith and hopes of his race rest" (*ibid.*: xi). While this claim is not really true, as I will show, Grey's work nevertheless represented a huge step forward in terms of immediacy and power – a fact not lost upon his readers.

4. A Taste for the Exotic: Grey's Reading Public

The reading public Grey was translating for needs some consideration, for its taste undoubtedly exerted a strong influence on *Polynesian Mythology*. As Dulcie Gillespie-Needham (1971) has shown it was a middle-class public, with a penchant for religious and historical works. It had a lively curiosity, too, about foreign lands and cultures; in particular, it had a decided taste for the exotic. Earlier in the century the Irish poet Thomas Moore had published his pseudo-oriental verse romance *Lalla Rookh* (1817) to huge applause, while Edward FitzGerald's *Rubaiyat of Omar Khayyam* (1859) would soon enjoy vast popularity. The myths and legends of 'primitive' indigenous peoples such as Native Americans or Maori were even less familiar to this readership than the stories of Mughal India or medieval Persia, but the enthusiastic reception accorded to Longfellow's *Song of Hiawatha* (1855) suggests that it found such material, however altered and edited, fascinating. One English reviewer, for example, stated that he thought *Hiawatha* "the noblest piece of legend it has been our lot to read or hear" and opined that "henceforth the Odjibway and Dacotah are to us realities, men of like minds to ourselves" (*Oxford and Cambridge Magazine* 1856: 49). It was a readership, in other words, that was going to be receptive to a book like *Polynesian Mythology*.

It was a public, however, that had a distinct leaning towards the sentimental (witness the huge popularity of Dickens) and a strict, even prudish morality, particularly when it came to reproductive and sexual matters. It had, in addition, little understanding of the beliefs and traditions of other cultures (especially non-Western cultures), and little knowledge of or patience for their sometimes different literary traditions and narrative methods. Any translator addressing this readership would have had to take into account these characteristics; judging by the way he translated his Maori material in *Polynesian Mythology*, Grey generally did. The influence of his readership, in fact, is a very important factor in any assessment of Grey's work, and provides, at one level, a convincing explanation of why *Polynesian Mythology* is as it is.

5. *Polynesian Mythology*: The Book

Before discussing the text itself, it is worthwhile looking at the book (1971), the actual object itself, that Grey produced in collaboration with his publisher, John Murray. Physically, the 1855 edition of Grey's book is a handsome volume, bound in green cloth boards with an embossed 'Maori' motif round the edges. The front cover bears a gold tiki (or pseudo-tiki) figure, and the spine displays a crossed taiaha (halberd) and tao (spear), lending the book a faintly heraldic flavour. Inside, the frontispiece has a fantasy scene, showing a tall, snowy volcano, a pa (fort) situated picturesquely above a river, and a highly decorated waka (canoe) prow. Facing the frontispiece, on the title page, is a dramatic picture of a waka being paddled straight at the reader (as it were) by semi-naked indigenes. Scattered through the text are 14 engraved illustrations showing various aspects of Maori life and pastimes ('The Swing', 'Chief Lying in State'). Interesting as these illustrations are, they do not relate to the accompanying text, and seem to have been inserted in order to give the reader a general visual impression of Maori and Maori life.

The physical appearance of the 1855 edition of *Polynesian Mythology* tells us a great deal. The book was aimed, clearly, at a relatively affluent market, but one which had only the vaguest notion of what Maori, Maori art and even New Zealand looked like (the height of the volcano of the fantasy scene, for example, is vastly exaggerated, and the 'Maori' in the waka being paddled straight at the reader are more Native American in appearance than Polynesian). It emphasizes the exotic nature of its contents (witness the striking gold tiki figure on the cover), but does so in a way that recalls familiar European motifs (the taiaha and tao, for instance, are crossed rather like a halberd and a lance on a medieval coat of arms). In this respect, it can be said that Grey's book often reproduces at the level of design what it does at the level of textual organization and at the detailed level of the text itself. It offers the strange and the unfamiliar, the exotic and the exciting, but in a subtly refocused, edited form, one acceptable to a mid-nineteenth-century European reading public.

6. *Polynesian Mythology*: The Text

Most significant, however, and of greatest interest in terms of this essay, are the changes that Grey made to his Maori-language source text, *Nga Mahi a Nga Tupuna*, as he translated it into the English of *Polynesian Mythology*. *Nga Mahi* itself, as has long been noted by a number of scholars of Maori culture, is by no means a simple, transparent record of pre-European Maori mythology. As David Simmons showed (1966), it is, rather, a complex patchwork of different tribal traditions, with contributions from various tribes, from Te Arawa, Ngati Toa, Waikato, Ati Awa, Taranaki, Ngai Tahu and others.[9] It is a patchwork, moreover, which Grey freely edited. As Bruce Biggs noted (1952: 181), Grey rearranged and combined material from different sources, a practice that sometimes resulted in confusion. In addition, Grey removed passages that revealed his contributors were familiar with Christianity and European culture (*ibid.*); he also bowdlerized his material by removing or obscuring sexual references, for instance in the story of Maui's death (quoted above) where the original source material is explicit in its treatment of the *vagina dentata* motif (*ibid.*). While the obscuring of sexual references is to be expected from a mid-nineteenth-century editor like Grey (according to Bremer (Bremer 1987: 249-50), Schoolcraft behaved in a similar way with his Native American material), the removal by Grey of allusions suggesting his Maori contributors were familiar with European culture is intriguing. Grey, clearly, was anxious to present his Maori mythology as pure and ancient, untouched by European beliefs and attitudes. From what we know of Grey's ideas about the importance of 'ancient' languages and mythologies

---

[9] See Simmons. He identifies contributions from Te Arawa, Ngati Toa, Ngati Raukawa, Waikato, Ati Awa, Taranaki, Ngati Kahungunu, Ngai Tahu, as well as contributions from Northland and Auckland sources.

(see above), his editing in *Nga Mahi* becomes comprehensible, if not acceptable according to modern translation theory.

If *Nga Mahi* departs in some ways from its sources, *Polynesian Mythology* departs in many ways from *Nga Mahi*, despite Grey's claim that it was, broadly, a 'close and faithful' translation (Grey 1855: xi). At the level of general textual organization, for example, Grey's book differs in being substantially shorter than its Maori-language source text. It has only 23 chapters, and these chapters are themselves contracted versions of their counterparts in *Nga Mahi*. In 'The Legend of Rupe', for example, matter relating to the death of Kaitangata is left out, a fact Grey admits in a footnote (*ibid.*: 89), while in 'The Voyage to New Zealand' the priest Ngatoroirangi's long chant is omitted (*ibid.*: 141). *Polynesian Mythology*, in fact, generally lacks the many waiata (songs) and karakia (incantations) that punctuate the prose narratives of *Nga Mahi* (some of the songs, it is true, are given in highly abbreviated form). Their absence deprives the reader of an important dimension of *Nga Mahi*, and of a significant aspect of pre-European Maori oral culture.

More than just songs were omitted in Grey's translation. Much of the material in *Nga Mahi* was excised *en bloc*: all the taniwha (monster) stories, for example, were left out, as was the long Paoa legend, material relating to Tutanekai's birth in the Hinemoa story, and the Te Huhuti tale (a legend from the East Coast about a young woman who swims across water to reach her beloved). Grey's thinking behind these abbreviations and excisions is sometimes clear, sometimes opaque. The loss of the taniwha legends is hard to explain, since these stories are vivid, entertaining, free of embarrassing (i.e. sexual or reproductive) material and – to European readers familiar with stories of dragon-slaying – intriguingly familiar. At other times the reasons for abbreviation and excision are less hard to guess. The Paoa story was omitted probably because of its very length, while the Te Huhuti legend was eliminated no doubt because it reduplicated, or appeared to reduplicate, the theme of the longer, more detailed Hinemoa legend. Matter relating to Tutanekai in the Hinemoa story (see below) was undoubtedly dropped because it dealt in part with childbirth, a subject it was not possible at this period to discuss in polite literature.

Whatever the reason or reasons behind these large-scale textual changes, they had an important effect on *Polynesian Mythology* and on the image conveyed of Maori mythology. The element of the picturesque and the romantic (even the sentimental) was strengthened; the element of the violent and the monstrous (and the sexually explicit) was reduced Jane McRae (2000: 7), alternatively, finds an increase in the romantic and the picturesque "at the expense of the explanatory and the educative". This alteration in emphasis may have come about through a kind of unconscious selection by Grey (he valued Maori poetry for its 'romantic glow', after all); alternatively, Grey may have deliberately calculated that his changes would endear his book to a sentimental Victorian readership. Certainly the whimsical and romantic aspects of his material are emphasized by Grey's chapter titles, which underline the magical and sentimental elements in the legends ('The Magical Wooden Head', 'The Loves of Takarangi and Rau-Mahora'). The notion that Grey was carefully tailoring his translation to suit the tastes of his readers is supported by the fact that he provides a certain amount of help, in the way of background information, for his European reader. The simple, austere chapter titles of *Nga Mahi*, for example ('Ko Hatupatu') are expanded ('Hatupatu and his Brothers'), and footnotes, sometimes quite elaborate, explaining Maori and Polynesian customs are added. An example is found in 'The Emigration of Turi', where Grey explains at length the common Polynesian topos of discovering a plot by overhearing a song (Grey 1855: 205).

Polynesian Mythology, in fact, is very clearly a book designed for the general reading public of Grey's day. This was a public which had a decided taste for the romantic and the sentimental but which, despite a curiosity about remote, exotic peoples like Maori, had little real knowledge of indigenous, non-European cultures or traditions and only a limited ability to cope with difficult or explicit material. The influence of this public's taste is especially apparent, I believe, in Grey's translation of the Hinemoa legend, which, for various complex cultural and literary reasons I will describe, struck a particularly deep chord with the readers of *Polynesian Mythology*. It is useful, I believe, to consider Grey's translation of this legend in detail at this point, for doing so will reveal very clearly how deftly Grey adapted his material for European consumption.

7. Governor Grey and the Maiden of Rotorua: *The Hinemoa Legend*

The Hinemoa legend, which recounts the swim of a beautiful young aristocrat across Lake Rotorua to join her lover, Tutanekai, on the island of Mokoia, has a complex, revealing translation history. It was first recorded, in Maori, at the very end of 1849, while Grey was travelling through the

Rotorua region in his capacity as Governor (according to George Cooper, Grey's secretary, Grey wrote down the legend as it was dictated to him by 'an inhabitant' of the island of Mokoia (Cooper 1851: 190).[10] The first translation of the legend appeared as early as 1851, when an English version of the story was printed side by side with a Maori source text in the bi-lingual *Journal* that Cooper published in Auckland that year. Interestingly, Cooper's claim (*ibid.*) that the story "here subjoined verbatim" represents the original account jotted down on Mokoia Island in Lake Rotorua is inaccurate; as an examination of the relevant manuscripts in the Grey Collection in the Auckland Public Library shows, the Maori text in Cooper's *Journal* is in fact a longer, more rhetorical (and arguably a somewhat Europeanized) expansion of the original Mokoia island notes, one which Grey seems to have written down at a later date, drawing, apparently, on another Maori source.[11] Who this other Maori source was is unclear; it may have been the Te Arawa chief Te Rangikaheke, one of Grey's main Maori informants, who was living in Grey's house and working for Grey at this time.[12] The possibility that Te Rangikaheke may have been involved in the production of the second, longer version of the legend is supported by the fact that he subsequently annotated Grey's new transcription, clarifying narrative points and adding geographical and genealogical detail.[13] In addition, Te Rangikaheke wrote out his own, separate account of the story, an account which appears to function as something akin to a commentary on Grey's second version, and which has since been published (Biggs *et al.* 1967). Exactly *why* Cooper, for his part, claimed the later, longer version written down by Grey was the original one recorded on Mokoia Island is a matter for speculation. Possibly he did not know that it wasn't; possibly he did know, but wanted to pass off the later version as the original. If the latter is the case, it is an intriguing example of an 'original' source text turning out to be not so 'original' after all. As translation theorists such as (Barnstone 1993: 81-5) and

---

[10] See GNZMMSS 70 in the Grey Collection in the Auckland Public Library.

[11] See GNZMMSS 60 in the Grey Collection in the Auckland Public Library.

[12] Wiremu Maihi Te Rangikaheke (18??-96), also known as William Marsh, was a chief of Te Arawa who provided Grey with a great deal of his Maori material (see Biggs 1952; Simmons 1966; Curnow 1985). He started writing for Grey c. 1846, and was living in Grey's house in 1849. As a member of Te Arawa (the local Rotorua tribe) he would have been in an excellent position to give Grey further details of the Hinemoa legend.

[13] See GNZMMSS 60, where Te Rangikaheke's annotations are clearly visible.

(Kálman 1986: 117-121) have noted, the nature and status of source texts in translations is often a complex matter. Careful analysis of such 'original' texts can be both surprizing and illuminating.

Who translated this longer, more rhetorical version into English for Cooper's *Journal* is equally unclear. It may have been Grey, or it may have been Charles Davis, a Maori-speaking European who had accompanied Grey on his gubernatorial expedition as an interpreter, or it may have been a third party.[14] Whatever the truth, the story in its English version excited some approving comment in the local colonial press. It then effectively disappeared till 1855, when it reappeared, with some changes, in *Polynesian Mythology*. It is this translation, which Grey claimed as his own, as he did all the translations in his book, that I would like to consider here.

As I have already noted, at the large-scale level Grey's translation of the Hinemoa legend differs considerably from its claimed *Nga Mahi* source text, notably in the excision of material relating to Tutanekai's birth, material which seems to have been supplied by Te Rangikaheke.[15] But it is at the detailed level of word and phrase that the differences between the two stories become particularly striking. Often it is a matter of euphemism, with a sexually explicit word or phrase being replaced in the translation by something more acceptable to a Victorian readership. Tutanekai's mother Rangiuru is described, for example, as having 'run away' with her lover Tuwharetoa (Grey 1855: 235); in the Maori text she is said more straightforwardly to have slept with him adulterously ("'ka moea tahaetia a Rangi-Uru e Tuwharetoa'") (Grey 1854: 127)). In the English translation, to take another example, Tutanekai is described by his brothers at one point as a 'low born fellow' (Grey 1855: 238); in the Maori text he is termed simply a 'poriro' ('bastard') (Grey 1854: 131). That said, it must be admitted that Grey's bowdlerization here is subtle rather than gross. He does not attempt, for example, to hide the basic fact of Tutanekai's illegitimacy, something that later European re-tellers of the story, anxious

---

[14] C.O.B. Davis (1817/18-87) was employed as an interpreter and translator by the colonial government at this period. He was later responsible for putting together *Maori Mementoes* (1855), a collection of Maori speeches, sayings, stories and reports addressed to or relating to Grey.

[15] See GNZMMSS 42 in the Grey Collection. This material was later printed in *Nga Moteatea* as an appendix (Grey 1853: lxxii-lxxiv), before being incorporated into the *Nga Mahi* version of the Hinemoa legend.

to transform Tutanekai into a kind of Polynesian Prince Charming, were apt to do.[16]

At other times Grey expands his source text, particularly in the direction of the romantic and the sentimental. The story's title in the Maori source text had been simply 'Ko Hinemoa' ('Hinemoa'). Grey's title in *Polynesian Mythology*, 'Hinemoa, the Maiden of Rotorua', carries by contrast a suggestion of innocence; to a mid-nineteenth-century reader, indeed, it would have underlined, more or less, Hinemoa's virginity. In the text, too, Grey's English translation uses a similar strategy. The sound of Tutanekai's and Tiki's music, for example, is said by Grey to have been 'wafted by the gentle land breeze across the lake' (Grey 1855: 236). In the Maori source text it is more prosaically 'carried by the shore wind to Owhata' 'ka kawea atu te tangi e te hau-whenua-a-po, ki Owhata' (Grey 1854: 130). During her swim to Mokoia island, in the English version, Hinemoa is described as being guided by the 'soft measure' of Tutanekai's instrument (Grey 1855: 240). In the Maori text she is guided simply by the 'tune' ('rangi') of his flute (Grey 1854: 132). It is not that the Maori source text is un-romantic, merely that its language is relatively more straightforward and less coloured by sentimental connotations than that of the English translation.

Perhaps the most striking characteristic of the English text, however, is its subtle but persistent archaicization. By 'archaicization' I mean the tendency, marked throughout *Polynesian Mythology*, to use language that is distinctly old-fashioned, even quaint. Grey's Maori source text, as far as I can tell, does not archaicize in this manner; in fact it happily uses a neologism such as 'marenatia' ('married') (*ibid.*: 134) that clearly reflects the linguistic borrowing from English that was occurring in mid-nineteenth-century Maori (see below). Grey's English translation, by contrast, is full of medievalisms, or pseudo-medievalisms. Hinemoa was 'a maiden of rare beauty'; fame 'attended' her; she 'ever said to herself' and so on (Grey 1855: 236; 237). It is not hard to trace the literary origin of such language; it is to be found in the 'medieval' writings of early nineteenth-century British men of letters such as Scott, Chatterton and Keats, which Grey would certainly have known. Its use here, in a mid-nineteenth-

---

[16] Grey's translation of the Hinemoa story spawned a vast array of imitations and adaptations, especially after the 1885 reprinting of *Polynesian Mythology*. In general these versions tended to sanitize the story, removing, for example, references to Tutanekai's illegitimacy.

century translation of a Maori legend, is an attempt to suggest the antiquity and venerability of the Hinemoa story. As such, it can be paralleled by similar pseudo-medievalisms in other texts from the period, notably in Alfred Domett's *Ranolf and Amohia*, which often uses archaic, 'medieval' imagery and language when dealing with its Maori characters (especially in battle scenes) (Domett 1872: 374-97).

A similar motivation lies behind the employment of stilted, somewhat Biblical phrases and syntax in the English text. In the Maori version of the story, for example, the final moments of Tutanekai's and Hinemoa's encounter at the hot pool are described in simple, vivid language:

> Ka tae a Tutanekai, ki tetehi ona kakahu, ka whakahoroa atu ki a ia, ka mau ia. Na, ka haere raua, ka tae ki te whare, ka momoe, ko to te Maori ritenga tawhito tenei, ana ka marenatia. (Grey 1854: 134)

> [Tutanekai took one of his cloaks and slipped it off over her, and took hold of her. Then they went off and arrived at his house and slept together; according to the old Maori custom, they were then married.]

Grey's discreeter English version, by contrast, while not actually inaccurate, is decidedly archaic and Old Testamentary in tone:

> And he threw garments over her, and took her; and they proceeded to his house, and reposed there; and thenceforth, according to the ancient laws of the Maori, they were man and wife. (Grey 1855: 243)

The effect of such lofty, old-fashioned language is once more to distance the story, moving it into an exalted, ancient, semi-sanctified past. As a result, the Hinemoa legend is removed from its particular, tribal and oral context and is subsumed into the larger body of western mythological literature.

We today, of course, with our emphasis on fidelity to source texts and concern over questions of cultural ownership and identity, would regard translation of this kind as questionable, even illicit and unethical (Venuti 1998). Grey, however, who in this respect was very much a man of his time, seems to have been untroubled by such considerations. He knew his readership and gave them, essentially, what they could understand and relate to.

8. Hinemoa as a Hit: Literary-critical Reaction

Grey's translation of the Hinemoa story proved enormously popular. All the reviewers of *Polynesian Mythology* mentioned it, and most of the requests Grey received from readers for permission to use his work mentioned Hinemoa in particular (see William Satchell's letter to Grey, discussed above). A vivid example of a contemporary reaction can be seen in the review of Grey's book in the *Dublin University Magazine*, a magazine Grey had earlier contributed to while serving as an officer in Ireland. Hitherto Maori had been considered, when they had been considered at all, as fierce cannibals or (at best) worthy converts. Here however was evidence that Maori were in fact equal in their affections to the most sensitive Europeans. As a review it is rather gushing, but it serves to illustrate how deftly Grey had translated the story so as to make it appeal to Victorian taste:

> Who can read this simple tale without feeling how "one touch of nature makes the whole world kin?" The rude Maori with his war club, and his stone-axe, his tatooed skin, and his matted cloak, full of revenge on his enemies, reckless of life, fierce and savage even to cannibalism, slaying, killing and eating a man, on slight provocation, or perhaps none at all, has yet a soul and a heart open to all the beauties of nature, and accessible to the soft influences of love. Poetry and song are his delight – not only the war-chant, but the love song; and his love is not solely the mere animal impulse, but as evinced by the above poem, full of sentiment, delicacy and grace, natural and artless, but refined and modest, and blending easily with music and flowers, cherished by the soft sunsets and moonlit evenings of summer, the natural efflorescence of the youthful soul among the Maoris as among ourselves. Which of us men would not have loved Hine-moa, and felt for Tutanekai as for a friend and brother? (*Dublin University Magazine*, 1855: 36)

Equally telling is the response of a contemporary New Zealand artist, Charles Decimus Barraud. Like the reviewer of the *Dublin University Magazine*, he was clearly taken with the romantic, sentimental aspect of the legend, as retold by Grey, for in a series of charming pen-and-ink drawings (Barraud, 1850?) he produced sometime after the legend had appeared in translation (possibly preliminary studies for a book of Maori legends and verse that Grey had planned to produce with his friend Domett) the romantic, sentimental aspects of the tale are carefully emphasized. Mokoia island and its surrounds, for example, are depicted as a sequence of dreaming, misty vistas, while Hinemoa herself is drawn as an innocent yet voluptuous maiden.[17]

The public's strong response to the Hinemoa story, it has to be said, did not proceed exclusively from Grey's artful translation. The legend fascinated European readers in the first place because it dealt with love, rather than with tapu (ritual restriction) or utu (response or revenge), concepts that were either hard to understand, or off-putting for lovers of the romantic and the sentimental. It dealt, moreover, with a love that broke, or appeared to break, social boundaries, a theme very popular in the Romantic period, to which Grey's Victorian readers were the direct heirs. The Hinemoa story recalled, too, if only subconsciously, the classical legend of Hero and Leander, while adding an intriguing, antipodean twist: in this case it was the woman, not the man, who did the swimming. The fact, too, that a naked or semi-naked, wet, young, indigenous woman lay at the centre of this story must have given the legend an extra erotic attraction, at least to male readers. As several critics, among them Rod Edmond, have noted (1997: 75), the figure of the naked, wet, female indigene (especially the naked, wet, *Polynesian* female indigene) is one of the abiding fantasy images of nineteenth-century colonial/imperial literature.

That said, Grey's deft translation undoubtedly contributed to the story's popularity, and stands as a prime example of how great an impact a translation can make when tailored so artfully to the taste of its target readership. What is true of the Hinemoa translation is also true, to a lesser extent, of the other translations in *Polynesian Mythology*, which were read with considerable interest, if not with the breathless enthusiasm accorded to the Hinemoa legend (the creation myth of Rangi and Papa, and the stories of the Maui cycle, especially, excited comment and proved a fertile source of material for New Zealand poets). While we today regard Grey's kind of translation as problematic, an example, perhaps, of 'colonizing romanticism', we can still study it with fascination. Nineteenth-century translations of Pacific indigenous material as a whole, indeed, deserve closer attention than they have, generally, received, preserving and encoding as they do the complexities of cultural encounter in the region.

---

[17] For a discussion of the book of Maori legends and poetry planned by Grey and Domett, and for an extended examination of subsequent visual depictions of Hinemoa by European artists such as Nicholas Chevalier and Gottfried Lindauer, see Bell 1992: 47-8, 140-6, 210-15.

References

Alpers, Anthony (1964) *Maori Myths and Tribal Legends*, London: John Murray.
------ (1987) *The World of the Polynesians*, Auckland: Oxford University Press.
Awekotuku, Ngahuia (2001) 'Hinemoa: Retelling a Famous Romance', *Journal of Lesbian Studies* 5 (1,2): 1-11.
Barnstone, Willis (1993) *The Poetics of Translation*, New Haven and London: Yale University Press.
Barraud, Charles Decimus (1850?) 'The Legend of Hinemoa', BL Add. ((1954) 1983), London, British Library.
Bassnett-McGuire, Susan (1980) *Translation Studies*, London: Methuen.
Baxter, James K. (1980) 'East Coast Journey', in J. Weir (ed) *Collected Poems*, Wellington: Oxford University Press.
Bell, Leonard (1992) *Colonial Constructs: European Images of Maori 1840-1914*, Auckland: Auckland University Press.
Biggs, Bruce (1952) 'The Translation and Publishing of Maori Material in the Auckland Public Library', *Journal of the Polynesian Society* 61: 177-91.
------, P. Hohepa and S. Mead (eds) (1967) *Selected Readings in Maori*, Wellington: Reed.
Bohan, Edmund (1998) *To Be a Hero: A Biography of Sir George Grey*, Auckland: Harper Collins.
Bremer, Richard (1987) *Indian Agent and Wilderness Scholar: The Life of Henry Rowe Schoolcraft*, Mount Pleasant: Central Michigan University.
Brown, John Macmillan (1907) *Maori and Polynesian*, London: Hutchison.
Collier, James (1909) *Sir George Grey – Governor, High Commissioner, and Premier*, Christchurch: Whitcombe and Tombs.
Cooper, Charles (1851) *Journal of an Expedition Overland from Auckland to Taranaki*, Auckland: Williamson and Wilson.
Croker, Thomas (1828) *Fairy Legends and Traditions of the South of Ireland*, London: John Murray.
Curnow, Allen and R. Oppenheim (eds) (1960) *The Penguin Book of New Zealand Verse*, Harmondsworth: Penguin.
Curnow, Jenifer (1985) 'Wiremu Maihi Te Rangikaheke: His Life and Work', *Journal of the Polynesian Society* 94 (2): 97-147.
Domett, Alfred (1872) *Ranolf and Amohia: A South Sea Day-Dream*, London: Smith, Elder & Co.
Earle, Augustus (1832) *A Narrative of a Nine Months' Residence in New Zealand in 1827*, London: Longman Rees.
Edmond, Rod (1997) *Representing the South Pacific: Colonial Discourse from Cook to Gauguin*, Cambridge: Cambridge University Press.
FitzGerald, Edward (1859) *The Rubaiyat of Omar Khayyam*, London: (nP)
Gillespie-Needham, Dulcie (1971) 'The Colonial and his Books' (unpublished

diss.), Victoria University of Wellington.

Grey, Sir George (1832) Annotations to *Fiesko; or the Conspiracy of Genoa* by Friedrich Schiller, trans. G.C. D'Aguilar, Dublin: Richard Milliekn, G34a36, Grey Collection, National Library of South Africa, Cape Town.

------ (1837) Letter to Richard Owen, 22 July 1837, BL Add. 42583, f.125, British Library, London.

------ (1840) *A Vocabulary of the Dialects of South Western Australia*, London: T. and W. Boone.

------ (1851) *Address to the Members of the New Zealand Society*, Wellington: The Spectator.

------ (1853) *Ko nga moteatea, me nga hakirara o nga Maori* (Poems, Traditions and Chaunts of the Maories), Wellington: Robert Stokes.

------ (1854) *Ko nga mahinga a nga tupuna Maori* (Mythology and Traditions of the New Zealanders), London: George Willis.

------ (1855) *Polynesian Mythology, and Ancient Traditional History of the New Zealand Race*, London: John Murray.

------ (1857) *Ko nga whakapepeha me nga whakaahuareka a nga tipuna o Aotea-roa* (Proverbial and Popular Sayings of the Ancestors of the New Zealand Race), Cape Town: Saul Solomon.

Hamlin, James (1842) 'On the Mythology of the New Zealanders', *Tasmanian Journal of Natural Science* 1: 254-64, 342-58.

Kerr, Donald (2000) 'Sir George Grey and the English Antiquarian Book Trade', in R. Myers, M. Harris and G. Mandelbrote (eds) *Libraries and the Book Trade: The Formation of Collections from the Sixteenth to the Twentieth Century*, New Castle, Delaware: Oak Knoll Press.

Langloh-Parker, Katherine (1896) *Australian Legendary Tales; Folklore of the Noongahburrahs, as Told to the Piccaninnies*, London: D. Nutt.

McRae, Jane (1998) 'Maori Literature: A Survey', in T. Sturm (ed) *The Oxford History of New Zealand Literature in English*, Auckland: Oxford University Press.

------ (2000) 'Maori Oral Tradition Meets the Book', in P. Griffith, P. Hughes and A. Loney (eds) *A Book in the Hand*, Auckland: Auckland University Press.

Meek, Allan (1990) 'Grey Mythologies', *Antic* VIII: 16-20.

Milne, James (1899) *The Romance of a Pro-Consul: Being the Personal Life and Memoirs of the Right Hon. Sir George Grey, KCB*, London: Chatto and Windus.

Moore, Thomas (1839) *Lallah Rookh*: *An Oriental Romance*, Philadelphia: Lea and Blanchard.

Orbell, Margaret (1995) *The Illustrated Encyclopedia of Maori Myth and Legend*, Christchurch: Canterbury University Press.

Polack, Joshua (1840) *Manners and Customs of the New Zealanders*, London: James Madden.

'Polynesia' (1855), *Dublin University Magazine* 46 (July): 18-37.
Pratt, Mary Louise (1986) 'Fieldwork in Common Places', in J. Clifford (ed) *Writing Culture: The Poetics and Politics of Ethnography*, Berkeley: University of California Press.
------ (1992) *Imperial Eyes: Travel Writing and Transculturation*, London: Routledge.
Rutherford, James (1961) *Sir George Grey – A Study in Colonial Government*, London: Cassell.
Satchell, William, letter to George Grey, date unknown, Grey Letters NZ S3 (1), Grey Collection, Auckland Public Library, Auckland.
------ (1914) *The Greenstone Door*, London: Sidgwick and Jackson.
Schirren, Carl (1856) *Wandersagen der Neuseeländer und der Mauimythos*, Riga: R. Kimmel.
Schoolcraft, Henry Rowe (1851-7) *Historical and Statistical Information Respecting the History, Condition and Prospects of the Indian Tribes of the United States*, Philadelphia: Lippincott, Grambo and Co.
Shortland, Edward (1856) *Traditions and Superstitions of the New Zealanders*, London: Longman, Brown.
'Short Notices' (1857), *New Zealand Quarterly Review*, Jan. 1857.
Simmons, David (1966) 'The Sources of Grey's *Nga Mahi a Nga Tupuna*', *Journal of the Polynesian Society* 75 (2): 177-88.
Snell-Hornby, Mary (1995) *Translation Studies, An Integrated Approach*, 2nd ed, Amsterdam: John Benjamins.
'The Song of Hiawatha by H.W. Longfellow' (1856), *Oxford and Cambridge Magazine* 1856.
Stocking, George (1987) *Victorian Anthropology*, New York: Free Press.
Taylor, Richard (1855) *Te Ika a Maui* [The Fish of Maui], London: Wertheim and Macintosh.
Thornton, Agathe (ed) (1992) *The Story of Maui by Te Rangikaheke*, Christchurch: Canterbury University Press.
Thornton, Robert (1983) *The Elusive Unity of Sir George Grey's Library*, Johannesburg: Witwatersrand University Press.
Venuti, Laurence (1998) *The Scandals of Translation. Towards an Ethics of Difference*, London & New York: Routledge.
Wattie, Nelson (1998) 'Grey, Sir George', in N. Wattie and R. Robinson (eds) *The Oxford Companion to New Zealand Literature*, Auckland: Oxford University Press.
------ (1998) 'Moteatea, Ko nga...', in N. Wattie and R. Robinson (eds) *The Oxford Companion to New Zealand Literature in English*, Auckland: Oxford University Press.
White, John (1874) *Te Rou*, London: Sampson Low.
Yate, William (1835) *An Account of New Zealand*, London: R. Seeley and W. Burnside.

Interpreting as a Tool for Empowerment of the New Zealand Deaf Community*

RACHEL LOCKER MCKEE
Victoria University

Abstract: *Interpreting has been an enabling mechanism in the New Zealand Deaf community's assertion of their identity and agenda as a linguistic minority. This chapter examines sociolinguistic impacts of interpreting and interpreters on the New Zealand Deaf-world[1] over the period 1985 – 2002, in which professional interpreting services have been available. Also considered are ways in which interpreting has the disempowering potential to create an illusion of access or independence that has not been actualised. As one of the first group of sign language interpreters trained in 1985, the writer bases the analysis on her involvement in the development of the profession and her observation of the Deaf/hearing interface since that time. Although written from an interpreter's point of view, the chapter also draws upon Deaf people's accounts of their experiences regarding interpreting.*

> The advent of interpreters marked a radical change for New Zealand Deaf. The Deaf could speak for themselves, the hearing could understand, and they in turn could make themselves understood to the Deaf. It was the beginning of learning about each other.
>
> Hilary McCormack (2001: 22)
> former president of Deaf Association of New Zealand

---

* I thank the following Deaf persons for use of material from unpublished videotaped interviews (cited in the text as Personal Communications): Pam Croskery, Susan Hamilton, Anne Holt, and particularly Tony Walton, who was interviewed more extensively for this paper. The Deaf Association of New Zealand provided statistical information and permission to use it. Pat Dugdale, Megan Mansfield, Tony Walton, Kaye Bird, Wayne Bird, and Wenda Walton provided helpful comments on a draft, for which I am grateful. Apart from direct quotations from identified sources, the views expressed in this chapter and any errors of omission or commission remain the responsibility of the author.

[1] 'Deaf-world' is a term commonly used by Deaf people in many countries (cf. Lane, Hoffmeister and Bahan 1996) to refer to the activities, ways and relationships that comprise the community and culture of the Deaf collective. Deaf-world members

Deaf people the world over are born into a situation of language difference, since the spoken language that surrounds a Deaf child from birth is not automatically absorbed as a mother tongue. Most Deaf[2] people acquire sign language informally from other Deaf people at various stages of their life and come to use it as their primary language because it is easily comprehensible through the eyes where spoken language is not. Without hearing, mastery of speech and lip-reading is elusive for the born-deaf, and even those who do have clear speech usually find it difficult to understand the speech of others. Since Deaf people, unlike immigrants, do not acquire access to the majority language through time and natural exposure, they are in the unique situation of potentially using interpreting services regularly from childhood until death, in a wide range of private and public communication situations. While the role and work of sign language interpreters parallels that of community and conference interpreters in other spoken languages, there exist some significant differences which amplify the role of sign language interpreters within the Deaf community. Whereas immigrant and indigenous minority language groups may achieve cultural and political recognition in society through the majority language, (often through bilingual leaders who have achieved in mainstream education), the Deaf community must access higher education and negotiate their advancement in society through their own language, mediated by interpreters. Sign language interpreters therefore have significant relationships with and impacts upon the individual and collective lives of Deaf people. This chapter examines how the development of interpreting over the last two decades has accompanied the New Zealand Deaf community's emergence from a history of linguistic oppression, educational under-achievement, and the ensuing low self-esteem and social status (cf. Moskovitz and Walton).

An interpreter (an outsider) writing about the impact of interpreting on a minority community risks valorising interpreters as 'liberators of the oppressed'. I take the view that interpreters are not in and of themselves

---

characteristically have strong social bonds with each other based on shared life experiences and use sign language to communicate most comfortably.

[2] The capitalized spelling of 'Deaf' denotes cultural and linguistic identity with other Deaf people, in contrast to the adjective 'deaf', which has the more general meaning of impaired hearing. Since Deaf is used as a label of cultural identity, it is not used in this article to refer generally to deaf children, who may or may not have formed a connection with the Deaf-world. Nor is it used to refer to 'deaf education', which is a construct of hearing society rather than of the Deaf-world.

'change agents', although they have been key participants in and witnesses to the New Zealand Deaf community's change process. This phenomenon is reflected by the World Federation for the Deaf's advocacy for the development of interpreting services as a high priority in achieving the advancement of Deaf people around the world (Bergmann and Scott-Gibson 1995). Deaf and hearing people are enabled to represent themselves and to relate in new ways when language and cultural gaps are mediated (albeit not always perfectly) by interpreters, engendering change in Deaf people's lives at many levels. These changes collectively fit with descriptions of empowerment as upward mobility, self-assertion, and political activity (Jankowski 1997: 6). Such positive developments have necessarily been accompanied by new tensions in the relations between Deaf and hearing people where interpreting has enabled the Deaf to articulate their experiences and in so doing to challenge the existing power imbalance between themselves and the hearing majority. Moreover, the recent presence of interpreters in many settings, such as courts, mental health, education, has illuminated the extent of educational and cultural gaps between deaf and hearing people. This in itself is not empowering, but has in many cases had the effect of focusing attention on how such issues can be addressed in accordance with the expressed needs and desire of Deaf people.

The account presented here focuses specifically on the interplay between interpreting and the Deaf community's 'coming out'. In fact this process has occurred within the wider context of sociocultural changes in the lives of Deaf people which have originated both within and outside New Zealand; these include greater societal tolerance of language and cultural diversity, technological developments that lower barriers to information for the Deaf, educational policy changes, human rights legislation, and importantly, new definitions of the Deaf self and culture that have permeated thinking in the international Deaf-world. These factors arise in this discussion but are not explored to the extent that each would merit in a comprehensive account of changes in the Deaf community over the last two decades.

To understand interpreting as an instrument of empowerment, some historical background about the era before 'interpreter' entered the New Zealand Sign Language (NZSL) lexicon is necessary. The next section will summarize the linguistic and educational situation of Deaf people in New Zealand up until the 1980s, when a process of linguistic de-colonization began within the Deaf community.

1. Historical Background to Language Use in the Deaf Community

People born deaf in New Zealand, as elsewhere, have historically been viewed as individuals suffering from impaired hearing and speech, and concomitant educational and social (and by implication, intellectual) disadvantage. In this paradigm, (known as a pathological or 'audist' view of deafness, cf. Lane 1992), the focus of educational, medical, and social responses to deafness is habilitation or assimilation to hearing sociolinguistic norms, through technological interventions and intensive efforts in speech and aural training. The associated educational approach is 'oralism', which advocates the exclusive use of speech and lip-reading for academic and social communication; this has traditionally been in opposition to 'manualism' – the use of a natural sign language, or signing combined with speech. Although sign language is more physiologically accessible to the eye and brain of a Deaf person, spoken language is comprehensible to hearing society and has therefore been more socially acceptable to them. Oralist education practically excludes Deaf people as teachers and role models, and is generally eschewed by Deaf people as an oppressive and difficult experience, while the use of sign language is positively valued as a 'natural' medium for social interaction and learning (Townshend 1993; Baynton 1996, McKee 2001).

Despite two preceding centuries of sign language being used effectively by Deaf and hearing teachers in European and American deaf schools, sign language was officially banned in New Zealand Schools for the Deaf from their establishment in 1880. This policy was in keeping with the infamous resolution of the 1880 International Congress on Education for the Deaf in Milan, that "...considering the incontestable superiority of speech over signs for restoring deaf-mutes to social life and for giving them greater facility of language... the pure oral method ought to be preferred" (Lane 1984: 394). As Sacks (1989: 25) observes, the educational treatment of Deaf people in Western countries stemming from this period was characteristic of the Victorian tendency to "oppressiveness and conformism, intolerance of minorities, and minority usages of every kind: religious, linguistic and ethnic ... at this time... the 'little nations' and 'little languages' found themselves under pressure to assimilate or conform". In colonial New Zealand, the oralist/assimilationist doctrine was enthusiastically taken up, as reflected in Sir Julius Vogel's letter, in 1879, regarding the proposed method of instruction at the first

New Zealand School for the Deaf at Sumner:

> ... we are convinced that under the French [signing] system there is a far greater danger than under the German [oral] system that deaf mutes should shun the society of those who are not deaf, and thus by congregating together should in many cases increase the natural and inevitable disadvantages arising from their affliction. (Allen 1980: 11)

The prospectus for the new School for the Deaf at Sumner set out two main goals that remained essentially unchanged in deaf education for the following century:[3] to train deaf children in spoken articulation and lip-reading, and to then use this as the means of instruction (*ibid.*). Although the director's 1898 report claimed "that the clearly spoken word was and is our only means of communication and that finger signs have no place and no meaning amongst us", (Appendices to the Journals of the House of Representatives, cited in Collins-Ahlgren 1989: 17) in fact the residential school (and the two others that followed) enabled a Deaf collective to form, where the roots of New Zealand Sign Language (NZSL) took hold and flourished outside the classroom for generations to come. A Deaf woman who attended a residential school during the 1970s describes how NZSL was transmitted informally between children:

> At school we learned signing from the older children and in turn we taught it to the little ones. [In the hostels],we looked after those children in a way that the staff didn't, even though I didn't have a clue how to.... I never thought about what it was at the time: I was passing on the language the same way it had been passed on to me from older ones – it was something that was just done naturally. (Pam Croskery, personal communication)

The chief legacy of the oralist century was that sign language and thus Deaf people themselves were socially stigmatized. The other equally

---

[3] Although most pupils of deaf schools used signs outside the classroom, signs had no official place in deaf education until 1979 when an artificial signing system, Australasian Signed English, was introduced as part of the new 'Total Communication' approach that aimed to improve deaf children's persistently low literacy levels. It was also seen that signing from an early age might reduce psycho-social problems stemming from the frustration of limited communication with parents and family.

oppressive outcome was that the majority of Deaf people in New Zealand – who did not successfully 'acquire facility in speech' – failed to gain an education, or even functional literacy in many cases. Even after the stranglehold of oralism officially loosened from 1979 onwards, hearing ideology still officially controlled deaf children's language use, as illustrated by this Deaf woman's recollection of her primary schooling during the 'Total Communication' era of the 1980s:

> The teacher separated the class into two different groups. One half were using lip-reading and speaking, the other half were the ones who relied on signing... I could do both, but the teacher put me in the signing group and we could carry on signing to each other. But the oral children weren't allowed to sign at all. The teacher wanted the oral kids to be able to communicate with hearing children. Despite that division we still all signed together whenever we were out in the playground ... There were a lot of problems. Children would go home upset that they weren't allowed to sign. (Anne Holt, personal communication)

Oralism was conceived through the world view of adult, hearing authorities; it worked against Deaf people's social orientation to their own kind and gave no credence to deaf children's spontaneous inclination to communicate with their hands and eyes (Monaghan 1996). Signing allowed easier access to information through social communication which enabled deaf children to make some sense of the world; it also forged identity with peers and social ties that generally spanned a lifetime. Bonds formed at school created the networks of the adult Deaf community which in time became formalized into organizations; these have brought together successive generations of Deaf people who identify with each other through a common mode of communication. In this context, NZSL has developed into its present form, but was not acknowledged either inside or outside the Deaf community as a 'language' until the mid 1980s.[4]

---

[4] Although there is scant documentary evidence of how NZSL evolved into a language which is today closely related to British Sign Language (BSL), Collins-Ahlgren's (1989) account of the likely origins of NZSL in the early Schools for the Deaf posits that signs were probably derived from a combination of the children's own creations at school, gestures used for communication with families, as well as BSL signs transmitted by a small but linguistically significant number of Deaf adults and children who were educated overseas and subsequently came into contact with young Deaf people at school and social settings.

In the earliest generations of the New Zealand Deaf community, the values and practices of oralism were hardly challenged. This is reflected today in the 'double-speak' of elderly Deaf people who do not acknowledge themselves as signers (even as they sign), and sometimes express concern about the more fluent and open signing of younger generations.[5] This parallels the experience of other oppressed groups who, for survival or through lack of an articulated alternative, internalize and espouse the belief system of the dominant majority.

Given this history, most Deaf people in New Zealand prior to the 1980s did not publicly identify themselves as 'signers' or signing as a 'language', and therefore did not articulate a demand for interpreting services. Interpreting, however, was a necessary function in their lives. Many first experienced 'interpreting' by peers as a survival strategy at school: those children who could hear, lip-read, or understand better than the others would (at the risk of reprimand), interpret for them on the sly. Della Buzzard was one such 'interpreter' as a student at school in the 1960s:

> At Deaf school, all the pupils signed ... Everyone helped each other by surreptitiously explaining when someone didn't understand. Most of the children couldn't understand what the teacher was saying or what they were supposed to be doing, but I could usually understand quite easily so I was always explaining to the others in sign language what the teacher had said ... I had a big advantage at school because my family was Deaf and so we absorbed a lot of information from talking [*signing*] at home. (Della Buzzard in McKee 2001: 163-164)

In adulthood, using a go-between (usually a family member or other helpful person known to the Deaf) to communicate with hearing people was a familiar experience to Deaf New Zealanders, but the notion of 'interpreter'

---

[5] For example, Kathleen French (educated in the 1920s) says her generation only did 'simple' signing at school, and comments (while signing and speaking): "I might be wrong, but it doesn't seem right to have Deaf people teaching Deaf children. There's far too much signing now. And the Deaf teachers can't hear the children's voice. How do they learn to talk? It's better to have hearing teachers who can hear their voices, and if their speech is bad they can help the children improve. I think it's harder for the children when they grow up if they use signing. I want the best for them... When I'm with my friends at Deaf club we sign a little bit in our old way, but not waving our hands around flat out like the young ones" (Kathleen French, in McKee 2001: 64).

with a defined role and set of skills was not part of the common vernacular. Unlike countries such as the United States and England, New Zealand did not have a robust tradition of voluntary or paid interpreting services supplied by the hearing offspring of Deaf adults, who in New Zealand, had generally internalized their parents' negative or ambivalent perception of signing and were thus not actively encouraged to become proficient signers, or at least not to sign openly in public. This parallels the experience of Maori (the indigeneous people) in New Zealand, whose language was also suppressed by assimilative education policies for more than half of the twentieth century, with the result that several generations of Maori parents discouraged their children from speaking Maori, leading, in turn, to language loss and high levels of cultural alienation in younger generations. For Deaf parents, this pattern has recently begun to change as sign language has become more acceptable, and even intriguing, to hearing society. In such a social climate, Deaf parents are more likely to recognize that signing skills are an asset to their children and themselves both inside and outside the family. Until the mid 1980s, interpreting was usually done on an ad hoc 'bring your own' basis, with the exception of welfare workers for the Deaf who often acted as interpreters when Deaf people came into contact with the law or other serious situations (Dugdale 2001). Interpreting (or 'communication') support was seen as a need stemming from Deaf people's handicap in spoken English, rather than a recognition of their different language status (which, in truth, is probably a perception that still prevails in society).

2. 'Interpreter' Enters the Lexicon of New Zealand Sign Language

The American sign for 'interpreter'[6] was borrowed into New Zealand Sign Language in 1985, when the first professional interpreters were trained. It took some time for the sign, and for the concept of using sign language to talk not only in front of, but *to* hearing people, to take hold in the Deaf community. This section outlines the development of professional interpreting services from the first training course until the present.

---

[6] The sign for interpreter is formed by two inter-linked circles of the thumb and forefinger of each hand (denoting 'connection'), with the right hand swivelling rhythmically from the wrist in an up and down movement (denoting the 'activity' of interpreting/connecting).

From the mid 1970s members of the emerging New Zealand Association of the Deaf became aware that Deaf people abroad, particularly in the United States where oralism had not been quite so omnipotent, had achieved better education and greater political autonomy. A group of American Deaf academics visiting New Zealand in 1981 advised the Deaf Association that interpreting services and sign language research had played a critical role in the advancement of the American Deaf community, and that the training of interpreters and sign language research should be a priority here (*ibid.*: 135). From a long tradition of amateur interpreters (mainly the offspring of Deaf parents), the early professionalization of sign language interpreters in the United States was supported by funding for their training and employment that was made available under legislation passed during the 1960s and 1970s which mandated the rehabilitation rights of people with disabilities (Frishberg 1990); this was motivated initially by the large-scale return of disabled Vietnam veterans and then strengthened by equal access principles achieved by the Civil Rights movement. New Zealand, by contrast, lacked legislated equal access until much later (e.g. the Human Rights Amendment Act of 1992), and the initiative to provide interpreting services always came from the consumer group, the Deaf Association, with support from parents of deaf children and the Department of Social Welfare.[7]

2.1 The First Interpreter Training Course, 1985

In 1985, after nearly a decade of discussion and negotiation, the New Zealand Association of the Deaf mounted a four-month training course in Auckland, funded by the Department of Social Welfare and the charitable J.R. McKenzie Trust. An American interpreter trainer, Dan Levitt, was recruited for the task of teaching this 'crash course', which he did with flair under pioneering conditions. At the time, New Zealand Sign Language (NZSL) was not named as such; it was referred to by Deaf people as 'old signs' (in contrast to the new Signed English system introduced into deaf education in 1979), and was widely regarded as an inferior form of communication that was less than literate, since it was not English. The interpreting course thus began with eight students and one teacher who did not know the language, and no existing 'teaching resources' in

---

[7] For a detailed account of the lead-up to interpreter training, see Chapter 10 in Dugdale 2001.

NZSL – although the first linguistic description of the language was simultaneously being conducted by another American, Marianne Collins-Ahlgren, as a doctoral thesis at Victoria University of Wellington. Her work was vital in demonstrating the integrity of NZSL as a bona fide language with a rich lexicon and the first interpreting course was an important vehicle for beginning to disseminate and apply this new knowledge. (How the course proceeded, in terms of language learning, is described in section 3) At the conclusion of the course, three graduates were employed as full-time interpreters by the Deaf Association in Auckland, Wellington, and Christchurch. While the new interpreters had a great deal yet to learn about their job, ripples from the new perspectives on sign language generated by this new initiative reached perceptions within the Deaf community, deaf education professionals, and the awareness of the general public.

2.2 Development of the Interpreting Profession and Services

Between 1985 and 1992, no further interpreters were trained, and provision of appropriate and adequate services over this period became problematic as the demand for interpreting quickly surpassed supply. The Deaf Association tried to meet needs by short-term contracts with interpreters from Australia and the UK who used related sign languages,[8] but there was still no local expertise available to provide ongoing training. Initiatives by the Deaf Association and the National Foundation for the Deaf, with support from government departments, finally led to the establishment of a two-year undergraduate diploma course at the Auckland Institute of Technology, appropriately positioned in the School of Languages alongside training for spoken language interpreters, and taught by academically and professionally qualified Deaf and hearing lecturers. This course has enrolled approximately 14 students per year, and in the decade since 1992, 52 interpreters have graduated with the Diploma. It is estimated that approximately 45 qualified interpreters are currently working

---

[8] Comparative analyses of NZSL, BSL and Auslan lexicons reveal an overlap of between 62% to 82%, depending upon the criteria used for sampling and determining distinctiveness of signs, (Johnston 2000; McKee and Kennedy, 2000); they are considered by signers to be distinct but mutually intelligible.

in the field,[9] including a few trained in the U.K. (AUT 2002); an unknown number of untrained people (known in the Deaf community as 'Communicators') also undertake paid and unpaid interpreting where qualified interpreters are not available. A professional association of sign language interpreters was formed in 1996, (SLIANZ Inc.), establishing a Code of Ethics and complaints procedure, and working to enhance the profile and professional development of interpreters through conferences, workshops, and mentoring. As the range of contexts in which Deaf people are participating has expanded, and as Deaf and hearing consumers of interpreting services become increasingly sophisticated in their expectations, the need for advanced training of interpreters in more refined and specialized skills (e.g. legal, mental health, academic interpreting) has become apparent (cf. Scott-Gibson 1998). There is a wealth of experience in training overseas in such areas, but local delivery of training opportunities within such a small population and professional pool present some challenges which have yet to be met.

Government recognition of the right to interpreting services (in any language) in New Zealand has developed piecemeal through diverse pieces of legislation, often in a weak form qualified by the wording, 'wherever practicable'. These include the following: 1987 Transport Regulations (driver's license tests: applicant pays for interpreter); 1987 Mäori Language Act (right to interpreter in legal proceedings); 1989 Children Young Persons and Their Families Act ('wherever practicable' for child, parent, or guardian in contact with youth and family services); 1990 NZ Bill of Rights (accused has right to an interpreter in criminal court case); 1992 Mental Health Amendment Act (Compulsory Assessment and Treatment: interpreter for patient 'wherever practicable'); 1994 Health and Disability Commissioner Act (Code of Health & Disability Consumer's Rights: right to interpreter in public healthcare institution 'wherever practicable'); 1993 Electoral Act (right to interpreter assistance to vote); (*Source:* Office of Ethnic Affairs 1995).

Deaf people have benefited somewhat from these provisions in principle, although arrangements for funding and supply of interpreters have not always been straightforward, particularly outside of the main centers here public agencies rarely encounter a Deaf person or an interpreter. Most

---

[9] These interpreters serve a population of NZSL signers of approximately 7,700 according to the 2001 New Zealand Disability Survey, conducted by Statistics New Zealand.

sign language interpreting is arranged through local offices of the Deaf Association, which for the most-part contracts freelance interpreters for interpreting assignments. Between 1996 and 2001 the number of interpreter assignments fulfilled by the Deaf Association annually increased from 5,454 to 5,986. Changes to government funding mechanisms in welfare and health sectors in the early 1990s precipitated a reduction of salaried interpreter positions in the Association's branch welfare offices and a shift to employing freelance interpreters from bulk-funded contracts with government agencies. Although full-time staff interpreters offered the advantages of availability and continuity of service, and of course stability of employment for interpreters, it was uneconomic in many areas with small Deaf populations. There were also disadvantages from clients' perspective regarding lack of choice of interpreters, and some concerns about potential lack of confidentiality if information was shared between interpreters and other staff within Association offices (Scott-Gibson 1998). Reliance on freelance contracts increases individual interpreters' power to determine the kind of work they will accept or not – raising potential problems in coverage of difficult or unpopular jobs – although on the other hand it offers more capacity for the service to match differential interpreter skills and backgrounds to particular assignments.

The following sections of the chapter turn to a closer examination of the impacts of interpreting on the Deaf community, which are grouped into six areas as follows: (1) language status and identity, (2) Deaf political leadership, (3) individual autonomy, (4) participation in education, (5) Deaf-interpreter relationships in the Deaf community, and (6) Deaf relationships with hearing families. I will then discuss how interpreting may create an unwarranted illusion of empowerment or access, and finally comment on the changing role of interpreters in relation to the process of Deaf community empowerment.

3. Language Status and Identity

3.1 Impact of Interpreting on the Status of Sign Language

The first training of sign language interpreters in 1985 (as described above) propelled the profile of NZSL 'out of the Deaf club'[10] and into the public

---

[10] Deaf Clubs (which are formally incorporated 'Deaf Societies') are found in most cities, and are run by and for Deaf people for recreational and social purposes. They usually hold regular social nights, and have committees that organize a range of sport-

arena. Ten years prior to this, the Deaf Association had, on paper, adopted Total Communication (TC) as the 'official' means of communication for Deaf people, in preference to oralism and in the absence of evidence that their own form of signing was in fact a language. Dugdale (2001: 134) notes that the Deaf Association also felt compelled to support educational policy of the time (which was TC) in order to secure government funding. But plans to actually train interpreters sparked considerable debate within the council over the realities of language use in the Deaf community. While some favoured 'modernization' in the form of the Australasian Signed English system, others argued that as most Deaf people could not use it, interpreters must learn to communicate in 'the old' or 'informal' signs, which at that time had not been named as NZSL (*ibid.*: 136).

Arriving from America in 1985, Levitt (the first interpreter trainer) expected to find an indigenous sign language extant in the New Zealand Deaf community that paralleled the well-established language of the American Deaf Community. Aware of Collins-Ahlgren's seminal work in progress describing the language of Deaf New Zealanders, but without recorded evidence of the language to hand, Levitt began by observing Deaf people socializing together at the Auckland Deaf Club. On the basis of what he saw there, he ignored suggestions that he train interpreters in the new Australasian Signed English, which clearly did not correspond to the language in use by Deaf adults. Instead, with the help of dedicated Deaf volunteers he restored Deaf people to visit classes daily, and sent trainees out to Deaf events to immerse them in the vernacular. Levitt and the trainees also carefully recorded descriptions of each sign they discovered in the process. This culminated in the first published lexicon of 'NZSL', as it quickly became known (Levitt 1989). The fact that the book was illustrated by 1,500 photographs of local Deaf people performing their signs had a profound impact on Deaf and hearing people's recognition that they indeed had a language. Deaf historian Pat Dugdale (2001: 140) states that, "One of the greatest benefits from Dan Levitt's appointment was that the question of which language to use – TC or NZSL – was finally decided. (...) While Marianne Collins-Ahlgren proved academically that NZSL was a true language, Levitt proved it in practice... Levitt [worked] on the basis that NZSL was the language to be used and that NZSL came from Deaf people". The extensive involvement of grassroots

---

ing and other social events in the Deaf community.

Deaf people in this unique interpreting course (cum linguistic laboratory) provided practical validation of their language to themselves as well as to the interpreting students.

With the availability of interpreters, Deaf people are now in a position to use NZSL more freely outside of their private social settings (Deaf homes, clubs, sports). Although this was initially – and sometimes still is – uncomfortable for many Deaf people and probably startling for hearing people, exposure to sign language interpreting in many settings has contributed to the gradual acceptance of signing as the rightful language of Deaf people. It is not unusual for Deaf people to request organizers of major political or entertainment events to provide a sign language interpreter, sometimes as much for the value of public awareness of NZSL and Deaf people's right of access, as for the actual benefits of participation in the event.

Whereas sign language had historically been a tool of oppression, from the mid- 1980s the perception of signing has reversed to a sense of pride on the part of Deaf people, and positive interest on the part of the hearing public. This process echoes the experience of many linguistic minorities for whom the language takes on symbolic significance as an embodiment of a distinct cultural identity during their struggle for social recognition. This process has been further underpinned by ongoing linguistic research on NZSL, and the teaching of NZSL as a community language, which is outlined below.

3.2 Development of the Teaching of NZSL: Deaf People as 'Language Experts'

The 'outing' of NZSL following interpreter training led to a boom of general interest in learning NZSL from the late 1980s, creating new professional opportunities for Deaf people as teachers of NZSL. McCormack (2001: p. 21) notes that the 1985 interpreter training course "brought to light the fact that learning sign language is not easy and ... had shown that the Deaf themselves could become teachers...". In 1992, an association of sign language tutors was formed (NZSLTA Inc.), most of whom at that time had no teacher training but some experience and a strong motivation to improve their teaching skills and the quality of NZSL classes available. This was felt to be especially important in preparing a greater number of hearing people to enter interpreter training. The Deaf Association obtained government funding for introductory training workshops for NZSL tutors in 1991 and 1992, and then in 1997 a permanent one-year course in teaching NZSL was established at Victoria University of Wellington. The emerging professionalization of NZSL teaching and its acceptance in academic institutions have opened new doors for Deaf people, who in some cases have acquired a new status as 'experts' in sign language, in a reversal of their community's former image as inept speakers of English. During the 1990s, the number of hearing people enrolling in community education classes in NZSL burgeoned, increasing the pool of potential interpreter trainees, although as yet, still not in sufficient quantity or quality. Males and Mäori, in particular, are still under-represented in the interpreting profession which is a particularly important issue for Mäori, who are over-represented in deafness statistics (National Audiology Centre 2000).

In recent years the interpreters' association and the NZSL teachers' association have convened joint annual conferences, reflecting mutual recognition of an important connection between the development of NZSL teaching and the training of interpreters. Politically, this cooperation represents opportunity for formal dialogue between Deaf professionals and interpreters about common interests, goals and issues.

3.3 Interpreting vis a vis Variation in Language Use and Identity

Where language can be a bonding force in a minority group, its usage can also be a source of tension as a marker of internal boundaries within the community. As well as making Deaf people publicly visible as signers, the provision of interpreting services has, perhaps for the first time, held up a mirror to the range of language use and linguistic identities inside the New Zealand Deaf community. As described earlier, the initiative to start interpreter training in 1985 was a catalyst for impassioned debate in the Deaf Association about the actual and ideal nature of signing used in the community; whilst a decision was made in favour of NZSL, in reality the forms of sign language used between Deaf people, interpreters and hearing people is variable, and this interface itself has stimulated consciousness of language variation and identity issues in some quarters of the Deaf-world.[11]

---

[11] In a similar vein, the training of interpreters (and teaching of NZSL to hearing people) has stimulated discussion and definition of what 'Deaf culture' means in the

Interpreters expect to encounter lexical and grammatical variation in the use of NZSL that stems from age (era of NZSL used), region, and the type of schooling attended – (residential deaf school, deaf unit, or mainstream) – which affects the timing and extent of a Deaf person's exposure to fluent sign language models.[12] Variation of sign language use in interpreted situations can also arise from situational variables (e.g. who the participants are, the nature of the setting) and the Deaf person's degree of bilingualism which condition code switching behaviour – namely the use of 'contact language', in which signs are used with English-like syntax and sense, and/or with voice. Furthermore, some Deaf people describe themselves as 'oral' and do not sign at all, yet in group situations they cannot follow speakers and need an interpreter to relay speech by silent lip-patterns that are more lip-readable (a practice known as 'oral interpreting' in New Zealand, and 'lip-speaking' in the U.K.). It is not uncommon for an NZSL interpreter to find themselves interpreting to a mixed audience of an oral Deaf person and a fluent NZSL signer.

Interpreters, the majority of whom are second language learners of NZSL, try to accommodate this diversity as well as they can. In each interpreting situation, interpreters must assess the Deaf client's style of signing and communication, taking into account factors such as age, fluency, degree of code-mixing with English, and likely level of 'hearing-world' knowledge – and then attempt to provide interpretation in a language style that is acceptable and comprehensible. In doing so, however, they face the possible accusation of linguistic bias, by virtue of

---

NZ context; for instance, the interpreter training programme at Auckland University (formerly Institute) of Technology has established a tradition of holding regular panel evenings at which invited Deaf community members respond to questions about their life experiences and perspectives on various Deaf/hearing cultural issues, for an audience of both Deaf and hearing people. Such events have created a new forum in which familiar experiences are externalised, articulated, and examined – a process which has surely contributed to gradual change in grassroots consciousness of cultural identity and distinctions from hearing people.

[12] Fewer than 10% of Deaf people are 'native' signers in the sense of having acquired NZSL from Deaf parents. The majority acquire NZSL from older peers upon entering a deaf school situation anywhere between the ages of 4 to 17 years. While some deaf people spend their entire childhood in a deaf school which comprises a community of signers, others may only attend for a few years either early or late in their childhood, or not at all. These varying circumstances result in a wide range of sign language fluency and acculturation into the Deaf community among the community of Deaf adults. Currently, most deaf children individually attend mainstream schools, in which they have limited and delayed exposure to NZSL; this will further alter the linguistic profile of future generations of Deaf interpreter users.

their choice of communication style – especially when interpreting for an audience of more than one Deaf person, as frequently happens. Mairian Corker (1997), an orally-raised Deaf person who signs, contends that sign language interpreter training in the U.K. is falsely based upon the translation ideal of two distinct languages rather than on the continuum of contact varieties of signing that exists in the Deaf community. In New Zealand, some older Deaf people do not identify with the NZSL style of younger Deaf generations, upon whom interpreters in training are more likely to model their language use. Deaf people who were educated in mainstream schools and acquired sign language as young adults may be less familiar with NZSL than English, yet still need access to communication through interpreters who use NZSL. It could be argued from these perspectives that the focus on NZSL as a target language in interpreter training and interpreting services amounts to linguistic suppression of Deaf consumers who prefer a literal transliteration of English. An anonymous consumer complaint received by the Deaf Association about the NZSL interpreting at an international conference illustrates such a perspective:

> There were times when we felt "short-changed" – language was too simple and too much left out. We are aware that there was a wide range of needs to meet but it was felt that sometimes interpreters are too judgmental in deciding what we can understand. How can Deaf people increase our knowledge and understanding of English if what we are given is always limited? (Deaf Association 1996)

The writer(s) of this letter express the view that the interpreters' language choice was disempowering to Deaf participants such as themselves. (The reference to simplification is quite possibly based on a common misapprehension about structural differences between NZSL and English). Conversely, interpreters are equally liable to receive unhappy feedback from NZSL- dominant Deaf consumers who feel disempowered when interpreters transliterate in a more English-influenced signing style that is less comprehensible from an NZSL point of view.

Linguistic variation in the Deaf community may pose dilemmas for interpreters in choosing an appropriate and acceptable target language form in particular situations; their choices may also reflect Deaf people's own language characteristics back to them, potentially raising tensions around linguistic and attitudinal boundaries within the community, and questions about the definition and ownership of NZSL.

3.4 Coining New Vocabulary

Interpreters work at the interface between new information and NZSL users in educational, community and political situations. Deaf people's recently expanded sphere of participation in public life means that the lexicon of NZSL is currently being stretched to mediate ideas and experiences that are new to the signing community as a whole. Whereas the Maori speaking world in New Zealand has a Maori Language Commission (Te Taura Whiri) which is officially charged with coining and disseminating new vocabulary, sign language interpreters usually find themselves at the crucible of this process. They have to make split-second decisions about devising equivalents for unfamiliar concepts and so inevitably, signs to translate new concepts are coined between interpreters and Deaf clients, giving interpreters considerable potential influence on the creation of new vocabulary. The creation of academic and technical vocabulary is currently a problematic issue, as Deaf people are now enrolling in tertiary education in unprecedented numbers. In educational settings it is sometimes possible for decisions about new vocabulary to be negotiated in advance, using complementary linguistic strengths of Deaf people and interpreters. This has two notable limitations however: firstly, that students may not always understand the meaning of new terms until after they have been taught in class, and thus cannot always devise adequate translations in advance; secondly, a large proportion of Deaf students entering tertiary education to date have grown up in mainstream schools in which English has been their chief mode of communication and, as such, they may not be fluent users of NZSL. Since interpreters are potentially key agents in the transmission of new coinages to subsequent Deaf clients, they need a heightened awareness that the NZSL community remains the arbiter of the eventual adoption, rejection, or modification of new vocabulary.

4. Impacts of Interpreting on Deaf Political Activity

4.1 Changes in Leadership

The emergence of NZSL as a respectable language and the availability of interpreters through which Deaf people can engage directly with the hearing world has indirectly influenced the characteristics of leadership in

Deaf organisations. Early hearing leadership (the first president of the Deaf Association was the hearing son of Deaf parents) gave way to 'intercultural' leaders in the 1980s (Deaf people who had strong oral/literacy skills which enabled them to negotiate both hearing and Deaf worlds), followed more recently by the emergence of 'grassroots' leaders ('full Deaf' who are NZSL users and identify culturally with the Deaf world).[13] A prominent grassroots leader, Tony Walton (former president of the New Zealand Deaf Sports Association and the Deaf Association of New Zealand) explains the impact of professional interpreters in this change:

> Without interpreters, I couldn't have become president of Deaf Sports and organised the World Games for the Deaf in 1989. It would have been impossible for me to liaise with hearing sports organizations. We knew that Deaf leaders used interpreters in the USA, but we'd never had interpreters in New Zealand. Hearing people would 'communicate' [interpret] for us in meetings, and they always kept us on the sidelines, taking control of what we could say .... It was a similar progression with the Deaf Association: there had been a hearing president until the first interpreter training course which coincided with the election of the first Deaf president. Deaf societies (clubs) in the past didn't need interpreters because they organised activities within the Deaf world, and they still don't use interpreters much. But when national Deaf organizations developed and became more active in lobbying, needing more contact with the hearing world, interpreters became very important for Deaf leaders. Interpreters are also important within the running of the Deaf Association services, to communicate between the Deaf Council and executive and the hearing employees. (Walton, personal communication)

Walton's final sentence indicates that interpreting enables more appropriate power relations between Deaf and hearing people in the running of their own affairs. However, he added that, even with interpreters, hearing and Deaf people in these contexts still frequently talk past each other, with respect to deeper cultural values and goals.

---

[13] The terms 'intercultural' and 'grassroots' leaders are borrowed from Lane, Hoffmeister and Bahan 1996.

4.2 Positioning as a Language Minority, and Participation in the Disability Lobby

Agitating for, and using interpreters in public has been an element in the process of politically aligning the Deaf community with other language and cultural minorities in New Zealand. Although New Zealand lacks coherent government policy or provision for community languages, Deaf people have discovered over the past decade that arguments for equitable access to services, resources, and culturally appropriate education can be made appealingly from a minority language-culture standpoint. Emphasizing parallels with cultural groups (a stance successfully adopted by Deaf empowerment movements overseas, cf. Jankowski 1997; Parasnis 1996) is essential to changing public perception of what deafness is about. A recent media statement by Jennifer Brain, the first Deaf person to be employed as Chief Executive of the Deaf Association, illustrates the explicit positioning of Deaf people as a linguistic-cultural community:

> Deaf children need to have a sense of pride in who they are. Look at other people in other communities – Croatian, Italian, Greek, Maori. They are raised with a sense of their cultural group plus they mix as New Zealanders. They've got both sides and therefore a more positive self-image. Why is it different for Deaf people? (Quoted in Calder 2002: B5)

Parallels between Deaf and Maori situations have been drawn, not only through sharing histories of linguistic suppression, but also both having a claim to indigenous status, as recognised by a government office for the first time in a National Language Policy discussion document which states: "NZSL is a language endemic to New Zealand, that is, it is not used as the first language of any Deaf community outside New Zealand" (Waite 1992: 51). Unfortunately most of this report's practical recommendations were not implemented, although this acknowledgement in principle encouraged the Deaf Association to keep the recognition of NZSL high on its political agenda.[14]

---

[14] At then end of 2002, a Private Members Bill to parliament seeking official recognition of NZSL was due to be drafted under the auspices of the Office for Disability Issues. Scott-Gibson (1998) comments that while legislation may not be the most effective way forward for the Deaf community to achieve language recognition and support services, the detail of such a bill might usefully highlight parallels with the

During the period that the Deaf community has re-framed itself as a cultural-linguistic minority, their increased connection to the general disability movement has also strengthened Deaf advocacy efforts. Deaf delegates to the New Zealand Disabled Person's Assembly since the late 1980s have boosted the profile of Deaf needs within the disability sector, and connected the Deaf-world to the practical gains and strategies of disability advocates from whom they were previously cut off by communication barriers (McCormack 2001). The letter of complaint cited above (section 3.3) in fact came from some of the Deaf participants at an international rehabilitation conference held in New Zealand in 1996, at which one of the keynote speakers was a Deaf political activist from England. Interpreting has enabled Deaf leaders here to increasingly have a voice in shaping government disability policies and funding mechanisms that affect them, particularly in welfare, health and education. Interpreters have played a facilitating role in both avenues of advocacy – Deaf people positioning themselves as a language minority, while also making pragmatic gains through a strategic alliance with the disability sector.

5. Individual Autonomy Impacts

Perhaps the impact of interpreting provision that comes to mind most readily is the potentially increased independence and control available to Deaf individuals through using an interpreter to interact with hearing people (especially 'authorities' and professionals) – compared to partially understanding through speech, lip-reading, or writing, or being spoken for by another. The experience of powerlessness and lack of autonomy expressed in these recollections of two Deaf people who entered the workforce in the 1970s would be less likely to happen today, when interpreters would be an expected part of these scenarios.

> The practical aspects of the [draughting] course were easy enough because it was pretty visual but the theory I was not able to understand at all. There were no interpreters, no support, nothing! A

Maori situation and legal provisions thereof. The parallel with Maori, however, is not completely accurate, since the demand for Maori translation and interpreting is largely socio-political in motivation, and optional rather than absolutely necessary for communication purposes, whereas Deaf people's need for interpreting access is not optional.

month later I got a job. My father came with me to the job interview. I sat there twiddling my thumbs while they had a conversation between themselves. I was applying for the job, so it should have been me they were talking to, not my jolly father! He didn't know what was right or wrong for him to be doing - he was speaking to the employer on my behalf. There were no interpreters. (Susan Hamilton, in McKee 2001)

When I was in 4th form we were sent off to various places for work experience. One August holidays I was sent to a shoe factory that made heavy duty footwear. A week went by, then two and finally the third week. They approached me then and asked me to sign a form – which I realize now was a tax form – asking me to become an employee. I didn't know what it all meant so I just signed it. The following Monday I was up ready to go to school as usual. Mum said to me that I wasn't going to school, I was going to work. 'What!?' I'd never said that I wanted to go to work. I was only in 4th form, I wasn't finished at school. It ended up that I did work there (…) for seven months doing my apprenticeship, and this meant regular training sessions with the manager in his office. He tried his best to help me, but …(t)he communication problem was too difficult and I was fired in the end. (Douglas Croskery, in McKee 2001: 120-121)

The Deaf Association's records show that in the five years between 1996 and 2001, the use of interpreters in three key areas has doubled, indicating that Deaf people in New Zealand now have considerably more autonomy in their dealings with employment, the legal system, social and medical services, public information (e.g., election campaigns, census information, community consultations), recreational and religious activities.

Setting	1996 interpreter bookings	2001 interpreter bookings
Employment	482	957
Legal	288	527
Social & medical services	995	1983

What these figures do not reveal however, is the extent to which Deaf people still do not use interpreters when needed, for reasons of lack of availability (perceived or real), ignorance of, or resistance to, the possibility (more often on the part of hearing parties). Understandably, reluctance to involve a professional stranger in personal matters remains a factor. In a 1997 survey of 100 members of the Wellington Deaf community that investigated a wide spectrum of aspects of their lives, Dugdale (2000) found that a minority of respondents used an interpreter for purposes such as visiting the doctor, participating in staff or supervisory meetings at work, or accessing other public services. The greater proportion reported relying on relatives or friends to help out, or getting by independently with writing, or speech with gestures/mime as needed; these methods were all reported as problematic. In other words, twelve years of the availability of professional interpreters have not entirely surplanted the historical tradition of 'bring a helper' or 'get by on your own'. The minority who did report using interpreters (and being able to secure one when requested) mentioned recurring problems with interpreted situations not proceeding in an enabling way – for example: *"they* [hearing person] *interrupt interpreter"*, *" they talk to the interpreter not me, laugh behind back"*, *"don't allow time for interpreter to explain words"*, *"I don't trust interpreter"*, *"interpreter better* [than writing] *but hard to get one in time"*, *"interpreter booked – but get sign communicator [*untrained interpreter*]"* (*ibid.*: 291-292). A number of Dugdale's respondents reported that they did not use interpreters because they did not know about them. The majority of problems described were located in hearing consumers who don't understand the role of an interpreter, some within interpreting service provision, while others indicate reservations about the characteristics or role of interpreters themselves.

6. Educational Impacts

6.1 Increased Participation in Higher Education

As mentioned previously, the availability of interpreting has led directly to an increase in Deaf people's participation in higher education and vocational training. Whereas this process took off during the 1970s in the U.S.A., in New Zealand up until the late 1980s, only Deaf people who were 'oral successes' could have hoped to enter or succeed in higher education. Even for them, communication in the classroom was a minefield; hence the first Deaf (signing) teacher of the Deaf was not trained until 1992.

A Deaf person who attended mainstream schooling and university without interpreters, and who learned NZSL as a young adult expresses the advantages of using an interpreter, even for a person who expresses himself fluently in spoken English:

> When I didn't know sign language well, I couldn't use an interpreter. But one day, I had a kind of epiphany at a staff meeting. Before this, I'd try to listen and watch the interpreter because I didn't feel confident about the information I got from the interpreter. But that day, I decided to just watch the interpreter. I switched off my hearing aids so I wouldn't be bothered with trying to match speech and signing (because they're different languages and it doesn't work). I just sat there, and suddenly - bingo, it happened. I could understand perfectly what was going on! It was an incredible feeling ... It had such a big impact on me... it made me wish I'd had interpreters at university... in a tutorial or in a lecture where the teacher asks questions and you have to respond. It would have been so good to have an interpreter there to get the feedback of what's going on around the room, because it's impossible to lipread that. The contrast made me realize how much I'd been using the 'jigsaw process' ... and how much I'd missed. It's very tiring because you're just thinking all the time about the different possibilities and which one fits and where it goes, and sometimes you get it wrong. I've been doing that all my life. When I use a sign language interpreter I get 100%. (Alistair Appleby in McKee 2001: 183)

Tertiary education now appears to be the fastest growing area of interpreter use, which will certainly have a long-term impact on the upward mobility of the Deaf community, as it already has elsewhere, such as the USA. In 1996, the Deaf Association booked 908 educational interpreting assignments, and 1194 in 2001; however, because tertiary institutions began to employ freelance interpreters directly during this period, rather than through the Deaf Association, this modest recorded increase does not reflect the actual growth, and anecdotal evidence from interpreters suggests that it may have almost doubled.

Access to higher education has led to wider employment options for a small proportion of the Deaf community, which in turn opens the door to higher incomes and social status. Deaf people with higher education now have greater power to access information and benefits of the hearing world, which has flow-on benefits for the wider Deaf community; for example, a few Deaf professionals are now providing services to their own community in education, welfare, mental health, and policy writing.

6.2 Sharing Power and Perspectives within Deaf Education

The setting and language(s) in which deaf children are schooled are crucial in determining the language and cultural socialization they experience, and the quality of their access to learning. Choices made for deaf children are shaped by cultural beliefs about what it means to be a Deaf person, and as such, are of paramount interest to Deaf adults who view deaf children as their future community. Their interest is also motivated by that knowledge that they, better than anyone else on the scene, understand the journey that Deaf children face in negotiating school, family life, and the hearing world in general. One important outcome of Deaf adults' access to higher education through interpreters is that they have finally achieved some professional influence on the education of deaf children – though not yet enough, if one imagines a parallel with Kura Kaupapa Maori (Maori language medium) schools being run 95% by non-Maori staff.

Deaf input into Deaf education began in the late1980s when the use of interpreters allowed the Deaf community, who were overwhelmingly dissatisfied products of the education system (cf. Townshend 1993, McKee 2001), to express their perspectives in their own language to hearing authorities (often their former teachers). Gradually, recognition of a consumer perspective became formalized in ways such as Deaf representatives on the board of trustees at schools for the Deaf, symbolizing a breakthrough in dialogue with Deaf people about issues of great import to their own community. Previously, both psychological and language barriers to Deaf participation in such forums were high. As a veteran Deaf advocate puts it, "(A)fter 100 years of dictatorial hearing people making decisions for the Deaf, (f)inally, Deaf are now becoming part of the decision-making process. They are speaking out and being listened to about the things that affect their whole lives" (McCormack 2001: 34).

> The status quo has inched from just 'being listened to' towards more genuine power sharing, as Deaf professionals who have completed higher education via interpreters, are now actually providing deaf education services and leadership in some areas. Today, 48 Deaf people are employed in various roles in deaf education, although only 13 of these are qualified teachers (Smith 2003). These Deaf professionals, para-professionals and Deaf parents are increasingly active participants in the planning and delivery of deaf education. Interpreters, as mediators of linguistic and cultural differences, have a pivotal role in facilitating this process. However,

the fact that formal interactions must still be interpreted (i.e. English prevails unquestioned) and that Deaf people remain in the minority in the field tends to maintain their position at the margins rather than at the locus of control.

The participation of Deaf adults in professional roles and the success of deaf children in mainstream schools is still largely contingent on the availability of competent interpreters. Since demand outstrips supply, that condition is not yet being adequately met. There are still Deaf staff and a large number of deaf children in education settings who are stranded for satisfactory communication access (for example, in classroom instruction, or in staff meetings) because the cost (or indeed the very notion) of interpreting is not provided for within mainstream educational structures.[15] This causes stress and constrains the ability of Deaf students and teachers to achieve or contribute to their full potential.

7. Deaf-interpreter Relations within the Deaf World

Whereas interpreters who work between minority and majority language groups are usually cultural members of the minority community, sign language interpreters are by necessity not Deaf, and are thus identified by Deaf people as outsiders and members of the dominant culture (although perhaps less so if they have acquired sign language from Deaf parents). Interpreters are, nevertheless, expected to exhibit the linguistic characteristics of insiders, be insightful about Deaf experiences and ways, and to demonstrate an understanding of Deaf values and goals. The specter of paternalism in Deaf people's interactions with hearing people ensures that some tension is always present in this relationship. This tension is reflected in the emphasis that the sign language interpreting field places (in literature and discussions) on the relationship between interpreters and Deaf people, and in particular, issues of power and control as the inter-

---

[15] The norm for Deaf children in mainstream classrooms is for interpreting and tutoring to be performed by Teacher Aides, who have largely unassessed skills in NZSL and no training in interpreting (McKee 2002).

[16] Some have even asserted that sign language interpreters as a group have experienced a degree of oppression through their affiliation with a downtrodden linguistic minority – manifesting in a lack of recognition of professional status and working conditions. Writing as an interpreter in the American context, Duffy (1987:5) sug-

preting profession and the Deaf community have respectively struggled for recognition.[16] This is illustrated in the following extract from a paper co-presented by a Deaf leader and an interpreter trainer at the World Federation for the Deaf in 1995:

> Sign language interpreters are a crucial mechanism by which deaf individuals obtain equal access and opportunities as the hearing individuals in any society ... [*Around the 1980s*] the number of sign language interpreters all over the world was increasing. However ... some national associations of the deaf and deaf individuals were frightened of this positive development. They were afraid that the new professional group of sign language interpreters would take over and control the life of deaf people. They were opposed to the establishment of independent organizations of sign language interpreters, since they were convinced that all interpreters should be placed under the national associations of the deaf, and that all decision making concerning interpreting issues (training, assessment, working conditions, etc) should only be done by deaf people themselves. Why should this be? In recent years the composition of sign language interpreting has changed. Sign language now has a commercial value, and those who can use it have a marketable skill; those who enter the field of sign language interpreting want an interesting career, and one from which they can earn a reasonable living. Often they have no previous connection whatsoever to the Deaf community... (Bergmann and Scott-Gibson, 1995: 5)

A popular Deaf joke expresses the ambivalence that Deaf people may feel about whose 'team' interpreters are on:

> A party of delegates to a disability conference are travelling together in a small plane. Mid-flight, the pilot announces that one engine has died and the plane is losing altitude. He explains that it will be necessary to off-load some baggage to reduce the weight so they can fly safely. All the luggage is thrown out of the hold, but

---

gests – in direct counterpoint to Deaf people's concerns about the potential power of interpreters – that the lack of recognition and status of interpreters "makes interpreters an attractive prey to the ambitions of the Deaf community in taking control of their destiny. To confront the medical or educational professions at this stage of their liberation would be unreasonable. Interpreters, however, are ripe for the picking". While this may or may not have been a widely representative view of the situation, it does evidence the jostling for position and appropriate relations between Deaf people and interpreters during the emergent stages of Deaf liberation.

the pilot announces that still more weight must go. The paraplegics reluctantly toss out their wheelchairs. Next, the blind passengers nobly fold up their white canes and throw them out. Finally, the Deaf group solemnly agree that their contribution will be to sacrifice their interpreters, and so overboard they go.

This scenario (told to best effect in the company of interpreters) always produces hearty laughter from a Deaf audience and usually interpreters too, both recognizing true sentiments expressed in jest, which can be summarized as follows: (i) Interpreters, though human, are ultimately a tool or an 'adaptive accessory', even analogous to white canes and wheelchairs. Interpreters are visible evidence of 'disabledness', having the double-edged value of being liberating yet also appearing to others as a symbol of dependence, and perhaps being experienced as a burdensome appendage. (ii) Good interpreters are often liked and valued as allies, but given their dominant/oppressor group identity, some Deaf people feel ambivalent about them as participants in their community and in their personal lives. In various renditions of the joke, the final phrase meaning 'throw out the interpreters' may be rendered with gleeful, resolute, or regretful affect, depending on the desired effect on the audience. The joke is a playful reminder to interpreters that as outsiders, their co-existence with the Deaf-world is at the behest of Deaf people. Appreciation of this joke in New Zealand is a sign of the Deaf community's self confidence compared to pre-1985, when the sign and social category 'interpreter' was hardly a part of the lexicon, and those who did provide communication assistance were unlikely to be publicly challenged.

Interpreters are a modern category of hearing participants in the New Zealand Deaf-world. Because they are not Deaf themselves and so do not enter the community through the usual avenues (of which the most important is the shared experience of being Deaf, cf. Higgins 1980), their presence has altered the traditional range of identities, relationships, roles, events, and information found in the Deaf-world. Walton (personal communication) considers that the presence of hearing interpreter trainees and interpreters at social events at the Auckland Deaf Club has brought a wider range of people to interact with, new information and ideas, and potentially useful links to the hearing world. Not all club members might share this positive view.

However, interpreters' social participation in the Deaf community is generally regarded by Deaf people as necessary because non-native signing interpreters (i.e., those without Deaf parents) often lack depth of sign language skills and/or the cultural insight gained from prolonged contact with Deaf people. Walton (personal communication) emphasized the importance of social contact in the Deaf-world for interpreters' contextual knowledge and rapport with Deaf consumers:

> If I get an interpreter that I haven't met socially in the community I feel nervous that they won't have background knowledge of the issues I want to talk about, they won't know my signing style and the kind of vocabulary I use. When someone I don't know arrives to interpret for me, how do I know what their comprehension skills are like?

Such gaps in linguistic or contextual knowledge can show up in both social and working situations and negatively affect outcomes in subtle or obvious ways. For instance, at a work meeting an unfamiliar interpreter could not accurately interpret some of Walton's signing, and as a result he felt that he lost the authority of his role as a manager in the situation. He attributed this breakdown to the interpreter's lack of personal familiarity with him, rather than to a generalized lack of interpreting skills.

On the other side of this coin, interpreters feel tension between the need for distance between their personal and professional lives, and an expectation of social involvement with Deaf people. Interpreters know that social contact after hours is important to improving cultural and linguistic skills, and for maintaining knowledge of current issues and a trustworthy rapport with the community. From a Deaf perspective, it is expected that interpreters will share at least some of their personal lives with Deaf consumers who have no choice but to expose much of their private lives to the interpreters who accompany them on personal business (see Lee 1997 on this point). Declining to spend time in the Deaf social world is not understood by Deaf people as ethical professional distance but as cultural and social distance, implying a lack of reciprocity in sharing time and personal information – valued commodities in the Deaf-world (Mindess 1999). However, it is also realistic to acknowledge that there must be limits to the relationship, since interpreters are not Deaf, and "their professional and personal selves need to have the space to maintain a sense of their own identity ... especially when they spend huge chunks of their waking hours taking on other personas ... in order to do their job properly as interpersonal mediators" (Turner 2001: 31-32).

8. Interpreters as an Element in Deaf–hearing Family Relationships

The dynamics of communication between Deaf people and their families are shaped by the "90-percent rule" – that is, 90 percent of Deaf children have hearing parents, approximately 90 percent of Deaf people marry another Deaf person, and 90 percent of children born to Deaf couples have normal hearing (Schein 1989: 106). This pattern of discontinuity between generations creates unique issues of communication, socialization, identity and emotional connection within Deaf-hearing families. Most hearing parents who give birth to a Deaf child are naturally unprepared for the ensuing linguistic and cultural challenges, because the parents' own experiences do not provide much of the information that would be most relevant to raising their deaf children" (*ibid.*: 107). Some parents take years (sometimes the entire childhood) to develop adequate communication skills and to come to terms with the fact of deafness. Deaf people's identity and role within a hearing family are thus often a product of constrained communication, the family's 'hearing' perspective on deafness, and their fundamentally different experiences of the environment. Many Deaf people eventually develop their strongest emotional ties with Deaf peers, simply because communication is easier and based on a similar physical and cultural orientation to the world. Families in which Deaf adults raise hearing children may face different communication dynamics, in particular, reliance on hearing children to act as interpreters and intermediaries for their parents. The advent of interpreters has had at least a small impact on these traditional patterns, as discussed below.

8.1 Changing Perceptions of a Deaf Family Member

It is a generalization, but fair, to say that many Deaf people have most often played dependent or subordinate roles within their families, typically being spoken for in interactions with the hearing world. They become accustomed to exclusion from much everyday conversation, and cannot always fully reveal their true 'Deaf persona' in a non-signing family where communication is limited to routine or superficial interactions. The possibility of using interpreters outside the family to manage their own affairs increases Deaf people's independence and can also lead to a family's more positive perception of a Deaf family member as a competent individual.

This is illustrated by a Deaf person's description of the impact on her relatives of witnessing her communicating through an interpreter for the first time:

> Linda [*an interpreter and friend*] came over to interpret a phone call to my parents in England. That was a real eye opener for my aunt and uncle, who were staying with me at the time. Whenever Linda visited, she would always interpret all of our conversations, making sure I was included. This made a big impact on my aunt and uncle, and since then, whenever the family is together, they always make more effort than anyone else to make sure that I am not left out. (S. Hamilton, personal communication)

Seeing her communicate fully in her own language through an interpreter, this family realized that the Deaf person could operate in a more sophisticated and 'normal' way than they had previously perceived. This new insight led them to consider how she was usually excluded from family communication, and thus to positively alter their behaviour.

Over the past 17 years, many hearing families have first experienced interpreted communication with their Deaf adult family member and their friends at a formal occasion such as a funeral, wedding, or twenty-first birthday party, where personal anecdotes are likely to be told by Deaf friends. Deaf people and interpreters have told me of many situations where hearing family members were surprised to learn about the 'hidden' personality or exploits of a Deaf person in their Deaf-world context, revealed in stories interpreted from NZSL into English. Listening to Deaf-world views of a Deaf person can be a revelation that alters a family's perception of the Deaf person's character and capabilities, and to reconsider their status within the family. Sadly, this sometimes does not happen until a funeral. A Deaf friend told me of attending a funeral where the parents of a young person who had died were moved to learn for the first time that she was known in the Deaf community for a sharp sense of humour and as a very loyal helper of others, qualities that weren't apparent within the family because they did not have enough depth of communication, and because at home her role was a 'disabled' one. Conversely, at the funeral of a hearing person, a Deaf family member, through an interpreter, expressed in frank detail some unpleasant truths and bitterness about the way the deceased had treated the Deaf person. To the discomfort of everyone present, this occurred only because an interpreter was, unusually, available within the family setting and the Deaf person was determined to seize this rare, if not entirely timely, opportunity to voice their feelings.

Historically, it has been relatively common for Deaf children to be silent victims of abuse in family or residential school situations, abusers being able to exploit their inability to communicate such experiences to outsiders (Dugdale, 2000; Townshend1993). The use of interpreters for the purposes of disclosure, counselling, and legal proceedings is now revealing a backlog of such grievances in the adult Deaf community, and the possibility of deaf children communicating outside the family or the school through interpreters makes abuse slightly more difficult to hide.

Insightful dialogue between hearing parents and their deaf children can now also happen in formalized ways with the presence of interpreters, a good example being a panel of young Deaf people who described their experiences of education at the 2002 Annual General Meeting of the NZ Federation of Parents of Deaf Children. Five of the six panellists (aged 10 – 23 years) made their presentations in NZSL, which were simultaneously interpreted into English; both the content and their chosen manner of delivery articulated a clarity of perspective and sense of identity that was compelling for the audience of parents. One of this group, Amanda Everitt (19), interviewed later in a newspaper article, challenges society's perceptions of her as a Deaf person, asking: "Why do I have to conform? Why can't you accept me as part of another culture?" (Calder, 2002: B5). This kind of cross-cultural, cross-generational dialogue did not happen pre-interpreters, and Deaf people's lack of voice about their experience has contributed to parents' and educators' pursuit of some fruitless and painful paths on their behalf.

8.2 Decreased Dependence and Burden on Hearing Family Members

It can be a relief for hearing families to be able to call on an interpreter. Reliance on family members to interpret can create stress all round, as this Deaf person recalls:

> My grandmother died three years ago and my sister got up and interpreted for me. (Her signing had improved due to a Deaf friend overseas teaching her...) But although it was good that she was interpreting for me, it was a bad time for her because while everyone else was crying she restrained herself – and I had to as well, not wanting to affect my sister. It wasn't until afterwards that we

let it out and just cried. It was terrible of my family to do that; it should have been a stranger interpreting. (Pam Croskery, personal communication)

Yet Deaf people sometimes encounter resentment when they request the presence of an impartial interpreter in important family discussions to do with medical matters or distribution of an estate, for example. A hearing family's sense of intrusion may stem from the fact that an interpreter alters the expected roles that participants can take in the discussion and thus changes the accustomed power balance – usually in the Deaf person's favour. The Deaf person's request for an outsider to facilitate communication may also be felt as implied criticism of the family's ability to communicate with their own kin, or of their 'fair' treatment of them. Interpreters working in such emotionally charged situations need to be alert to these tensions and tread carefully in maintaining their role in a diplomatic fashion.

Since the advent of interpreters, adult children of Deaf adults (who call themselves CODAs) describe a sense of relief not to feel that each time they visit their parents they will be asked to interpret. Knowing that their parents can use professional interpreters to meet their communication needs, they can now have a different kind of relationship.[17] Although many CODAs still interpret for their parents in the course of daily life, Deaf parents now have the option of privacy and adult level communication for adult matters without involving or burdening their children. Through exposure to community discussions about interpreting, Deaf parents are now more aware of the emotional and psychological burden on children who are expected to interpret. Using professional interpreters instead maintains a more appropriate adult-child power balance in the family, in contrast to the broker role that many CODAs assume with precocious maturity (and sometimes undue control) in acting as the buffer between their parents and the hearing world.

9. Interpreting as an Illusion of Access to Participation

Inserting an interpreter into a Deaf-hearing encounter does not necessarily equalize the communication situation, for a myriad of reasons to do

---

[17] These observations are based on numerous personal communications with CODAs.

with cultural experience, education, language difference, and discourse processes. When the presence of an interpreter is assumed to have closed the gap but in fact has not, this maintains a disempowering situation for the Deaf party. The nature of miscommunication and effects of participation constraints that arise in interpreted interactions with Deaf people have been studied in medical settings (e.g. Metzger1999), courtrooms (e.g. Reed, Turner and Taylor 2001), and education settings (e.g. Winston 2001, Johnson 1989), among others. The interplay of contributing variables is complex and beyond the scope of this chapter to detail; however, several common sources of disempowering situations in community interpreting in New Zealand can be identified.

9.1 Interpreter's Situational Knowledge

The first common cause of unsatisfactory (and thus potentially disempowering) interpretation is a mis-match of an interpreter's skills or knowledge – or sometimes personal style – to the situation and/or the clients. This is exacerbated by the short supply of interpreters and a small employment market which results in necessarily generalist coverage; this is exacerbated by a lack of specialized or advanced training available in New Zealand. As Fenton (1991) comments, inadequate interpreting may "cause frustration, resentment and often outright hostility, and rightly so". Sign language interpreters, it must be noted, are expected to undertake a hugely varied range of assignments, since Deaf people at every strata of society require interpreters everywhere that they want to communicate in depth with hearing people, on a lifelong basis. Ozolins (n.d.) notes that expectations of sign language interpreters exceed those for any other group of spoken language interpreters, since they are regularly in the unusual position of having to meet the contextual and linguistic demands of everyday community settings right through to specialized professional meetings, university lectures, and conferences. This means that interpreters commonly find themselves working in a context they know less about than the Deaf and/or hearing participants, and struggling with the language and content of the communication. Particular difficulty arises in the transfer of English technical, academic or political terms and concepts that are not used in NZSL discourse outside of interpreted situations, or perhaps are new to the interpreter even in English. Greater understanding of the importance of preparation, by consumers especially, would make some difference. More diversely and highly educated interpreters are also needed in the profession to meet such challenges.

9.2 Consumers' Unfamiliarity with Interpreted Interaction

Consumers' inexperience or discomfort in managing interpreted communication also typically obstructs effective interaction. This is disempowering for all involved, including the interpreter who is hampered from functioning properly when clients communicate to rather than through her, and when they have little understanding of the communication norms and expectations of the other party in the situation. Seventeen years of consumer education efforts have seen some improvement in this, but interpreters work daily with first-time interpreter users, as well as with experienced consumers of interpreting who persist with the same ineffective behaviours and attitudes. Because of the frequency of their use of interpreters, Deaf people tend to be more au fait with interpreted situations than the hearing party, although sometimes superficially so. It has not been an easy transition for many Deaf people to assume ownership of communication responsibility in interpreted encounters in the way that interpreters would think ideal, after a lifetime of being spoken for and spoken about, and uncertainty about 'the system'. It is clearly still necessary to make more explicit the mechanics of how interpreted communication works (or can go wrong) for both Deaf and hearing consumers of interpreting. With respect to educating Deaf consumers about managing interpreted communication effectively, the best role models are Deaf people who are sophisticated interpreter users who know what works and what doesn't. Walton, for example, comments: "I realize now that presentations are much more successful if you prepare in detail with the interpreter beforehand – it's very important for getting your message across clearly. But some Deaf people don't realize this, and don't bother" (personal communication).

Interpreters, who work in relative isolation and often with people who do not share an understanding of their role, frequently struggle with maintaining ideal role boundaries, and making decisions about facilitating communication in an empowering way. The express reason for tightly circumscribing the interpreter's role as a neutral communication facilitator (rather than spokesperson or advocate) is to vest decision-making power with the two parties who need to communicate with each other. On the other hand, a potentially hidden source of disempowerment for consumers is when interpreters take an overly mechanistic or rigid view of their role in situations that require some communication 'trouble-shooting'. In a British study that explored sign language interpreters' application of what they understood as 'ethics', Tate and Turner (1997) found that interpreters sometimes limit effective communication by taking an inappropriately constrained role – for example, failing to intervene to clarify an obvious language or culture-based misunderstanding, or interpreting confidentiality to mean withholding knowledge of potential physical harm to a client, counter to common-sense about the person's welfare. Such choices are not ultimately empowering, and if interpreters feel they are breaching their role to deal with such contingencies sensibly, this works against reaching good communication outcomes. Debate continues to rumble about whether or not, and the extent to which, interpreters should expand their 'prescribed' role to act as cultural facilitators or information brokers in instances where the Deaf participant is clearly disadvantaged by more than just language difference.[18] Tate and Turner suggest that, given the variability in practice, there may be a need to formalize a 'non-mechanistic' understanding of how ethical and role considerations might apply in problematic situations. The participation of interpreting consumers in discussion of their experiences in relation to principles would bring important insights to this.

9.4 Gaps Beyond the Scope of Language Transfer

Interpreters may be called upon to bridge gaps that are patently wider than just language, i.e., in situations where there are significant differences between the hearing and Deaf clients in terms of literacy, situational knowledge, power status, cultural experience, and familiarity with the

---

[18] Speaking from outside the profession as a CODA, Forman (2002) criticizes interpreters for rejecting the 'helper' model, claiming that NZSL interpreters actually disempower Deaf people in medical situations in particular, in which, he argues, the interpreter should intervene as "a companion and perhaps advisor" where necessary to ensure a good outcome from the Deaf person's encounter with an unfamiliar health system and new information. While they certainly recognise the sometimes unsatisfactory scenarios that can result from neutrally mediated communication, most interpreters and probably many Deaf people would view this recommendation as potentially paternalistic and counterproductive to developing greater autonomy in the long run.

structure of the communication event. For instance, interpreters may be expected to facilitate complex communication (such as in a legal or medical situation) with a Deaf client who has limited language skills due to childhood experience of language deprivation and minimal education. In such cases, the type of conceptual communication that is possible, or needed, may be beyond the interpreter's expertise,[19] while the exact nature of the problem is not apparent to the hearing party. This can lead to serious communication breakdown or an incorrect assumption that the interpreter has achieved understanding, sometimes with an escalating chain of consequences.

Gaps deeper than language difference arise in other circumstances too: whereas Deaf people were previously excluded from events such as vocational training, public meetings, and political consultations, they now attend these events expecting to fully access the face-to-face talk via an interpreter. However, printed information is usually heavily embedded in such contexts, with discussion often being structured around written materials. This can present three important barriers to inclusion, even in the presence of an interpreter. Firstly, many of the first generation of Deaf people to pioneer participation in such forums, through the circumstances of their language and educational histories, may be on a different footing from their hearing counterparts with regard to literacy and general background knowledge, which can present invisible comprehension gaps that an interpreter cannot easily bridge on the spot. Even if literacy itself is not an issue in such situations, Deaf participants face the physical constraint of trying to visually follow references to written materials at the same time as watching the interpreter constantly; some information in one modality or the other is inevitably lost.

Secondly, the structure of communication events – the unspoken 'script' for how interaction (such as a job interview) proceeds – may be automatically understood by hearing participants but unfamiliar to Deaf participants. Thirdly, simultaneous interpreting (the most frequently used mode of sign language interpreting) can give the illusion of instant access to a stream of information, when in fact, simultaneous interpretation of

---

[19] In such situations, a Deaf person who has a depth of cultural and linguistic experience with the whole spectrum of deaf people can be called upon to act as relay interpreter, breaking down concepts to a more 'non-verbal' form that may be more comprehensible to the client than standard NZSL. A small number of interpreters, particularly CODAs, may also have such specialised skills.

talk in groups creates the frustration of being one speaking turn behind, making it difficult to contribute with confidence of being timely. This dynamic has not and will not change over time, except where participants recognize that interpreted interaction is not a 'natural' process and take deliberate steps to facilitate Deaf participation differently, taking account of interpreting lag time and visual strategies for turn-taking.

10. The Changing Role of Interpreters in Relation to Deaf Empowerment

During the first years of professional interpreting services in New Zealand neither the grassroots Deaf community nor the hearing people with whom they interacted perceived interpreters as a necessity or as a right. Deaf people were accustomed to incomplete and unequal communication in the hearing world, and hearing people generally didn't expect that anything more was possible. In this context, the newly trained interpreters consciously took on responsibility as change agents in order to achieve public understanding of Deaf people's right to use interpreters, and also to pave the way to interpreted encounters with some cross-cultural awareness. This ally or facilitator role supported early progress in the Deaf community to the point where it is now appropriate for interpreters to step aside from it. As Walton commented (Personal Communication, 2002), "Now with interpreters, Deaf can do their own P.R. and answer hearing people's questions themselves – it's fantastic! Deaf people are much more confident in the way they present themselves and take the lead. Interpreting has made this possible".[20] Although interpreters in the course of their

---

[20] Tony Walton's story (2002) is a good encapsulation of the transformation of opportunity that has evolved in Deaf lives since the 1980s. By trade, Walton was a cabinet-maker who by dint of skills and personality achieved senior foreman's status at his company, while also excelling as a participant and organizer of Deaf sports, becoming the president of the NZ Deaf Sports Association soon after the training of the first interpreters (as explained in his account earlier in this chapter). As well as intelligence and exceptional leadership qualities, Walton has the typical characteristics of a core member of the Deaf community: he attended a residential deaf school, uses NZSL as his primary language, identifies as culturally Deaf, does not have very intelligible speech, and lacked school qualifications. These features no doubt constrained his vocational and higher education opportunities in the hearing world. However, with the political savvy gained through years of sports leadership, Walton moved on, a decade later, to head the Deaf Association of NZ, a more complex advocacy and service organisation that intersects significantly with hearing-world

work continue to witness barriers, injustices and ignorance , there is now more opportunity to work within the interpreting role alongside Deaf leaders who are addressing these problems on their own terms.

Reflecting on the development of the interpreting profession in the United States, Lou Fant (1990) advises that interpreters must "learn to walk the narrow path between advocacy as individuals, and objectivity as professional interpreters". He contends that while interpreters naturally feel a commitment to the Deaf community's interests, retaining public neutrality on issues affecting that community is necessary for interpreters to be trustworthy for both hearing and Deaf parties. This implies that the interpreting profession should maintain some autonomy from Deaf political organizations and causes, for example considering carefully whether, or how, it is appropriate for an interpreters' organization or its members to comment on issues such as the Deaf community's right to a phone relay service, or controversy surrounding cochlear implants in Deaf children, since interpreters with professional distance will be needed as a communication bridge in any such debates.

Interpreters are content when they can function virtually unnoticed, which usually indicates that their clients are communicating successfully with each other – a form of consumer empowerment that interpreters generally aspire to. In a book titled *Deaf Empowerment* Kathy Jankowski (1997), a Deaf American sociologist, analyses the rhetoric and communication strategies that emerged in the successful 'Deaf President Now' uprising at Gallaudet University in 1989, which became a focal event in the empowerment of Deaf people everywhere. It is telling that interpreters as participants, and interpreted communication as a phenomenon, do not figure in the analysis of how events unfolded and aims were achieved, although interpreters were present at every interface between the Deaf protestors and their opponents, and played a crucial and visible role in Deaf leaders' articulation of their cause in the public media. The implication

---

bureaucracy. Walton's work in these two leadership roles entailed frequent use of interpreters, and also exposure to accomplished Deaf role models overseas (and their interpreters). In recent years, Walton left his trade to take up a white-collar position as a residential social worker at a deaf school. In the wake of a Deaf 'cultural renaissance' and a policy shift to bilingual education, his cultural and language skills and his mana (prestige) as a Deaf role model had become sought after. Walton is now one of a handful of Deaf people in a managerial position within deaf education, in which he often observes, with frustration, the cross-cultural complexities of interpreted interaction across differences of power and hearing status.

is that within the sociocultural environment which exists in this (middle-class) Deaf milieu in the United States, effective and on-tap interpreting goes without saying. The model of Deaf empowerment represented by Jankowski implicitly ascribes to interpreters and interpreted communication the invisibility and insignificance of a window through which negotiation with the hearing world passes directly – as indeed is also the norm in the case of spoken language interpreters who interpret political negotiations and media appearances of world politicians. What this example points to in relation to Deaf empowerment is that interpreters – or the right of access to participation in the hearing-world, which they represent – assume a different level of importance or profile once they are available as of right, and reliably competent at a certain standard. Their existence can then remain unquestionably in the background as the Deaf community pursue their own agenda. The level of politicized self-determination of the American Deaf community contrasts with Deaf communities in many other countries, including New Zealand, which are still experiencing more freshly the possibilities and impacts of forging a bridge to the hearing world through interpreters.

11. Conclusion

For the more empowered members of the Deaf community in New Zealand, utilizing an interpreter as a tool for conducting their own affairs can be seen as a statement of confident linguistic identity and personal autonomy. For Deaf people who continue to lead less empowered lives, interpreters simply increase the amount of information available in some of the stressful circumstances they face, reducing (but not always eliminating) barriers to communication, and perhaps offering independence from other potential 'helpers'.

This article has identified some overall impacts of the training, use, and visibility of sign language interpreters in the New Zealand context. These outcomes are wide-ranging and are intertwined with the emergence of sign language as a marker of the Deaf community's private and public identity; they reach beyond the improvement of communication in individual situations to subtle alterations in the social fabric of Deaf community life – such as altering the face of Deaf political leadership, and facilitating the articulation of a linguistic and cultural identity – as well as the more palpable opening up of opportunities to participate in hearing world contexts. Interpreting has opened doors to fairer access to higher education, justice, health and welfare systems at a personal level; at a political level, the presence of interpreters has enabled self-representation about policies and services affecting the Deaf community, and supported Deaf people's entry to professional participation in the education of deaf children. Less directly, the activities of training interpreters and the visible use of NZSL in interpreted situations have raised the public profile of NZSL as a language worthy of study and respect, which in turn has generated new roles for Deaf people as teachers and experts on NZSL.

As the interpreting profession and the Deaf community move forward together into a new phase of maturity (perhaps akin to adolescence), it will be important to foster co-operation in the following areas: (i) strengthening Deaf participation in the interpreting field - in activities such as interpreter training, defining appropriate role and ethical behaviour, consumer feedback about interpreter performance, and the management of service provision; (ii) research on interpreting (who determines the important research questions, and who conducts the research?); (iii) raising the skills and the general education level of interpreters, through research, training and assessment of expertise, rather than through 'experience' (which is no guarantee of specialist skills); and finally, (iv), jointly taking stock of progress and of the impacts that interpreters and the Deaf community are having on each other, for better or worse.

Speaking a year before the 1992 establishment of a professional diploma course in sign language interpreting, Fenton (1991) suggested a parallel between the forthcoming era of wider access to the world via interpreters, and a "golden period in Deaf history" at the end of the eighteenth century when Deaf people in Europe and America gained formal education in their own sign languages and developed a sophisticated cultural and political life. The peaks of achievement in any historical period always conceal other less exemplary layers of life, and this is undoubtedly as true of the 'golden period' as it is of the current emergence of the New Zealand Deaf community. Nevertheless, interpreting – or rather, the liberation of 'voice' that ideally results from it - offers a potentially powerful tool for change (for the better) in the Deaf-world.

References

Allen, A. B. (1980) *They Hear with the Eye: A Centennial History of the Sumner School for Deaf Children*, Wellington: Schools Publications Branch, Department of Education.

Auckland University of Technology (2002) Unpublished information paper on interpreter training at AUT.

Baynton, Douglas (1996) *Forbidden Signs: American Culture and the Campaign Against Sign Language*, Chicago: Chicago University Press.

Bergmann, Asger and Liz Scott-Gibson (1995) 'Professional Interpreting: A Prerequisite for Full Access and Participation – From the Consumer/Trainer's View and the Interpreter's View', Unpublished plenary lecture presented at the *12th World Congress of the World Federation of the Deaf, Vienna, Austria*, July 13th 1995.

Calder, Peter (2002) 'Silent Revolution' *NZ Weekend Herald*, May 25-26, 2002, B5.

Collins-Ahlgren, Marianne (1989) *Aspects of New Zealand Sign Language*, PhD thesis, Victoria: University of Wellington.

Corker, Mairian (1997) 'Deaf People and Interpreting – The Struggle in Language', *Deaf Worlds* 13 (3) *Special Issue: Sign Language Interpreting – in Search of the New Breed*: 13-20.

Deaf Association of New Zealand (1996) Unpublished letter to Interpreting Systems Manager, 26.9.96.

Dugdale, Patricia (2000) *Being Deaf in New Zealand: A Case Study of the Wellington Deaf Community*, Unpublished doctoral thesis, Victoria: University of Wellington.

------ (2001) *Talking Hands, Listening Eyes: The History of the Deaf Association of New Zealand*, Auckland: The Deaf Association of New Zealand Inc..

Duffy, J. Trey (1987) 'The Sharing of Power', Paper presented at the 10th National Registry of Interpreters for the Deaf Convention, St. Paul, Minnesota, August 3-7, 1987.

Fant, Lou (1990) *Silver Threads: A Personal Look at the First Twenty-five Years of the Registry of Interpreters for the Deaf*, Silver Spring, Maryland: RID Publications.

Fenton, Sabine (1991) 'Interpreting: Bringing Two Worlds Together', Paper presented at the Deaf View Conference, Auckland, April 1991.

Forman, Wayne (2002) 'The Bias of Neutrality: The Role of Interpreters in Healthcare Settings', *Vision: A Journal of Nursing*, 8 (14): 20–22.

Frishberg, Nancy (1990) *Interpreting: An Introduction*, Silverspring, Maryland: Registry of Interpreters for the Deaf, Inc..

Harrington, Frank (1997) 'Agencies, Interpreters and the Deaf Community: Working in Harmony', *Deaf Worlds 13 (3) Special Issue: Sign Language Interpreting – in Search of the New Breed*: 3-8.

Higgins, Paul (1980) *Outsiders in a Hearing World: The Sociology of Deafness*, Beverly Hills: Sage Publications.
Jankowski, Katharine A. (1997) *Deaf Empowerment: Emergence, Struggle, & Rhetoric*, Washington D.C.: Gallaudet University Press.
Johnson, Kristen (1989) *Miscommunication Between Hearing and Deaf Participants Via the Interpreter in A University Classroom*, Unpublished Masters Thesis, University of California, Los Angeles.
Johnston, Trevor (2000) 'BSL, Auslan and NZSL: Three Signed Languages or One?', Paper presented at the 7th International Conference on Theoretical Issues in Sign Language Research (TISLR), Amsterdam, July 2000.
Lane, Harlan (1984) *When the Mind Hears: A History of the Deaf*, New York: Random House.
------ (1992) *The Mask of Benevolence: Disabling the Deaf Community*, New York: Alfred A. Knopf Publishers.
------, Robert Hoffmeister and Ben Bahan (1996) *A Journey into the Deaf World*, San Diego: Dawn Sign Press.
Lee, Robert (1997) 'Roles, Models, and World Views', *Deaf Worlds* 13 (3) *Special Issue: Sign Language Interpreting – in Search of the New Breed*: 40-44.
Levitt, Dan (1985) *Introduction to New Zealand Sign Language*, Auckland: National Foundation for the Deaf.
McCormack, Hilary (2001) 'Between Two Worlds – Breaking the Sound Barrier' (Interviewed and edited by Peter Beatson) *New Zealand Journal of Disability Studies* 8, 3-35.
McKee, Rachel (2001) *People of the Eye: Stories from the Deaf World*, Wellington: Bridget Williams Books.
------ (2002) 'Teacher Aides of High and Very High Needs Deaf Students: A Summary of Findings from the Project "Communication Access And Learning Outcomes for Deaf Learners in the Mainstream"', unpublished paper, Deaf Studies Research Unit, Victoria: University of Wellington.
McKee, David and Graeme Kennedy (2000) 'Lexical Comparison of Signs from American, Australian, and New Zealand Sign Languages', in K. Emmorey and H. Lane (eds) *The Signs of Language Revisited*, London: Lawrence Erlbaum.
Metzger, Melanie (1999) *Sign Language Interpreting: Deconstructing the Myth of Neutrality*, Washington D.C.: Gallaudet University Press.
Mindess, Anna (1999) *Reading Between the Signs: Intercultural Communication for Sign Language Interpreters*, Yarmouth, Maine: Intercultural Press.
Monaghan, Leila (1996) *Signing, Oralism, and the Development of the New Zealand Deaf Community: An Ethnography and History of Language Ideologies*, unpublished PhD Dissertation, University of California, Los Angeles.
Moskovitz, D. and T. Walton (1990) 'New Zealand Sign Language and Deaf

Mana', unpublished paper presented at the Second National Community Languages and ESOL Conference, Wellington.
National Audiology Centre (2000) *New Zealand Deafness Notification Data, January – December 2000*, Auckland.
Office of Ethnic Affairs (1995) *Let's Talk: Guidelines for Government Agencies Hiring Interpreters*, Wellington: Department of Internal Affairs.
Ozolins, Uldis (no date, c. 1999) 'Sign Language Interpreting: Like All Other Interpreting? Like Some Other Interpreting? Like No Other Interpreting?', Unpublished paper, Centre for Research & Development in Interpreting and Translating, Deakin University, Melbourne.
Parasnis, I. (ed) (1996) *Cultural and Language Diversity and the Deaf Experience*, Cambridge: Cambridge University Press.
Ramsey, C. (1997) *Deaf Children in Public Schools: Placement, Context, and Consequences*, Washington DC: Gallaudet University Press.
Reed, Maureen, Graham Turner and Caroline Taylor (2001) 'Working Paper on Access to Justice for Deaf People', in F. Harrington and G. Turner (eds) *Interpreting Interpreting: Studies and Reflections on Sign Language Interpreting*, Gloucestershire: Douglas McLean, 168-216.
Schein, J. (1989) *At Home Among Strangers: Exploring the Deaf Community in the United States*, Washington DC: Gallaudet University Press.
Scott-Gibson, Liz (1998) *Review of Sign Language Interpreting Services, Summary Report*, unpublished paper, Deaf Association of New Zealand.
Smith, Eileen (2003, forthcoming) *Deaf Ways: Literacy Teaching Strategies of Deaf Teachers*, Unpublished Masters Thesis, Victoria University of Wellington.
Sacks, Oliver (1989) *Seeing Voices*, Berkeley/Los Angeles: University of California Press.
Tate, Granville and Graham Turner (1997) 'The Code and the Culture: Sign Language Interpreting – in Search of the New Breed's Ethics', *Deaf Worlds* 13 (3) *Special Issue: Sign Language Interpreting – in Search of the New Breed*: 27-34.
Townshend, Suzan (1993) 'The Hands just Have to Move': Deaf Education in New Zealand – A Perspective from the Deaf Community, Unpublished masters Thesis, Massey University, Palmerston North.
Turner, Graham (2001) 'Rights and Responsibilities: The Relationship between Deaf People and Interpreters', in F. Harrington and G. Turner (eds) *Interpreting Interpreting: Studies and Reflections on Sign Language Interpreting*, Gloucestershire: Douglas McLean, 22-33.
Waite, Jeffrey (1992) *Aoteareo: Speaking for Ourselves – Part B: The Issues*, Ministry of Education, Wellington.
Walton, Tony (2002) Personal Communication (by interview with the author), Auckland: New Zealand
Winston, E. (2001) 'Visual Inaccessibility – The Elephant (Blocking the View) in Interpreted Education', *Odyssey: New Directions in Deaf Education, Winter/Spring*, 5-7.

New Caledonia

Background : New Caledonia was settled by both Britain and France during the first half of the nineteenth century. The island was made a French possession in 1853 and became an Overseas Territory of France in 1956.
Land Area : 19 060 sq km
Capital : Noumea
Population : 207 858; 42.5% Melanesian. 37.1% European
Languages : French (official), 33 Melanesian and Polynesian Dialects

Translation in New Caledonia
Writing (in) the Language of the Other
The "Red Virgin", the Missionary, and the Ethnographer

RAYLENE RAMSAY
The University of Auckland

>Abstract. *This study turns on the centrality of translation in New Caledonian culture. It traces the interaction between two cultures, European and Kanak, through the translation work of major figures: the translation of Kanak tales at the height of the colonial enterprise by Louise Michel, deportée from the Paris Commune; the pioneering work of the first French Protestant missionary, Maurice Leenhardt in the early twentieth century, and the contemporary work on texts in Paicî and Cemuhi by the ethnographer Alban Bensa. More than half of the texts of indigenous Kanak oral literature exist only in translation. In its turn, the translation of these texts has influenced the emergence of literature by a settler population of European origin. We follow the contributions made by Michel, Leenhardt and Bensa to a translated and hybrid culture considering the distinctive value and particular character of the 'third spaces' created by very different modes of translation.*

Translation is central to the history and literature of Kanaky/New Caledonia. This article examines the contribution of three of its most significant translators against the background of the colonial and missionary histories and the postcolonial contexts that shaped their work. As François Bogliolo puts it, a place of transportation became a place of intersections, the stage of one world for another (Bogliolo: 2000). No other literature in the French speaking world, he claims, has used translation so extensively. Translation constructed new and exotic ethnographic discourses. It served as a mediator not only between languages considered in a hierarchical relation but also between two literary worlds. Kanak[1] [Melanesian] oral

---

All translations are my own unless otherwise indicated.

[1] The earliest term used for the indigenous peoples was the word Kanak (or Kanack) signifying 'man', borrowed from Hawaian. In the nineteenth-century the term was generalized and given a French spelling, 'canaque', most often used with pejorative connotations, coming to designate, after settlement, the uncivilized Melanesian. (Boulay 2002: 52-56). The contemporary re-use of Kanak was an outcome of the

literature was translated into written medium and more than half of the oral literature available today in print form is in translation. Written French, it can be argued, served the conservation and dissemination of a culture in translation, a literature haunted by the ghosts of its indigenous informants.

The translations of Louise Michel (1830-1905), Maurice Leenhardt (1878-1954), and the contemporary ethnographer, Alban Bensa, all produce new, mixed and different spaces out of the encounter between Kanak and European cultures. This study considers the usefulness of Homi Bhabha's theoretical concepts of 'hybridity' and 'third space', and the associated idea of 'untranslatability', elaborated within subaltern studies, for evaluating these texts in translation that have helped to form the substratum of an emerging Caledonian literature. As Douglas Robinson (1997: 27) points out, for Bhabha, culture is not 'untranslatable' because each culture is unique but because, particularly in migrant cultures or border areas, it is mixed and overflows the artificial boundaries that nationalisms set up to contain it. Do the very particular 'third spaces' created by this New Caledonian literature in translation, seeking to bridge the gaps but also to take account of the power imbalances between languages and cultures and to 'move the center', begin to transcend nationalisms and to create a dialogue of equals? At another level, is the space of articulation of cultural difference created a space of change and incompleteness, of assimilation of opposites, akin to Bhabha's postmodern hybridity? Is it in any way the "Third Space of colonial or postcolonial provenance", the "split-space of enunciation" with "productive capacities", that, according to Bhabha, "may open the way to conceptualizing an *inter*national culture, based not on the exoticism of multiculturalism or the *diversity* of cultures, but on the articulation and inscription of culture's *hybridity*". This is *inter* or "in-between" space that "carries the burden of the meaning of culture" (Bhabha 1994: 38).

---

independence movement in the nineteen-eighties. The anglicized spelling of 'Kanak', linked to the founding ancestor and new state, Kanaké/Kanaky and formalized in the name of the FNLKS (Front National de Libération Kanak et Socialiste) connoted a political linguistic act. In opposition to the grammar rules of French, Kanak was to be invariable in number and gender, although some dictionaries, including *Le Petit Robert*, give the noun in the plural a plural marker (les Kanaks). I have retained forms with gender and number agreement where these are used in a quotation.

1. New Caledonian Contexts

The translation sites examined are, however, not all contemporary but from different periods of New Caledonian post contact history that dates from the visits of Cook in 1774 and d'Entrecasteaux in 1842. They include texts from different geographical areas of an archipelago become an administrative unit that includes the main island (Grande Terre, about three hundred miles long and fifty miles wide), the Loyalty Islands – Maré, Lifou, and Ouvéa and Belep, – the Isle of Pines and some very small islands to the South and to the North. We are concerned with the forms of mixing effected by translation as New Caledonia continues today to be characterized by two radically separate communities and histories, Kanak and European.

In contrast to postcolonial diasporas of the kind Homi Bhabha and Gayatri Spivak write of from North America, what is central to any contemporary account of New Caledonian history is the survival within a dominant French settler culture of an indigenous culture based on land-use rights and custom areas which, at 43% of the population, is close to being a majority. New Caledonian history is marked by the effects of a Melanesian settlement dating back two thousand years before Christ (around 1,400) and its oral histories. But it is characterized in the more recent past particularly by the radical impact of a century and a half of colonialism and written administrative French culture on a number of communities of quite unequal power – Kanak, convict, communard, free settler, indentured workers from China, Japan, Indochina, Indonesia, Vanuatu and more recently immigrants from the Polynesian islands to the North, the French Territory of Wallis-et-Futuna.

The indigenous tribal groupings (language communities and custom areas) were connected by marriage alliances and trade and divided by competition for land and status. Local varieties of a general 'custom' in which gift and counter-gift as symbolic exchange and creation of reciprocal ties and obligations, chiefly prestige, and retaliation for unmet obligations functioned to maintain both the commonalities and the conflicts.

In the colonial period, the Kanak were largely excluded from the European enterprise of development, exclusion given form by the notorious *Code de l'Indigénat* ('Native Law'). This remained in force until 1945 when the Melanesians acquired citizenship at the end of a war in which they participated actively as New Caledonia rallied to De Gaulle and became a major allied base in the Pacific. During the period of colonial expansion, indigenous groups were dispossessed of their customary lands and pushed back into the narrow valleys of the North and East coast lands belonging to others. These were designated as reserves that Kanak, now subject to new 'chiefs' appointed by the administration, could not leave without authorization. While this land dispossession limited mixing with the European world of 'Nouméa la blanche', it forced cohabitation on several traditionally separate Kanak groups, a process later encouraged by the political leader of the Independence movement, Jean-Marie Tjibaou, in the forming of a new and authentic Kanak person and a Kanak nation.

In another kind of mixing, Christianity was a further major new influence, forming but also to a considerable extent, formed by its Melanesian contexts. The 22,000 French convicts in the environs of Nouméa dependent on the all-powerful penitentiary authority constituted a further example of groups dominated and restricted, separated, in the colonial period. Assisted settlers from France, grouped in independent land concessions, most often in areas linked only to a distant Nouméa rather than to each other (Koné and Voh); the equally isolated farmer colonists disposing of a small capital, solicited by Governor Feillet in the last decade of the century, growing coffee in a largely failed plan for agricultural colonization; the landless liberated convicts who roamed the colony; the larger entrepreneurial landowners and run-holders such as the Irish-Australian, Paddon; and the administrators in Nouméa all constituted very different kinds of 'free' settler groups. Mixed race children were identified as either Kanak or European not by skin tone but by their upbringing *en tribu* or in the European community.

It is evident that translation in New Caledonia in the colonial period with its frames of irreducible difference between European and indigene, or indeed between convict and free settler might infringe taboo. It could erase boundaries constructed for political or ideological purpose or create suspect third spaces, to the extent the mixing it introduces is one of perceived contamination – a European 'encanaqué' (who 'goes native') or a Kanak who shares the forbidden secrets of a local patrimony with the outsider.

Theory, notes Alex Calder *et al.*, has taught us to scan the texts (and the translations) that emerged in the first contact period between Europe and the Pacific to detect 'eurocentric assumptions' and 'imperial designs'. The Pacific journals of explorers, scientists, missionaries and others most often conceal "the propensity to project European fears, hopes, or expectations in the place of the native" (1999: 15). The very debate on noble (natural or Edenic) savages and ignoble barbaric people in a state of non-civility, it is argued, derived less from a concern with knowing the other than a reflection on the nature of Europeans in a civil society. Was European civilization enlightened or fallen from natural goodness as Rousseau saw it? In the consideration of the nature of the savage as an innocent or as a violent and idolatrous non-being and of the contracts of civilization itself (the primitive being most often seen as the European past), "European consciousness is inevitably the subject" (*ibid*.: 4) and the object (the other, local histories) is altered by the European history or intertextualities and borrowed allusions that inscribe it.

Although the role eurocentric translation has played in the creation of a colonized subject is being re-examined, less work has been done on the role of translation in the modification of Metropolitan or settler understandings of the indigenous groups who most often remained socially invisible, isolated in their 'reservations'. Recent renewed interest in these texts reflects the new climate created by two major political agreements, the *Accords de Matignon* in 1998 and the *Accord de Nouméa* (Noumea Agreement) in 1998. The latter provides increasing autonomy and the possibility of an independent state within 20 years, access to educational development for all groups and a referendum to be held in 2013. The intent of the present study is to look particularly at the nature of the knowledge transmitted by the translations of the *Vierge rouge* [Red Virgin] as the revolutionary Louise Michel was commonly known, the missionary, Maurice Leenhardt, and the contemporary ethnographer, Alban Bensa, and to consider the value of the "third spaces" their translations create. Christopher Pinney has shown that European traditions were already themselves 'creolized' or hybrid at the time Europe imposed its hegemony on the Pacific, influenced for example by the classical world and by voyages to China and the Orient.[2] The translation of the legends of Cemuhi and Paicî speaking areas by Bensa and Rivierre (1982, c 1994) works from the premise that these texts are themselves also already hybrid, in this case, in their negotiations between different Melanesian languages and sets of cultural knowledge and particularly in border areas. Melanesian oral texts, too, are of course, hybrid over time, both changing internally to reflect evolving political and material realities and melding Western modernity, adopted and adapted Christianity, and tradition.

---

[2] Christopher Pinney, 'Creole Europe', Paper given at seminar on 'Unsettling Settlement: the new humanities and new world cultures', 22 March 2002, University of Auckland.

2. The Indigenous Tradition of Multilingualism and Translation

The socio-political stakes of translation in Kanaky/New Caledonian contexts, have always been high. Kanak have been engaged in the practice of translation from the depths of time. Twenty-eight indigenous languages are still spoken in this former Overseas Territory (*TOM* or *Territoire d'Outre-Mer* recently designated a *POM or Pays d'Outre-Mer*) where French has been the official language since a colony was established in 1853. Work on the transcription and translation of these languages of Austronesian origin, which arrived in the area from South East Asia (present-day Taiwan) around 2,000 B.C., was begun by the missionaries and continued by European linguists and ethnographers. Indigenous informants guaranteed authenticity. Despite an increasing participation of Kanak researchers in the new millennium, the recording of existing oral knowledge is still limited and far from complete.

From the 1960s on, the early ethnographic work of Maurice Leenhardt and Jean Guiart had been followed by work by trained linguists – A.G. Haudricourt, Jean-Claude and Françoise Ozanne-Rivierre, Moyse Fauré, Jim Hollyman, Jacqueline de la Fontenelle, among others – who transcribed a number of vernacular languages. More recently, the research team composing the Oral Tradition Laboratory (*Laboratoire de Langue et Civilisation à Tradition Orale*) of the French research institution, the *CNRS*, has also published a number of texts. Translations with the aim of giving "readers a better approach to the living history of Melanesians" have also been done by the South Pacific Commission, but these are criticized by Ihage for not giving attention to oral tradition and for "erasing local details that give stories their real significance" (1991: 39). Ihage is also critical of the publication of sixty or so Melanesian stories translated directly into French by the Historical Society (*Société d'Etudes Historiques de la Nouvelle-Calédonie* SEHNC) which abandons "the scientific presentation of vernacular, literal translation and gloss", using the arguments that "these days the indigenous people use more French anyway and it is impossible to locate an original text among the vagaries of oral transmission" (*ibid.*: 38).

The *Centre de Langues Vernaculaires*, founded in 1979, has been accelerating the collection and publication for educational purposes of the oral material of more and more of the language groups of the archipelago. Maurice Lenormand's doctoral thesis defended in Nouméa in 1995 and establishing a lexicon for the Drehu language and ethnographic notes on customs, beliefs, daily life, and legends of Lifou, for example, is contemporaneous with the offering of Drehu as a language subject that, along with three other indigenous languages (Paicî, Nengone, and A'jië) can be taken for the Baccalauréat.

3. Louise Michel: A Woman's Early Translation/ Transposition of Oral Literature and Encounter with the Silenced Other

Louise Michel's 1875 translation into a poetic literary French imitating orality of Kanak 'songs' and 'heroic legends' (Chants/chansons et légendes kanaks)[3] against the colonial grain is a form of reconstruction. Constrained by the tastes of her Parisian editor and readers in New Caledonia and in France, the 'translation' of the Red Virgin and *deportée* is a product of her French education, her contexts of political revolt, and her unique utopian personality and idealism. I would argue nonetheless, that, like Leenhardt and Bensa after her, this exceptional woman and generous translator created something new in her enthusiasm for Kanak culture, her attempts to write outside the known and at least partially (in) the language of the other. In the context of her own exile, Michel's encounter with Kanak culture was also the pretext for a voyage in time and space to the roots of Europe in the Middle Ages, the origins of mankind, and through her own experience as a woman. It reflects and conserves aspects of the Kanak culture of her time largely ignored and unrecorded: it is also a vehicle for her own emotional closeness to the other and to the earth. Michel's *Légendes et chants de geste canaques* are among the earliest published translations of Kanak stories into French. In 1853, the Marist missionary, le père Gagnière, sent a collection of "fables et contes calé-

---

[3] The first manuscript published in Nouméa in 1875 *Légendes et chansons de geste canaques* was reworked and modified by Michel for the 1885 Paris edition, *Légendes et chants de geste canaques* (Paris: Kéva et cie.), re-edited in 1900 and 1988. Hachette Calédonie published *Légendes et chants de gestes canaques: avec dessins et vocabulaires* in Nouméa in 1980. The most recent edition, established in 1996 by François Bogliolo (*Aux amis d'Europe, Légendes et chansons de geste canaques* Nouméa: Éditions Grain de Sable) is a compilation of texts from the 1875 and 1885 editions.

doniens" [fables and folk tales], to his superior, as his fellow Marists at Balade, the site of the first European landings and the first Mission would continue to do some ten years later. Le père Gagnière observed that he had neglected to follow up on an earlier request by the late Monseigneur Amata, believing that "cela ne pouvait avoir aucun intérêt pour des Français" [such a work would be of no interest at all to the French] (Bogliolo 2000). Le père Gagnière, notes Bogliolo, later acknowledged the existence of a Kanak literature but judged this to be 'pale' and 'defective'. New Caledonian literature, he claims, thus emerged under the triple sign of transfer, the typology of fables and tales being part of a European cultural tradition, translation, and dependency, that is, a relationship of comparative value with French literature that would last a century and a half ("Ainsi émergeait la littérature calédonienne sous le triple signe du transfert, de la traduction, et de la dépendance" *ibid.*: 32). Written text transposed oral texts within a different system of signs and in translations destined for the bourgeois capitalist France of Napoleon III. In his Anthology of New Caledonian literature, Bogliolo (1994) also documents two stories published in 1862 in *La Nouvelle-Calédonie et ses habitants* by a Noumean doctor, Victor de Rochas. The first is a variant of the Père Lambert's now 'classic' 'Chef de Touho' and the pastor Leenhardt's 'Maître de Koné' (a narrative of the vengeful lizard) and the second, the story of a chief helped by the good spirits (a friend of the French aided by the missionaries in Rochas' reading) accompanied by notes on the ghosts, warriors and magic battles. Rochas also quotes the translation by the explorer and discoverer of New Caledonian nickel, Jules Garnier, of the 'hoot' or farewell speech of the Chief of Arama in April 1864. Garnier had quite simply shortened this text for his reader by cutting out the repetitions and lists of names, replaced by the word 'etc.'! The problems of translating vernacular texts, most particularly, the issue of the loss of its rhetorical functions, the texts vital patterning repetitions and recital of names, are made evident by these two earliest flawed literary adaptations. So, too, is the importance of the different 'horizons of expectation' of listeners/readers. As Bogliolo points out, what is at issue is not simply the linguistic or ethnographic search for equivalence of different schools of translation, le père Lambert, the pastor Leenhardt, and more recently the translations of the research institutions, but translation as transposition with the translator serving as intermediary at the intersection between two literary worlds.

Louise Michel's texts, which first appeared in print in 1875 in Nouméa, perhaps lost on the voyage back to France after the general amnesty and re-published in 1885 in Paris, substantially rewritten, use the brevity of the fragment selected, dialogue, repetition, rhythm, metaphor and poetic voice to reflect something of the unusual movement in time and narrative focalization of the oral histories she encountered. Although there is relatively little information on her informants (the Kanak Daoumi and his 'more savage' brother in 1875 and the *déporté*, Charles Malato, in 1885), given the conditions of her imprisonment within the fortifications ('enceinte fortifiée') of the peninsula of Ducos, her experience of Kanak culture must have been quite limited. One of the fifteen women deported to *l'Ile Ducos* close to Nouméa in 1873 for their 'unwomanly' militant role on the barricades of the first proletarian revolutionary movement, the Paris Commune – Louise Michel bore arms and once dressed in male clothing as she admitted to the tribunal – Michel claims to have quickly become accepted by the local indigenous community, holding a school for twenty or so Kanak children on Sundays. She recounts in her introduction that when the administration of the penitentiary demanded she close her school hut, she continued to teach the principles of freedom and justice in the open. On Ducos, Louise describes how she met Daoumi, whom she described as an exceptional Melanesian from 'Sifou' who spoke French and worked in the canteen for the administration. Michel writes in her later *Memoirs* that Daoumi, son of a chief of Lifou, and almost European through being with Whites, was practising European life to take his knowledge back to his tribe. In her biographical text she claims that Daoumi was assimilating foreign knowledge through a thousand difficulties for the sake of his race. He knew how to read perfectly. His writing, she notes, was no worse than anyone else's (Michel: 1886). At her request, Daoumi sang a Kanak war song for her on their first meeting and Louise attempted to put on a Kanak play and to train a Kanak orchestra during her years on Ducos. These were years when few considered that the Kanak had a culture. Daoumi, notes Louise Michel, was also the informant who gave her the vocabulary lists for a number of indigenous languages appended to her published text and helped her translate the stories chosen for her book. She later also acknowledged the work of the Communard, Charles Malato, as the source, for example, of her translated version of the widely-known Pacific story "Le rat et le poulpe" [*The Rat and the Octopus*] (Malato, 1987).

Louise Michel's personal project was to recognize by translation the unrecognized power and nobility of an indigenous people carried by the 'myths' and folk-tales that had already interested her in Europe. It was perhaps inevitably (m)paternalistic, inscribed within a history dominated by a European notion of cultural progress from the childlike to the fully developed. Nonetheless, marking her sustained attempt at emotional empathy, Michel's preface speaks of 'your country' (France) as opposed to 'us' (the 'canaques'). In one of a number of her own (original and non-translated) texts in the collection, she identifies, very unusually for her time, strongly and emotionally with the proud and betrayed figure of the leader of the 1878 revolt, Ataï. Describing his death and particularly the transfer of Ataï's head to Paris where it is preserved as a specimen in the *Musée des Sciences Naturelles*, Michel asks her reader, "who are the barbarians?" Louise Michel participated in the work that would later make Ataï available as a hero of resistance and a figurehead for the Kanak independence cause in the nineteen-seventies.

Michel's introduction and translations integrate a number of untranslated Kanak expressions. Like her mixing of metaphor, these attempt to place her reader partly within the skin of the translated culture and convey Michel's own psychological and emotional identifications: "c'est à peine si à l'igname nouvelle, nous songeons à retourner le sablier" [We barely remember to turn the hourglass over at the new yam harvest, for the New Year] (Michel 1996: 64). Her work could be accused of appropriation, exoticism or of excessive idealism or sentimentality like Michel's life itself. Her linguistics are unscholarly and unsystematic. But the strength of her texts lie in their transmission of her intellectual interest in and sympathy with Kanak culture and dignity and of a courageous and relatively uncommon political critique of injustice against a people seen, says Michel, to be generally "despised by the Administration". Michel's introduction castigates the dispossession of "the poor Canaques". One of her fourteen *légendes* reproduces the lament of *Idara, la takata*, [healer-prophetess], recalling the coming of the Whites and despite the welcome given them by the Kanak, their subsequent taking of the productive land, the destruction of Kanak gardens by cattle, the 'selling' by the bad chiefs of young people and the most attractive women from the villages to work for the Europeans. The 1875 version seems to predict and vindicate the forthcoming Kanak revolt of 1878. Idara, as Bogliolo notes, speaks like Michel for the protection of a sacred relation between Kanak and the land that can be broken by the power of the Whites.

Michel's text is also eurocentric, presenting the legends she claims to have heard in New Caledonia to a French readership in relation to European literary traditions and to the concept of evolution. Where Europe has its Eddas, Sagas, Romancero, Niebelungen, she writes in her preface, "here we have black bards singing the *épopée* of the stone age", the tales of "the childhood of humanity" with their own "figures of Faust" and "of the Temple of Mars" (*ibid.*: 62). Bogliolo suggests in his preface to his 1996 edition that Louise addressed her work to 'Friends in Europe', to revolutionaries like herself rather than the bourgeois power she contested, that her stories tell of the evolution of the universal brotherhood and liberty she herself sought. Writing of the aptitudes of the 'canaques' and citing successful cataract operations carried out with pieces of glass, Michel seeks to resolve the question of violence and again has recourse to the paradigm of progress. She observes that the 'canaque' peoples have the "unconscious cruelty of children" often as a result of violent feelings of anger and vengeance. Doomed to extinction, this people has, she claims, the qualities and defects of children that include the emulation of the Europeans (what Franz Fanon will later call 'mimicry') and (hurt) pride. Despite his own major contribution to the valuing and conserving of Kanak culture, Maurice Leenhardt, speaks similarly of the 'neolithic poetry' of peoples of the late stone-age ('l'âge de pierre polie') (Leenhardt 1957: 56), situating Kanak culture close to early (primitive) periods of European history. Bogliolo suggests that primitivism is not necessarily pejorative for Michel, who, influenced by Victor Hugo, returns to a heroic and positively connoted Middle Ages or to the teller of traditional folk-tales around the fire to find what Europe has lost. Her project is rather, he claims, a return of the Other to the Human Condition in a universal progression of all peoples.

Courageous and open, resistant to the play and abuse of power in the politics of the colony, Michel's sensibility remains idiosyncratically romantic. She seeks to discover evidence of her own credo of the universality and brotherhood of all races in the tales she translates and the cultures she encounters. In her *Memoirs* Louise will liken the Kanak revolt to that of the Communards. "The same hope for liberty and bread was in the hearts of the Kanakas. They rebelled in 1878 seeking liberty and dignity" (Michel 1886). In her study of the language of the other, she encounters her own somewhat fantastic cosmogony. Michel rewrites, for example, the legend of Andia, the blue-eyed dwarf and bard/*takata*, killed alongside Ataï, leader of the rebellion, perhaps representing, she hypothesizes, a now lost early race of white (Indo-European) origin. Noting the development of a common language in the Pacific pidgin, Bichelamar, Michel asks her reader rhetorically whether one day, the tribes across all the oceans will mingle? "Faudrait-il qu'un jour les tribus se mêlent de tous les points du monde à travers toutes les mers?" (Michel 1996: 34). In a less than rigorous linguistic analysis, within what she identifies as the '35 dialects' of the country (there were in fact approximately 38 indigenous Melanesian languages), she lists words like 'popinée' (a pejorative term used to designate a Kanak woman) that recalls the French word poupée or doll or *Piquinini* from the Antilles, itself similar to Italian, to substantiate her hypothesis of links between all languages and her belief in the possibility of the development of a universal language not unlike Walter Benjamin's pure or original language, languages being the pieces of that broken vessel.

The "First Ouanith tells of the coming of cannibalism" – a topic of particular fascination for European readers. A closely associated story then recounts the origin of war and of evil. The bad brother in a search for power over his good brother and possession of his brother's wife may be the instigator of war, but, concludes the tale, without hunger and anger to tear them apart, men would not have been led to eat human flesh. Good triumphs when the tribe finally rises up against the bad chief and refuses exploitation (the depriving of food or eating of the women and children). After the bodies of those who resisted heroically but died are themselves not cut up and eaten but covered in green branches in a ritual of mourning, the text can come to the moral conclusion that great is a person's gratitude when he/she is treated as a person. The chief who wants to wage war merely for prestige and plunder is punished; the text claims that famine is no longer an acceptable excuse for eating one's fellow beings. The Kanak stories Michel is being told or is choosing to reconstruct in translation have evidently been influenced and transformed by missionary discourse. It would seem that Michel is translating stories permeated by a sense of Christian sin in relation to cannibalism for a European readership particularly curious about such exotic or different behaviour while at the same time transmitting her own personal investments in equality, human rights and dignity.

Her exile, concludes Bogliolo allowed the recognition of the Other rather than the knowledge of the Other. Her will to translate the Other moved between tradition reinterpreted and new utopias. Idara the prophetess announcing revolution and denouncing the injustice of the Whites, the struggle of the Other or the subordinate, for Bogliolo, is a portrait of Louise Michel's own struggle. The Kanak world is assimilated to the intuitive knowledge of the land, of nature and its languages to universal language(s). Michel's 'knowledge' is in the nature of poetic intuition, giving the first literary life to a 'Kanak' voice. Metaphors of wind, breezes, dream, that is of history, progress, revolt, those great cyclones of history, concludes Bogliolo, are primal energy, beginning, a poetics. Before the cubists and surrealists in Black Africa or Segalen in the Maori world, Michel, discovered that Europe can find its missing part in the Other. As Bogliolo (2000) suggests, the linear movement of her stories through flood and origins, cannibalism, war, suicide, the end of the world, is as much an extension of herself as mankind (Michel as 'canaque') as it is a portrait of the Other.

Beyond the stories of the Origin of War, Cannibalism, and Evil, and the coming of the Whites, a second surprising major thematic focus in the tales is women – women close to the earth as healers with special prophetic powers; women without men; warrior Princesses; women as poetic victims. "Idara (bruyère) prophétesse" praises woman's gifts as 'takala' (healer or 'magnetiser') and as story-teller. Although Idara who has "seen many yam harvests" is a mere woman, a 'nothing' or *nemo*, she knows how to heal wounds (Michel 1996). A *nemo* or *popinée*, adds Louise Michel with irony, is a useful object for carrying everything including the children and serving her lord and master. A woman 'doesn't count', yet Idara can put you to sleep with her magic songs. Another ironic comment on women's condition (of nothingness) reappears in the humorous 'Récits nocturnes' where a first person narrator observes that "my father took another wife who beat me every day, and ... I regretted my dead mother although she was only a woman" (1885: 104). Michel's presentation of Idara is a 'feminist' one before the letter, an early rehabilitation of the figure of the 'witch' in a text which compares kanak magic, the lizard, with the spells of the Middle Ages that cause the victim to be eaten up by fear or remorse.[4]

The dreaming of the old woman Nechewa goes back so far before the Whites, before the time when the dead were put into the branches of trees, that language cannot tell it, writes Michel in another portrait of a woman. Michel addresses her reader directly: "Savez-vous la légende de Faust? Elle existe chez les Canaques". [Do you know the story of Faust? The Canaques have their female version]. Michel proceeds to recount the story of the young and solitary Keidée, "Faust avide de science" [A Faust, hungry for knowledge] (Michel 1996: 'Le génie ondulé' [The Undulating

---

[4] This appears to be a story of the power and danger of the feminine not dissimilar to 'The Bride of Corinth', a story which has roots in antiquity, medieval versions, a nineteenth century re-telling by Michelet and a twentieth-century version in Robbe-Grillet's autobiographical *Romanesques* (1984). A fiancée who dies, returns in the form of a ghost or vampire and causes her betrothed to waste away and die.

Spirit] 53) who sings for the dead in the cemetery, eats wild fruit and refuses all fiancés. Wooed by a promise of privileges and delights – mats of bark softer than the fabrics of the Whites, layers of fat like those of the few women who are well served and stay at home instead of serving and carrying the axes and stones for the slings of the warriors – she prefers to remain single, choosing instead to fly back alone into the mountains. 'Les jeunes filles d'Owié' is a hymn to the link between women, magic or life-force, and peace-loving. The women must stand on the banks of the river, beating bamboo sticks and rubbing coconut branches together, singing songs to call the fish into the men's nets. In what are surely Michel's own conclusions, the daughters of Owié are brave, but they prefer to listen to the growling of the waves than to see the blood of their *tayos* [friends] (Michel: 1886). The genie Ondoué, likened to Mephistopheles, gives women power but takes away their 'souffle' or breath.

Women warriors appear with Mika and Kouira, who fought with the fighting men of Paimé, the good 'Théama' or chief against Téchéa, the bad 'Théama'. For Téchéa takes the food of the women and children for his warriors. The weaker and less powerful disappear periodically into the native oven as 'condiment' to give taste to the diet of yams and taro. Mika and Kouira refuse to hide in caves with the other women with the treasure – bracelets of jade and flying fox feathers – and choose instead to die in heroic battle. "Their hatchets were red, their arms were red, the red blood of the heart will flow today" (1885: 81). The song of the young women's mother accompanied the battle like a trumpet. "Long was the battle, long and terrible, the beautiful black women, Mika and Kouira, fell like warriors and their mother went on singing" (*ibid.*). Kaméa, also a daughter of the brave, but this time the self-sacrificial heroine rather than the warrior, had thrown herself onto the reef rather than allow Téchéa to take her from her husband, the (good) brother Kérou whom Téchéa had just killed and eaten.

Another form of self-sacrificial romantic heroism is evoked in the origin story, the 'Legend of the cyclone', a dramatic recasting of the story of the flood. As the rains fall, Paila, daughter and sister of warriors, and wife of warriors, watches the waters rise and does not tremble. Making her body into a canoe to save her sons, cast onto an outcrop and wounded by the rocks, she gives her life blood for her children's survival like the mother pelican in the romantic poem by Musset. From her heroism and sacrifice, through her surviving sons, *Grande Terre* [the main island of New Caledonia] will be founded. As well as refusing the feminine condition to become warriors, women may also turn out to be spirits, the dangerous and powerful daughters of the North Wind.

Michel's text is literary and uses the full range of French tenses; the passé simple marks the succession (as temporality and causality) of narrative events and conventions of literary dialogue create effects of narrative realism.

> Comme il était en train de se lamenter, passa un poulpe qui l'aperçut.
> – « Que fais-tu là, petit », lui demanda-t-il?
> « J'attends la mort », répondit tristement le rat….
> « Hélas, » murmurait-il, « tout à l'heure l'eau m'atteindra ici, et il faudrait bien que je meure » (1885: 122).

This translation of the well-known fable, 'Le Rat et le poulpe' (The Rat and the Squid] inspired by fellow communard, Charles Mulato, bears very little resemblance to the simple sentences in the present of the translations of the versions in Paicî, one from the East and one from the West coast, that appear in Bensa's *Les Filles du Rocher Até* (1995) more than a century later.[5]

Bensa and Rivierre tell a less ornate story in a familiar register close to the vernacular and the spoken in 'Le rat de Goropèto' (Narrator Henri Téa, 1973).

> 21. (le rat) s'installe dessus et pleure
> 22. Le poulpe l'entend
> 23. et demande: "Qu'est-ce qui pleure, les filles"?

Michel's literary style recreates a sense of the repetitions and personal address of the oral story, espousing the voice of the Kanak. At the same time, this nineteenth-century publication, which bears little trace of the earthiness ('verdure') that the later ethnographers Alban Bensa and Jean

---

[5] In its most common version, *Le rat et la poule sultane*, (The Rat and the Swamp Hen), this is a tale of 'false friends' that originated in the island of Tiga and was spread through the archipelago by the evangelists from the Loyalties. It tells the story of a rat and a swamp hen (or often a rat and a squid) who make a raft to go fishing on the reef. In Michel's version, the rat eats the raft while the hen is gathering food and is abandoned on the reef. A squid hears the rat weeping on the reef as the tide rises and saves him from death by carrying him on his back, only to be laughed at by the friend he rescues once he is safely back.

Guiart both remark on, recasts Daoumi's stories into comprehensible forms of 'good writing' models in French. It appears to have abstracted most references to physical bodily functions.

The 'third space' produced by Louise Michel could be described as early feminism or early anthropology. Ataï's death in 1878 has been seen as the last and failed attempt to challenge the increasing power of the colonial world by force of arms. Partially acculturated and seeking ways for his people of accommodating to the new colonial situation, Daoumi's stories of the flood, of the original sin of the eating of human flesh, of Cain murdering his brother may reflect an assimilating of the knowledge of the new arrivals, of the stories and taboos brought by the missionaries but may also reflect Michel's own imagination and mission. Louise Michel's version of *La Vierge de Neklai* tells the dramatized story of a young woman sacrificed to the dark waters of the sacred river by the local takata to ensure the favour of the god of traditional shell money. The wind rises and covers the cries of the victim. The spirit of her mother was not there to defend her, writes Michel. The story of the sacrifice of the virgin could also be seen to be a Kanak version of a more 'universal' mythology – the rites of Spring. Such a mythology close to the mystical quest and renewal of the kind that Joseph Campbell advances, or to the central originary sacrifice of propitiation (the sacred scapegoat who breaks the cycle of violence and revenge) of the kind René Girard's study of the violence and the sacred investigates, seems very abstract in relation to the stories translated by Leenhardt, Guiart, and Bensa. Here the marvelous is situated in the concrete detail of the everyday (food, mats, skirts, ancestors who take material forms). The single published Kanak woman writer, Déwé Gorodé, has always insisted that what Europeans call 'myths' are not at all 'myths' for the Kanaks but their history, a history integrated into daily social interactions.

Alongside stories of women as sacrificial victims to ensure the functioning of the social system, Michel evokes the frequent phenomenon of female suicide. In *Les Souffles* Kéa, Kéri and Lira, called by the spirits of the breezes, don't know why they jump from the cliff. In *Le Kouindio*, the reef calls the smiling Marek who seems to have no cares ("do popinées have time for cares?" adds Michel) but whose beloved has just died in battle into its caverns. Michel's Romantic representations of Kanak female suicide can be compared with Leenhardt's understandings of this phenomenon in his translations some decades later. Suicide in Leenhardt's analysis is linked to a whole mythico-social system (gods and totems) constructed with the help of anthropological concepts, a system in which death is not a void but rather a sometimes reversible passage from one state to another which gives access to a different kind of power. The mother and her three daughters who, admonished for eating the taboo taros reserved for dignitaries, commit suicide by hanging themselves with bark rope, notes Leenhardt, put on their best jewelry and adorn themselves with black powder like warriors, evidently in preparation for their entry to the spirit world. Suicide gives the betrayed wife power. She destroys herself to enter another timeless state where, ubiquitous, she can haunt her husband like the ancient furies. Bensa and Rivierre cast such tales less as mythical depth and cosmology than as narratives of social systems and local politics. The contemporary ethnographers focus on the fulfilling of social responsibilities to the group in the account of the mother who commits suicide and becomes a spirit but continues to nourish her unborn child.

Déwé Gorodé (1994), like Louise Michel before her, will produce a woman-centered work, and in *Uté Mûrûnû*, will put forward a rebellious Kanak goddess, anchored in tradition, like Michel's warrior women, as a model for women. Her characters in the long short-story that tells the tale of four generations of women named Uté Mûrûnû are all exceptional independent and strong women who refuse the marriages arranged for them. Both Michel's translations of the Other and Gorodé's writing in French in the language of the Other evoke a dramatic and poetic mode of living and feeling, a strong and even heroic life of the spirit, the link between language and the land, even if Gorodé's less Romantic text remains close to the detail of the everyday. Michel's translations as transpositions of her own preoccupations are open to criticism but her original 'third space' of empathy with the dominated culture, with the excluded subjectivity or gender bridges gaps and attempts to shift the center. It can be argued that Michel's work is a not wholly successful attempt to transcend nationalisms and create an in-between space of culture's hybridity.

4. Maurice Leenhardt and Translation: Between Missionary Discourse and Reverse Acculturation

The first printed document in New Caledonia was the translation of Mark's gospel in 1847 in the Loyalty Islands by the London Missionary Society. On *Grande Terre*, the *nata* [messenger and teacher], Joanné Nigoth (1866-

1919), had produced a Haouilou version of the Gospel of Mathew before the arrival of Leenhardt, sent by the *Société Evangélique des Missions de Paris*[6] in 1902 to establish a Mission on *Grande Terre*. The missionary had been requested both by the *natas*, discouraged by their powerlessness in relation to unsympathetic settlers and the colonial administration, and by Kanak chiefs interested in the new White protestant religion not directly associated with the colonial administration. Over the 15 years following Leenhardt's arrival in the region of Haouilou, the translation of the remaining New Testament into *A'jië*, the language of the populous Haouilou area, printed in 1917, was at once a collective enterprise and a major focus for Leenhardt's interest in ethno-linguistic research. Some of the Acts of the Apostles were also translated into neighbouring Paicî but this tonal language posed problems of transcription for the religious leaders. The translator Joané Nigoth, who wrote in three languages, also served as secretary to Mindia, the protestant chief of the Houailou valley in his negotiations with the colonial administration.

Despite its often negative press in current postcolonial theory as eurocentric and intolerant or destructive of non-European cultures, or, at best, patriarchal and condescending, the missionary work of evangelization of the heathen ('les païens') generally provided the earliest and most powerful motivation for the systematic transcription and study of oral languages with the primary goal, particularly in the case of the Protestant missions, of making the *Evangile* (New Testament) available in all vernaculars. The autobiographical texts of Leenhardt's militant daughter, Roslène Dousset-Leenhardt, suggest the doubts that some of the early Kanak informants may have had in respect to this translation process. Roslène recounts that when Tawa, a Melanesian *nata* came from New Caledonia to Fontfroide, the family estate in the South of France, to work with her missionary-father Maurice Leenhardt on the completion of his translation of the New Testament in the early twenties, the Kanak sought her out somewhat anxiously to ask whether it was really 'a good thing' he was doing.

According to Leenhardt, "God speaks to the heart of man in the language he has learned at the mother's breast" (Clifford 1987: 21). His goal was to limit European influence and bring an autonomous alliance of indigenous churches, using their own languages into being. As James

---

[6] The Société Evangélique des Missions de Paris took over from the London Missionary Society.

Clifford points out in his extensive work on the missionary-ethnographer, Maurice Leenhardt remained virtually the sole Protestant evangelist on the *Grande Terre* for over a quarter of a century. The teaching work was done by the native pastors or 'messengers', (*natas*), first from the Loyalty Islands and later, from *Grande Terre*, trained in the Do-Néva mission and pastoral school. The work of his informants, the first native pastor and translator at Do-Néva, Bwêêyöuu Erijiyi, or of Joanné Nigoth, or of Tawa Manéo, is acknowledged by Leenhardt as indispensable. Leenhardt's *natas* were encouraged to keep notebooks to record aspects of the culture they encountered in their work *en tribu*. For his part, their mentor was not inclined to allow this information to be shrouded by traditional secret or taboo.

Leenhardt fought with determination against the theories of those who wished to suppress native languages and impose a European language in the hope of "elevating an inferior people" (*ibid.*), observes Clifford. Although they retain an evolutionary perspective, and continue to make distinctions between primitive and civilized, his arguments work against the grain of the hierarchy of cultures and the ideology of progress that were self-evident tenets of the period. The natives, claims Leenhardt, will come to form their own new abstract concepts and general ideas by encounter with the second culture. They will thus arrive at self-awareness as individuals as well as at a social consciousness that would give them the possibilities of choice that the new contexts in which they found themselves required. The assumption that the 'natives' had little self-awareness would seem to cast Leenhardt as typically colonialist in his understandings. Yet Leenhardt's belief in the possibilities for autonomy of what he called paternalistically his 'pagano-christians', was also informed by developed Protestant beliefs in the individual conscience and, like his interest in using indigenous languages and teachers, was somewhat in contrast to the practice of the rival Marist missions with their fifty or so European priests using mainly Latin and French to catechize and teach. The first native priest, for example, was ordained in 1946. After a quarter of a century spent in the mission field in New Caledonia, Leenhardt would spend the next quarter of a century as an academic, an ethnologist in Paris, drawing on his lived experience and writing to counter those who would use French or English to refashion the thinking of the 'primitifs' and prevent the potential blossoming of their 'primitive' language. The term shocks a century on although Leenhardt's own imaginary references for the 'primitive' included in particular the patriarchal societies of the Bible documented in the Old Testament that he had studied so intimately. Jean Guiart, Leenhardt's disciple, argues in *Mwà Véé* (2002: 23), a volume dedicated to celebrating Leenhardt's centenary, that if Leenhardt used the word 'primitive' in his writings, this was because it was impossible otherwise to make himself understood by the ethnographic establishment in Paris at the time.

Leenhardt was accused by his family, his Mission, and many of the settlers who were very hostile to his influence, of being '*encanaqué*', of having 'gone native', being pro-native or being too affected by his new cultural contexts. He himself was well aware of the dangers of religious heterodoxy at the edge of Empire. But translation, claimed Leenhardt, as the creative inter-penetration of two cultures, should participate in the 'liberation' and 'revivification' of meanings latent in each. In the translation of the Bible, the source language is reborn in the encounter with other target languages.

Clifford reads Leenhardt's translation work as implying the preservation of an endangered Kanak expressivity or affectivity through the transcription and translation of documents that were not to be static ethnological recordings but writings in which words were 'acts of life' springing from experience. The missionary came to argue that Christianity itself, like translation, was a means of recovering a communal and affective Melanesian essence, a culture that was being lost. Although he never analyses the relations of inequality and the power imbalance between source and target languages explicitly, in *Gens de la Grande Terre* (1957) Leenhardt again makes the argument for necessary cross fertilization and indeed 'reverse acculturation' in the encounter between cultures and for all involved in the colonial situation. The language that he uses is nonetheless also influenced by his missionary origins and purposes and by his French mission audience, needed to pay the bills. One Leenhardt hides another.

"We must receive from the blacks, the means that correspond to the needs of their hearts, know how to use their pagan language and make of it the vehicle of the message of the Bible", explains Leenhardt in 1922. He continues: "It is true that these non-civilized people lack abstract terms that are familiar to us, but they possess a concrete vocabulary that is infinitely rich" (Clifford 1987: 13). Non-civilized, pagan, concrete rather than abstract thinkers – all the colonial stereotypes of the Other are present. But although Leenhardt's accounts of his translation of the Bible into Houailou for the Paris Mission and even the claim that the translator's role is to initiate thinking in his native-speaker informants and then to fix in writing the words he has aroused or overheard often has a moralizing or paternalistic ring and appears to take his own role as authority or necessary intermediary for granted, the idea that translation from a dominant language should proceed from native speaker practice is a modern one. To seek a meaningful concrete rendition for a concept or practice from a Houailou-speaker ('redemption', for example), Leenhardt would read completed chapters of Bible translations to an informant, or to his students, and ask for their reactions, reports Clifford. Thinking in Houailou would itself be translated in terms of emotion as represented by what was going on in one's 'insides'. A 'prison' in Houailou 'thinking' would thus give 'maison lier hommes' [house binding men] in the Houailou vernacular (A'jië). Clifford concludes that, for Leenhardt, translation was the location of meaningful rather than accurate expressions as these arose spontaneously in the speaker of the target language in a situation of dialogue. Europeans would learn from the Melanesians in this process. By the process of translating 'us into them', the missionary claims that he discovers what his Hebrew/Latin and particularly French source texts really mean. This is akin to Louise Michel's belief that translation provided access to what was missing or what had been lost (the 'primitive' in a positive sense) in Europe. For Clifford, Leenhardt is evoking Nida's 'dynamic equivalence before the letter.

In 2002 in the centennial year of Leenhardt's mission, the postcolonial debate around the political and social stakes of missiology and of the translation of the Bible into native languages is still open. For his part, Leenhardt speaks of the danger of a Christianity that would simply be an add on to a Kanak socio-religious system. This system, analyzed by Leenhardt, and identified as having valuable mythic depth, was no longer sufficient to deal with the new conditions created by the pressure posed by a technological, rational ideology that took itself to be universal and superior. For Leenhardt, as source of life and power, God could speak in the vernacular but the encounter with Christ would also require a change, formulated as a movement toward self-awareness and moral choice. In such a frame, much would ride on translation. Leenhardt's premise of the Kanak person as 'primitive', evolving in a universe of mythical social relations with a conception of self without physical boundaries, of myth as emotional thinking that did not class but juxtaposed, and of a journey to self-awareness (Leenhardt 1947) has since been put in question within a postcolonial ethnography. But in Leenhardt's own explicit analysis of the language situation, although an opposition can be made between the more concrete (New Caldonian) and the more abstract (European), no language has a superior status. "There are 60 Kanak terms for 'length' ['longueur'], and a separate verb for each food they eat – meat, vegetables or fibre"[7] he points out to radio listeners in Paris in 1935.

Leenhardt was among the first scholars in New Caledonia to see urgency in the recording and study of what he discovered to be ancient, complex languages and cultures, changing rapidly, one of the first to think about ways of reading/ translating landscapes and of understanding ways of being that had remained invisible to most Europeans. The Kanak, for him was not an essential or natural romantic savage waiting to be saved (or developed and made more rational) as European and mission myths proposed. Nor was he only the doomed primitive Other of a fatal impact, largely invisible to or ignored by the settler population. In the letters to his parents examined by Clifford, Leenhardt rejects the role of 'representative of a civilization' spreading 'a gospel of the whites'. He makes the claim to be seeking a gospel that, in translation, adapts itself 'to all people'.[8] Translation for Leenhardt, as we noted, would first and foremost require speaking in the not so simple language of the Other and identification with the Other's mythical system, an understanding of the strata of their culture.

The myth Leenhardt recorded, transcribed word for word and translated in his 1932 collection of significant oral texts that have become foundational, *Documents Calédoniens*, is seen less as an expression of the past, or less story as charter legitimizing the present order than as a form of knowledge arrived at by means of emotional participation in a material and mythical social and geographical space. Clifford (1987) argues that such knowledge could not be grasped by a continuous story told by a central subject where past and future were distinct as a standard translation into French would require. For the discontinuous series or cycles of lived socio-mythical spaces constituting the kanak 'person' and continuous with the person, as Leenhardt points out in his later and influential although contested ethnographic text, *Do Kamo* (1947), include both the living social being and the *bao* or ancestor-divinity that succeeds the putrefaction of the dead body. The boundaries of such a 'person' for

---

[7] Maurice Leenhardt 'La Bible en mission 2. La traduction de la Bible', Lecture given 23 May 1935, Poste national Radio-Paris. Quoted by Clifford (1987: 19).
[8] Private correspondence. Quoted by Clifford (1987: 11).

Leenhardt are quite different from those of the European 'I' with a distinct body or identity. Contemporary Kanak writers like Déwé Gorodé, continue to figure an 'I' that is both autonomous and restricted first person view combined with an omniscient third person narrator, and a tribal 'I' constituted in dialogue with others over a time that spirals back to the earth/ the past/ the *duée* or spirits and the ancestor, and into the future or the child to come. It is in fact the case that like the texts of the settler writer, Nicolas Kurtovich, Gorodé's writings of 'liberation', political and esthetic, have been influenced by Leenhardt's tales.

Again explaining problems of translation to his Mission readers, Leenhardt notes that in A'jië, the 'I' is both a first and a third person and the particle that indicates duration does not clearly demarcate the past from the future. European minds, he observes, are not well adapted to those formulae where invariable terms can be verbs or nouns or neither one nor the other. The central kinship terms posed evident problems for a language that did not make the same distinctions. 'Brother' must be specified, as elder or younger as must sister, for example. The translator must show that 'Mother' extends to all of mother's sisters. Even the native pastors have difficulty with the dual nouns that signify an 'us' that is inclusive – the maternal uncle **and** nephew *nya*, or the mother **and** child; or the 'homonym' from four generations back with his present namesake.[9] Abstract terms like passion and soul also posed problems – propitiation, for example, was finally translated by the name of the native plant used to heal wounds. Demons could be designated by the U, powerful spirits that dwelled in material forms in nature.

Leenhardt's translation of two essential terms into the language of Houailou, 'God' and the 'Word' are discussed at length by the missionary, and reported by Clifford, as central and exemplary. The European (name of) 'God' should not simply be imposed. Rather, the traditional name for gods and spirits *bao* (spirit, ancestor, or corpse) had to be 'brought to a new significance' beyond the original *Bao* given a capital letter by Leenhardt, and considered by him, indeed like all translations, to be inherently incomplete and provisional. Leenhardt translated an expression overheard in *A'jië*. "Tous les dieux à cause les hommes; d'autre part, tous les totems à cause venir selon femmes". [All the gods because of men, on

---

[9] One pastor translated a catechism confusing plurals and duals. Maurice Leenhardt, 'La Bible en mission 2. La traduction de la Bible', Lecture given 23 May 1935, Poste national Radio-Paris, cited by Clifford, (1987: 19).

the other hand, all the totems/life-force because come from women]. As Clifford understands Leenhardt's translation, this meant that Gods come from men and totems proceed from women. The authority of the *Bao* was masculine, associated with the male lineage, the ancestral heritage of the clan, and with the chief. It bore the virtue of power, he claims, and could refer to a magical spirit used in sorcery, an ancestor or very old person still alive, or to a deity identified with an element of nature. As Clifford continues to recount the story, Leenhardt discovered further that *bao* could itself be associated with a totem, become confused with an ancestor. A totem/life-force could thus also be God. In Leenhardt's argument, even chiefs had to give gifts to the *kanya*, members of the clan from whom they received their wives. These *maternels*, or uterine uncles, incarnated the principle of feminine totem (life-force) and were called upon to give the breath of life to their nephews and nieces on birth. "The long God who stretches out" from one named place to others, as God was described spontaneously by one of the *natas*, could also be identified with the 'femininity' of the sacredness of the features of the land. Clifford follows Leenhardt to the conclusion that feminine totemic language would therefore also need to be annexed to the term *Bao* in order to enable the term to conjoin masculine 'power' and the elemental feminine 'life force' emanating from the totem and passed on by the blood of the maternal lineage. As Clifford indicates, in Leenhardt's translation into A'jië, God had taken on unexpectedly modern androgynous forms!

To this back-translation from A'jië language and its understanding of the symbolic organization of the masculine and the feminine as complementary, Leenhardt adds a further hybridized notion. The immanence of what he perceives as the localized immediate mythic experience of an attachment to land and habitat (to the *maciri* or 'peaceable abode' of men and ancestors and to the *bao* as god/life-force) is conjoined with the European concept of the transcendent deity. Such 'rich' translation and its hybridizing impulse (in the sense of grafting one culture onto another) has aroused current debate, perhaps most particularly on the real (or indeed symbolic) equality of the masculine and the feminine in pre-colonial or in present Kanak culture.

Leenhardt observes that the reflection on the translation of particular words can provide keys for a reading of certain surprising aspects of Kanak behaviour in their earliest encounters with Europeans, in the person of Cook, for example. Among the attributes ascribed to Cook are a *kara bao* or 'skin of the god', the word subsequently used for 'European clothing'.

Despite the unwillingness of theorists working in the field of postcolonial studies to entertain the idea that indigenous peoples were naive enough to believe European explorers were 'gods' or 'goblins', there is some linguistic grounds in this instance for suggesting that the Europeans may have been initially identified as *bao* or beings not of this world.

Clifford's studies of Leenhardt conclude that his translation work was "the core of his evangelical practice", part of "a personal quest for religious authenticity" (1987: 3). Conversion itself, according to Leenhardt was "a complex and productive work of reciprocal translation" a movement of self-awareness but also an enlightened search for mediation between the old and the new, the pagan and the Christian, the mythical and the rational with old Melanesian terms taking on new meanings. Leenhardt was intimately concerned with third spaces articulating cultural difference, new places he also discovered in his work in the field. In Clifford's understanding, it was the resistances of his pastors that caused an increasingly relativistic Leenhardt to recognize the living nature of the culture he was translating and to come to characterize conversion in terms of various tribes looking for prestige, a means of becoming involved in the white world, having a better explanation of and control over a changing environment and being able to react better against what Leenhardt calls "the deadly breath of civilization".[10] What interested Leenhardt in his own translation work, argues Clifford, was the idea of a cross-culturally translatable Christianity. Such a new (third?) space, participating in the rational and in the mythic, in the unconscious and in self-awareness, the assimilation of opposites, seemed to offer the best hope for a Kanak future after colonization as well as insight into values that Europe has lost. Leenhardt noted that the French expression 'faire la paix' [to make peace] might best be rendered by the expression equivalent to 'donner le pays', that is, 'to give the land' back to the 'maîtres du sol' [guardians of the land], to those who had traditional responsibility for it. In the final instance, individual words that pose problems of translation are seen by Leenhardt as spaces of possible and positive encounter and action, spaces of change, rather than as differences in cultural codes to be bridged.

Both Leenhardt and Jean-Marie Tjibaou after him focus on the central function of the 'Word' in Kanak culture. Leenhardt was fascinated by the

---

[10] Leenhardt's private correspondence. This letter to Leenhardt's parents is quoted by Clifford (1987: 3).

kinship between the word for speech or word – the Word of God – (Greek *Logos* or French *parole*) and the A'jië word *no* which designates speech but also thoughts and action – as in Austen's theory of 'performative' language. An understanding of the biblical expression 'Word made flesh', the word as phenomenon, is thus improved, claims Leenhardt, by its 'living' Caledonian translation. The chief, the keeper or the reciter of the genealogies and the legends, the 'big son' or *orakau* as opposed to the *kamöyari*, the 'little men' or 'subjects' holds the Word. Back in Europe, arguing for his philosophy of translation, Leenhardt rejects the use by the Loyalty Island missionaries of the more abstract Greek terms, and in this case, of the word *Logo* for Word. A more practical understanding is given, he claims, by the use of the A'jië term for "word" in an expression such as "Il a commis une parole mauvaise" [He has committed a bad word] to describe the 'bad' action of adultery. 'Word' would thus designate both the thoughts and the acts of God.[11] The translation of the New Testament in A'jië claims to annex the original biblical texts (Hebrew, Greek, Latin, and French) to Kanak thinking, asserting thereby the power and action of the Kanak Word, while allowing the Melanesians to bring the missionary to better understand the power of the Gospel or of God as life force, immanent and participatory. Social, ecological and mythological attachment to the land, to the ancestor-god, could survive in this 'back' translation of Christianity.

It is difficult to say to what extent Leenhardt's vision inflects contemporary Protestantism, concludes Clifford. The *Documents néo-calédoniens*, obtained by encouraging pupils and informants who had just learned to read and write to keep notebooks and write down the songs and legends they remembered, and the extensive Haouilou dictionary published by Leenhardt have remained central documents in the corpus of indigenous texts to the present. *Do Kamo* is still a major influence on thinking and representing the Kanak personality. The October-November-December 2002 issue of *Mwà Véé*, the Kanak cultural review, devoted to "Maurice Leenhardt Cent ans plus tard", is predominantly celebratory. But with the hindsight of almost a century and in the light of the development of postcolonial theoretical analysis, gaps between what Leenhardt believed

---

[11] Clifford notes that on Lifou, Leenhardt's predecessor had translated 'Bible' as "container of the Word" until he discovered the islanders also used this term to describe their penis sheath.

he was doing (a form of back translation) and what he actually did are appearing.

An analysis of the metaphors and the discourse Leenhardt uses to communicate with the Mission or in his personal letters reveals an us-them split reinforcing the separation of observing (knowing) subject and (unknowing and obscure) object of observation. By "surprising the secrets of the native language" (surprendre les secrets du langage indigène), "the pagans will let us see the obscure pages of their hearts which the missionary cannot yet read" (1922: 194). The evangelical message cannot be compromised in a task not dissimilar to the imperial project. "The task is to succeed in penetrating the indigenous language sufficiently to not betray the Bible in the translation". This is a difficult task when what is seen to be in question is "a primitive language that does not lend itself to generalizations and is spoken by peoples from the stone-age" (*ibid.*). As Clifford concedes, the need to bring in funds for the mission by recounting the primitive state of the natives or telling moving or sentimental stories of conversion and indeed the religious vocation that made it impossible for Leenhardt to participate in, or encourage his flock to participate in, the last of the great *pilous* (ceremonial dances seen by the missionaries as orgiastic or pagan) which he nonetheless describes in detail in a now classic text, make the tone of the texts written by the missionary unpalatable to a postcolonial reader. To note a number of 'them and us' expressions in these mission texts that suggest that even for Leenhardt, difference remains a problem, and that make this reader uncomfortable, Leenhardt can speak in his letters of "the brutal passions of their primitive beings" ("les passions brutales de leurs êtres primitives"), of Kanak emotions as 'basic' ("sentiments encore rudimentaires"), and of a 'bestial odour'. He observes that 'primitive immorality' is characteristic of beings who do not have the long past of dominating the senses that constitutes the strength of Christian peoples. "We have the family and the ideal that constitutes; they have crude sexuality". His reference to his own deep but sublimated love for his puritanical wife and companion-co-worker, Jeanne, implies that Leenhardt is beyond such raw sexuality. Leenhardt again reveals his split allegiances, this time closer to empathy, but still the missionary, when he writes to his father in 1913 that the "greatest sacrifice demanded of the missionary is that of his own culture". He keeps this in reserve in order to acquire another, a native culture – one that the Sorbonne would call 'pre-logical'. The reason so little has been achieved is the lack of effort made "to penetrate their way of thinking and remake the givens of our concepts to produce concepts that are appropriate to them".[12] Leenhardt may distance himself here from the dominant anthropological concepts of the period (mystical pre-rationality or the primitive) but he is clearly also influenced by the thinking of his time. Leenhardt is not defining Others by what they lack to be like him – what Patrice Godin (2002: 15) lists as writing, the State, industrial technology, the body, individual conscience – or is he? In fact, the measure of his attempt to translate into another culture remains the 'universal' value. The facts or givens must be purified, states Leenhardt, so that only the 'legacy of humanity' remains. Like Michel, Leenhardt seeks out the 'universal' aspects of 'primitive thought' to give this thought added value. If it retained so much of the past in its very progress, he observes, it was because it possessed some very old elements within itself that are essential to mankind. To uncover these may be to find categories, even values, he claims, that we have allowed to diminish in ourselves.

But who has the cultural authority to define such a 'patrimoine de l'humanité' or pure origin? However strong his identification with and valorizing of the Kanak and the New Caledonian landscape, however broad or advanced Leenhardt's thinking, evidenced by his difficulties with an uncomprehending settler population, administration, and *Société des Missions*, his language is inevitably also constrained by a time which assumes the existence of universal or originary values. Postmodern critics like Baudrillard have argued that the supposed universal – for better or for worse – is European. On the other hand, contemporary Kanak political thinkers like Jean-Marie Tjibaou, as Godin points out in *Mwà Véé* (2002: 16) will use Leenhardt's work and the universal values it draws on to nourish their political thought. The paradox that for Godin is common to the work of all anthropologists, applies to Leenhardt, to his impossible attempt to overcome the hold the ideology of his own society has on him and to account at once for the radical otherness of Kanak culture and for its universality. A paradox that Baudrillard's work (2001) heightens in his assertion of the cycling of the singular, the universal and the global as competing forces for dominance that are also always co-existing.

Leenhardt was a liberal, a constant critic of the colonial administration, for example, its unjust land expropriations, requirement of compulsory

---

[12] Clifford (1987: 17), the personal letters referred to are quoted by Clifford unless otherwise noted.

labour that destroyed the life of the tribu, and tolerance of payments made in alcohol to the Kanak by the settlers. He supported the integration of the Kanak into the economy against an administration which had decided to restrict them to reserves and to a parallel (inferior and silenced) universe. He did not critique the colonial system itself (this will not come under full attack in Europe until after the second world war when Europe's civilizing mission began to look more fragile). Committed to his country, France, despite his suspect position as a protestant with a Germanic-sounding name (Swiss, in reality), he sent his pastors off to war in 1914, proud that two-thirds of the volunteers were protestant and believing they would enhance their image by their heroic action.

Unlike Louise Michel, Leenhardt denounces the 1878 (and also the 1917) revolt as rebellion.[13] He speaks of the 'cruelty and treachery' of the 1878 uprising and notes the 200 Whites killed by the 'canaque', 'true savage that he was',[14] while also criticizing the headhunting provoked by the bonuses offered by the administration for denouncing rebels – 50 francs for a dead head and 25 francs for a prisoner. These are perhaps the politics, respect for civil authority but refusal of injustice, that particularly characterize the French Protestant pastor/missionary.

Like Louise Michel's distinctive 'third space'. Leenhardt's construction of a 'third-space' of cultural dialogue in his translation work is original, but inflected by his contexts as a pre-eminent and solitary Protestant missionary reporting to Paris and as an early ethnographer writing for a European public of the time. Moreover, the 'horizons of expectation' of the publics addressed – by the description and analysis of *Do Kamo*, for example, or in his texts on the translation of the Bible written to attract support from the Paris Mission – are very different.

Leenhardt's later position as an ethnologist at the Ecole des Hautes Etudes (also the Institut d'Ethnologie and the Musée de l'Homme), after Malinowski, Lévy-Bruhl, and Marcel Mauss as mentors and before the structuralist Lévi-Strauss who will take over his Chair, will favor the development of the ethnographic over the missionary discourse. Leenhardt, the missionary become ethnographer, the European *encanaqué,* is hybrid, influenced both by his own European education and by the texts collected by the *natas* on whom he relied for much of his information. Like Michel,

---

[13] In 'De la Mort à la vie: l'Evangile en Nouvelle-Calédonie', Paris: Société des Missions Evangéliques, 1922: 193-218 (quoted Clifford, 1987: 9-10).
[14] *Ibid.*; quoted Clifford 1987: 10.

Leenhardt speaks in a voice often disconcertingly of his own time and yet places himself empathetically within Kanak language and understandings and there speaks of 'reverse acculturation'. His colonial translations, traversed by the voices and texts of Kanak Others, of other historical moments, retain a dialogic character. It could be argued that their pioneering and relatively enlightened third spaces where incompleteness and change predominate prefigure Bhabha's postcolonial hybridity and challenge Bhabha's tenet of untranslatability.

5. Bensa and Rivierre: Ethnographer and Linguist Translate the Hybridity in Kanak Narratives

It is evident that such translational or hybrid third spaces as we have identified in Michel and Leenhardt are neither new nor exceptional. A major criticism of hybridity (as of 'otherness') is that nothing is immune and everything can be seen to be migratory and mixed. Hybridization is also an internal aspect of a rapidly evolving and non-unified partly modern Kanak culture. This is the subject of our third case study, the contemporary contribution to translating and understanding Kanak oral literature and the socio-political messages it carries being made by the team of ethnographer and linguist, Alban Bensa and Jean-Claude Rivierre. In the Cemuhi and Paicî tribal areas of the North (Paicî with four and a half thousand speakers and Cemuhi with two and a half thousand are among the most commonly spoken languages), their recording and translation work discovers not a Leenhardtian 'mythic system' but local, formalized, and coded narratives that, says Bensa, we incorrectly call tales. The narratives selected recall and celebrate customary marriage alliances, commenting on the dangers of certain behaviours and on the 'unhappy fate' of children born from unions outside the rules. At the same time, these narratives constitute a 'metaphoric reflection' on the difficulties posed by customary alliances in changing contexts, and particularly in border regions. The ethnologists claim that the oral texts they are transcribing both uphold and contest the policy applied by the traditional authorities of the regions of Koné, Poinda and Poindimié. These authorities must maintain a balance between the restricted reciprocal exchange of brides between clans that constitute the body politic and a certain need for renewal from the outside.

Within Kanak retellings of the same story in a single language area or translations of the same stories from one linguistic zone to another (and Kanaks commonly speak three languages including the languages of the mother and the father), there is evidence of attempts to adapt the language of the Other to one's own system, needs and language. What could again be labeled third spaces, this time of historical competition for Kanak authority, exist in *Les Filles du Rocher Até* [The Daughters of Até Rock] (Bensa et Rivierre, 1995) between individuals (as in the thematics) and between the groups they emblematize. In the border region of Koné, for example, Paicî custom, with its two intermarrying halves, Dui and Bai, allowing marriage not only with cousins from the mother's *clan* as in contiguous groups, but with any of the *clans* from the mother's half, comes into conflict with Cemuhi custom. Bensa argues that the risks and stakes of matrimonial alliance and the search for wives is a particularly central theme in contiguous Cemuhi-speaking zones where restricted reciprocal marital alliances are the norm. What is important in terms of traditional Kanak rights, observes Bensa, is to establish the superiority of the system of marital alliances practiced by the group, and their efficacious magic or great matrimonial treasure (of ceremonial shell money).

In Bensa's reading of oral story, Leenhardt's notion of mythical thought is no longer useful; symbolic production, he claims, is a function of the situation of enunciation and a developing social system. Narrative is action, expressing rights and obligations and describing the alliances by which the political body is perpetuated or enlarged. The mythical-genealogical stories of marriage alliance are to be understood particularly in relation to other and also to changing central narratives, those that found the authority of the various *chefferies* [chiefdoms]. These stories and cosmologies serve both to establish rights and status and to contest Others' rights and status through the claims to direct links with the Ancestor through particular totems or self-identification with local natural features or places.

The origin myth of the Paicî (language area) ancestor who draws a tooth that he presents to the rising moon, told at Koné and transcribed by Guiart in *Structure de la chefferie en Mélanésie du Sud* (1992: 146), is told differently, for example, at Ponérihouen. In Guiart, the tooth placed on a rock produces the three worms, Te Kanaké, Dui and Bai that will fall into the sea and bleed on the beach to coagulate and produce the first man and the first woman. In the other version, the old people say that the earth, rolled into a spiral touched the moon and that the stone on the mountain was barely dry (from an indigenous or biblical flood?) when the land was divided on the mountain of Tyaumyê. When the sea left the first rock dry, the moon took a tooth from its mouth and placed it on the stone. The worms that emerged fell on the land, changing into lizards before they took a human form. The birth on the primordial mountain of the founding ancestor of the two groups of the area, Dui and Bai, is localized in both cases (the mountain and the ancestor are given local names), erasing the memory of arrival and establishing the more powerful status of first inhabitant rather than later 'immigrant' for the storyteller's group.

The mythico-genealogical stories that link a Kanak to the landscape by giving the child the name of the place or landscape feature, and also a name taken from a set stock of clan names, one not currently occupied, constitute a means of endowing the Kanak with certain local rights through toponym and patronym. Ways of rendering the central significance of these names in translation become vital in the present historical contexts where oral texts and genealogies can be used for political advantage. The 'Word' is able to create new rights over spaces in Kanak cultures that have always been both mobile (itineraries) and delimited, the property of a named individual who draws his identity from the clan and from allegiance to the *chefferie*.[15] Such naming is particularly useful in the present contexts of the claims for the return of areas of Kanak land taken in the colonial period from their 'original' or 'rightful' 'owners.'

The ethnographer's arguments create a picture of a rational social order constructing the history of its own origins and land rights, in which deviance serves overall to reinforce the norm of the group. But the stories where women take the initiative, refuse to move away from their clan, or take revenge on errant husbands are very numerous. The situation of enunciation (the importance of the interests of the informant's group and attachment to a space) and new developments in socio-political systems feed into and modify the stories recorded. Might it not also be significant, then, for example, that the stories in which women play assertive or vengeful roles are most often told by female informants? The hypothesis of the need to recall and renew essential links and maintain the established balance in exchange of wives, but also the need to renew through mésalliances or escape from rules does enable Bensa to explain both successful a-typical unions and also those stories where such unions lead to problems.

---

[15] The belief that Kanak land was owned in common or was a fixed territory over which the Chief had absolute jurisdiction that prevailed through the period of colonial administration is being deconstructed by historians.

Translation requires and perpetuates knowledge of the traditional and customary relations between *tribus*, clans and indeed individuals. It also requires an appreciation of the play of humor, memory, poetry and the art of telling stories as Bensa himself indicates in his preface; an understanding of the forms of rhetoric and an excellent command of French. The narratives constructed through Bensa and Rivierre's choice and organization of texts and interpretive commentary, however, are most often narratives of endogamy and exogamy and of politico-mythical genealogy embedded in what appears to be a dry and scholarly apparatus. Their frames derive from the European disciplinary discourses of anthropology and these contexts affect the scope and meanings of the translation. Bensa, himself affirms his support for the cause of Kanak independence, arguing that his discipline can no longer pretend to be neutral and objective and that its political positions must be assumed overtly.

In fact, the tales of the victories by cunning of the younger (less powerful) brother; the burning of Tibo, the devouring ogress with the withered breasts who steals from the banana plantation; the tale of revenge on a homonym, a trickster who pretends to serve up his wife's liver, and encourages his name-sharer to do the same with fatal consequences; fables of those who do not pull their weight in communal food-gathering tasks and who are cruelly punished (the dancer given his own cooked eyes to eat); of women's revenge for abandonment by their husbands are overdetermined and do not coincide fully with the readings/ translations given which can only be single and partial understandings. These tales remain open to readings from within a number of disciplines, psychoanalytical, structuralist, deconstructionist, comparatist, aesthetic, political, historical, feminist.

I would also suggest, in the tradition of Louise Michel, that some of these stories challenge the patrifocal and male-dominated structures of society, at least indirectly. As Bensa notes, one of the narratives appears to be making the modern case for finding a husband who will not require the wife to move away from her clan to his. In another story, a daughter who refuses a number of approaches from suitable partners in order to find her own husband in a distant group and give birth there is punished by her father who kills her son. But it is the daughter who will have the last word, following her stolen baby son to the underworld, succeeding in bringing him back to life, and to the husband and *clan* she has chosen.

These narratives portray a society in which women are subordinate to men who hold all public power and have almost absolute authority over the women and children for whom they share responsibility. Alone the eldest daughter of a chief has a certain latitude. Women have power only through their own marital and reproductive itinerary and domestic roles: to bring forth sons for their husbands; to feed the family community; to serve her husband's family. Women may have the symbolic power of life by association with blood, the totem, the earth, that Leenhardt claimed for them, but in everyday life, this is the indirect power within the family or the occult power interrogated by feminism as responsible for keeping women in their (secondary) place as the support persons or as dangerous (witches).

6. Conclusion

What constitutes the value in the different 'third spaces' created by our translators? The degree to which these spaces are still haunted by the Other; the degree to which the invisible substrata of the other language/culture can be detected and recovered? Or is it perhaps, paradoxically, at least in part the particular approaches they bring to the translations they produce and the openness of their texts, the space for further readings? In Leenhardt, translation of Kanak oral literature serves to fix a mythical universe of harmony and stability. His Kanak subject is on the path to self-conquest and knowledge of his god(s) as is Leenhardt himself. Michel naturalizes a Kanak subject, particularly the female, portrayed as a human being at an intermediary point on the evolutionary scale and idealized through the selection of scenes of human reciprocity, a revolutionary, heroic, or self-sacrificial subject decrying injustice and seeking liberty, not unlike Louise herself. Bensa, perhaps more modestly, certainly more self-aware of his intrusion, stages the socio-political structures of a particular tribe and time and the negotiating of power relations within and between them through narratives that cast particular light on the 'chemins des alliances', (geographical and bodily) pathways of tradition and contemporary challenges to the norms of such exchange.

In all of these translations, the grafted stem of Kanak oral stories, 'en langue' [in indigenous first languages] by the Kanak themselves, remains visible not as difference (exoticism) or as diversity but as an attempt to foreground another way of being in the world. Much of Leenhardt's translation and almost all of Bensa's involves the printing of the transcribed indigenous text and the word for word translations that mark the extent to which the difficult enterprise of thinking the Other language is encouraged.

Writing in the language of the Other then inevitably implies a critical reflection on the gaps, the fictitious creations of meaning in one's own. In all three cases examined, it is not only loss of self in translation or the extent to which the translation 'goes native' or situates itself at the borders of Empire, foreignized, that makes it effective. Nor the degree to which, domesticated, it maintains or speaks to French genre norms, to French as central or pure stock. The translation work of these three individuals is valuable to the extent that grafting one language on the other creates a third and new space of dialogic encounter, of cross fertilization, that does not detract from the role of translation as a sensitive and sentient instrument for showing forth Kanak culture, for transmission of endangered texts to future generations, and for redressing power imbalance. But it points to the impossibility of reproducing a text in all the truth of its original nature; to the already mixed character of the source text and of the translator; and to the inevitable (and often productive) transformations effected by committed and intelligent translators who write (in) the language of the Other.

References

Baudrillard, Jean, Public lecture, March 21, 2001, 'The Global, the Universal and the Singular', Auckland Town Hall.
Bensa, Alban et Jean-Claude Rivierre (1982) *Les Chemins de l'alliance*, Paris: Selaf.
------ (1983) *Histoires canaques*, Paris: Edicef.
------ and Jean-Claude Rivierre (c1994) *Les Filles du Rocher Até: contes et récits Paicî*, Nouméa: A.D.C.K. (Agence de développement de la culture kanak).
------ and Jean-Claude Rivierre (eds) (1998) *Le Pacifique: un monde épars*, Paris: L'Harmattan.
Bhabha, Homi K. (1994) *The Location of Culture*, London and New York: Routledge.
Bogliolo, François (1994) *Paroles et Ecritures: Anthologie de la littérature néo-calédonienne*, Nouméa: Les Editions du Cajou.
------ (ed) (1996) *Aux amis d'Europe. Légendes et chansons de gestes canaques*, Nouméa: Grain de sable. (Louise Michel's text of 1875 and extracts from text of 1885).
------ (2000) *Entre langues et terre. Emergence de la littérature néo-calédonienne (écriture et identité d'une île)*, Université de Paris III. Thesis (Habilitation à diriger des recherches).

Boulay, Roger (2002) *Kannibals & Vahinés: Imagerie des mers du Sud*, Paris: Musée National des Arts d'Afrique et d'Océanie: Seuil.

Calder, Alex, Jonathan Lamb, and Bridget Orr (eds) (1999) *Voyages and Beaches: Pacific Encounters, 1769-1840*, Honolulu: University of Hawai'i Press.

Campbell, Joseph ((c1949) 1968) *The Hero with a Thousand Faces*, Princeton, New Jersey: Princeton University Press.

Clifford, James (1987) *Maurice Leenhardt, Personne et Mythe en Nouvelle Calédonie*, Paris: éditions Jean-Michel Place.

------ (2001) 'Indigenous Articulations', *The Contemporary Pacific*, 13 (2): 468-490.

Dubois, Marie-Joseph (1973) Thèse de doctorat d'Etat, Paris V, Atelier de reproduction des Thèses, Université de Lille 111.

------ (1975) *Mythes et traditions de Maré, Nouvelle-Calédonie. Les Eleotok*, Paris: Publication de la Société des Océanistes, no. 35, Musée de l'homme.

------ (1977) *Les Chefferies de Maré, Nouvelle-Calédonie*, Paris: Librairie Honoré Champin.

------ (1984) *Gens de Maré*, Paris: éditions anthropos.

Dousset-Leenhardt, Roselène (1976) *Terre natale, terre d'exil*, Paris: Maisonneuve et Larose.

Fenton, Sabine and Paul Moon (2002) 'Bound into a Fateful Union: Henry Williams' Translation of the Treaty of Waitangi into Maori in February 1840', *The Journal of the Polynesian Society*, 111 (1), March 2002: 51-63.

Girard, René ((1972 1993) *La Violence et le sacré*, Paris: Grasset.

Godin, Patrice (2002) 'Le Paradoxe de l'ethnologue', *Mwà Véé*, 38 octobre-novembre-décembre 2002: 15-17.

Gorodé, Déwé (1994) *Uté Mûrûnû*, Nouméa: Grain de sable.

Guiart, Jean (1957) *Contes et légendes de la Grande Terre*, Nouméa: Editions des Etudes Mélanésiennes.

------ (1992) *Structure de la chefferie en Mélanésie du Sud*, Paris: Institut d'Ethnologie.

------ (2002) 'Avec Jean Guiart, etnologue', *Mwà Véé*, 38 octobre-novembre-décembre 2002: 18-27.

Ihage, Weniko (1991) 'The Current Condition: Texts on Orality in New Caledonia', *New Literatures Review*, 22, winter: 35-9.

Lambert, R. P. (1900) *Moeurs et superstitions des néo-calédoniens*, Nouméa: Facsimilé S.E.H.N.C., no 14, 1976.

Leenhardt, Maurice (1922) 'Notes sur la traduction du nouveau testament en langue primitive', *Revue d'histoire et de philosophie religieuses*, Université de Strasbourg, Faculté de Théologie protestante, 3, Mai-Juin: 193-218.

------ (1930) *Notes d'ethnologie néo-calédonienne*, Paris: Travaux et Mémoires de l'Institut d'ethnologie 8.

------ (1932) *Documents Calédoniens*, Paris: Travaux et Mémoires de l'Institut d'ethnologie, 9.

------ (1935) 'La Bible en mission 2. La traduction de la Bible', Lecture given 23 May, Poste national Radio-Paris.
------ ((1937) 1957) *Gens de la Grande Terre*, Paris: Gallimard.
------ (1947, 1960, 1971) *Do Kamo, la personne et le mythe dans le monde mélanésien*, Paris: Gallimard.
Lenormand, Maurice (1995) *Dictionnaire Drehu-Français*, Noumea: thèse de doctorat. Université de la Nouvelle-Calédonie.
Léonard, Sam and C. Lercari (1984) Ifejicatre no. 3, *Contes et Légendes de Lifou*, Nouméa: CTRDP.
------ (1980) *Littérature orale, 60 contes mélanisiens*, Nouméa: B.S.E.H.N.C, no. 21, 1980.
Michel, Louise (1875) *Légendes et chansons de geste canaques*, Published in Nouméa, in the newspaper *Petites affiches de la Nouvelle-Calédonie* 29 September to 15 December.
------ (1885) *Légendes et chants de geste canaques*, Paris: Kéva et cie. re-edited 1900, 1988.
------ (1886) Mémoires de Louise Michel écrites par elle-même, Paris: F. Roy.
------ (1980) *Légendes et chants de gestes canaques: avec dessins et vocabulaires*, Nouméa: Hachette.
------ (1996) (ed) François Bogliolo *Aux amis d'Europe, Légendes et chansons de geste canaques*, Nouméa: Éditions Grain de Sable.
Malato, Charles (re-edited 1987) *Contes néo-calédoniens*, Paris: L.-H., May.
Mwà Véé, 38 octobre-novembre-décembre 2002: 15-17.
O'Reilly, R.P. (1980) *Calédonien. Répertoire bio-bibliographique de la Nouvelle Calédonie*, Paris: Société des Océanistes, no 3.
Rivierre, Jean-Claude, Françoise Ozanne-Rivierre and Claude Moyse-Faurie (1980) *Mythes et contes de la Grande-Terre et des îles Loyautés*, Paris: Lacito, no 3.
Robbe-Grillet, Alain (1984)' Romanesques', *Le Miroir qui revient* Paris: Editions de Minuit.
------ (1987) *Angélique, ou l'enchantement*, Paris: Editions de Minuit.
------ (1994) *Les Derniers jours de Corinthe*, Paris: Editions de Minuit.
Robinson, Douglas (1997) *Translation and Empire*, Manchester: St.Jerome Publishing.
Sahlins, Marshall (1985) *Islands of History*, Chicago: University of Chicago Press.
Société d'études historiques de la Nouvelle Calédonie (S.E.H.N.C) (1980) *Littérature orale, 60 contes mélanisiens*, Nouméa: B.S.E.H.N.C, no. 21.
Wacquaint, Loic (1986) 'Communautés canaques et société coloniale', *Actes des Recherches en Sciences Sociales*, 61 mars: 56-64.
Wélépane, Wanir (1993) *Aux vents des îles*, Nouméa: A.D.C.K.

Fiji

Background: Fiji, an island group, became independent in 1970 after nearly a century as a British colony.
Land Area: 18 270 sq km
Capital: Suva
Population: 856 346; 51% Fijian, 44% Indian
Languages: English, Fijian, Hindustani

Foreigner Talk to Exonorm
Translation and Literacy in Fiji

PAUL GERAGHTY
University of the South Pacific

Abstract. *The linguistic diversity of Fiji was prehistorically midway between that typical of Melanesia, where there is great linguistic fragmentation, and Polynesia, with its largely monolingual island groups. When the missionaries arrived in the mid-nineteenth century, they found that a kind of standard Fijian already existed, and attempted to learn it in order to translate the Scriptures and other religious and educational works. They were however not totally successful in learning standard Fijian, and their translations were in 'Old High Fijian' – a mixture of foreigner talk and translationese with vocabulary from both standard Fijian and the Fijian of Lau, the eastern islands where they had begun their work. This written form of Fijian became the accepted literary form – an example of an 'exonorm', or standard language based on the speech of people outside the linguistic community. The translation of the Deed of Cession, by which Fiji was ceded to Great Britain in 1874, was written in Old High Fijian, but this does not appear to have greatly impeded the understanding of the terms of Cession by the chiefs who signed it. During the colonial period (1874-1970), particularly the last few decades, Fijian viewed as an obstacle to development, was used as little as possible in government, and was banned and denigrated in schools. The status of Fijian (along with the other major vernacular, Fiji Hindi) has improved a little since independence in 1970, and the Institute of Fijian Language and Culture worked to create a new written standard language based not on the Old High Fijian exonorm, but on spoken Fijian. Since 1997, both Fijian and Hindi have been designated official languages of Fiji, along with the colonial language English. Nevertheless, citizens who do not speak or read English are still greatly disadvantaged because literacy in Fijian and Hindi is not officially encouraged, and there are very few translators or interpreters, and none of them are professionally trained.*

Fiji is an archipelago in the South Pacific, large by Pacific standards, situated approximately 1,000 miles north of New Zealand, 1,500 miles north east of Australia, 3,000 miles south south west of Hawaii, and 2,200 miles west of Tahiti. It consists of two large islands, Vitilevu and Vanualevu, and numerous smaller islands, approximately 100 of which are inhabited, with a total land area about the size of Wales. The indigenous inhabitants, usually referred to as 'Fijians', are a physically impressive people who first became known to the western world through the reports of Captain Cook and his associates from neighbouring Tonga – some 250 miles to the south-east of eastern Fiji – where they were feared for their warlike disposition and admired for their craftsmanship and surgical skill.

While there are traits that are universally and uniquely Fijian, there is far more internal diversity than in comparable Polynesian island groups. Thus with language, 300 communalects can be discerned, in a population of about 400,000 Fijians, and can be assigned to 2 major and 27 minor communalect groupings, 12 in the West (approximately the western half of the main island of Vitilevu and adjacent islands) and 15 in the East. Generally speaking, western and eastern languages are not naturally mutually comprehensible, sharing only about 60% cognates on the 100-word Swadesh list,[1] and a similar level of difference is found between communalects at the extremes of the two major divisions. Nevertheless, the diversity is slight when compared to that found in more westerly island groups of the Pacific – New Caledonia, Vanuatu, the Solomon Islands, and Papua New Guinea.

1. Fiji before Literacy[2]

In pre-contact Fiji, the number of communalects was probably about the same as now, though their differences were probably greater, due to the more restricted movement of people. There was, apparently, a kind of lingua franca known to some extent in at least eastern parts of Fiji, based on the Fijian of the Bau-Rewa area, the political hub of eastern Fiji, and also a kind of 'foreigner talk' – a simplified version used with foreigners, originally Tongans, subsequently Europeans, who came to trade (Geraghty 1978).

---

[1] The Swadesh list is a list of word-meanings used by linguists as a rough indication of relatedness among languages. For two languages to be mutually intelligible, they generally need to show over 80% cognacy on the list.

[2] This is a revised, updated and considerably expanded version of Geraghty 1989.

Fiji was probably never completely isolated. Oral traditions record sporadic contacts with the Melanesian islands to the west, and contact between parts of eastern Fiji, especially Lau, and Tonga was commonplace. Contact also occurred with Futuna, Uvea, Samoa, and Rotuma, both directly and by way of Tonga. It was the Tongans, with their crowded islands and adventurous spirit, who were the great travellers of the western Pacific. They certainly had two-way contact with Kiribati, over 1,200 miles away, and probably also with Pohnpei, a distance of some 1,500 miles (Geraghty 1994). They came to Fiji mainly to build ocean-going canoes, suitable wood being exhausted in Tonga, and to take part in Fiji's internal wars. While they learned a great deal in Fiji, particularly pertaining to warfare, medicine, and canoe design, they also contributed. They probably introduced the wooden bowl for drinking yaqona (kava) which is now considered a typical Fijian artefact, though its Fijian name, **t~noa**, shows clearly its Tongan origin. Other probable prehistoric loans from Tongan into Fiji include **talanoa** 'chat, storytelling', **vÐtea** 'kind of body oil' (T. **pÐtea**), **veit~lia** 'never mind, regardless' (T. **fa'iteliha** 'please oneself'), and – surprisingly, since they were always present in Fiji – **vuaka/puaka** 'pig'.

Tonga was visited by the Dutch explorer Abel Tasman in the seventeenth century, and in the latter decades of the eighteenth century received extended visits from other Europeans – Cook, Mourelle, La Pérouse, Bligh, d'Entrecasteaux, Malaspina. During this period, Fiji was avoided by explorers, on account of its reputation for dangerous reefs and hostile inhabitants. Thus it fell to the Tongans to be the first modern language reformers in Fiji, as it was they, not Europeans, who were the bearers of the names of the many novelties from the western world. The earliest of these were from 17th century Dutch sources: Lauan **pua** 'wooden box, chest' (< T. **puha** < Dutch **bus**), **velekÐ** 'kind of narrow-bladed axe' (< Dutch **bijleken** 'small axe') (Geraghty and Tent 1997a, 1997b). Later came borrowings from English: **kote** < coat, **sote** < shirt, **tarausese** < trousers (T. **talausese**), **kapa** 'sheet metal' (< copper), **kÐpate** < cupboard, **pusi** 'cat' (< pussy), **loka** < lock, **m—tali** < medal, and Tongan coinages or loans from other Pacific languages: **pulumakau /pulumokau** 'cattle', **p~lagi** 'overseas' (originally from Malay **barang** 'goods' (Tent and Geraghty 2001)), **lilulu** 'shake hands' (T. **lulululu**, from **lulu** 'shake'), **ukamea/kaukamea** 'metal' (T. **ukamea**, probably from **uka** 'fishing-line' and **mea** 'reddish', originally referring to copper wire).

When eventually avarice overcame fear and the sandalwood trade began in the early part of the nineteenth century, to be followed by the bêche-de-mer trade, there was direct contact with English speakers and their world. In this pre-missionary era we see the Fijian vocabulary increasing naturally using both native and foreign material. Loans from English that probably date from this period include **veleti** < plate, **vinivÐ** 'dress' (< **pinafore**), **tavako** < tobacco, **bisikete** < biscuit, **kaloko** < clock, **paipo** < pipe, **vÐkete** < bucket, **t°kere** < tea-kettle, and **s—lÐ** < sail ho! But it was mostly by extension of meaning and compounding of indigenous elements that new things were named. 'Guns' were called **dakai ni v~lagi** 'bow from overseas', 'metal axes' **matau ni v~lagi** 'axe from overseas', 'iron pots' **kuro ni v~lagi** 'pot from overseas'. Eventually, as the native kind was superceded, it was the introduced form that became unmarked, so that soon 'gun' was simply **dakai**, and 'bow' **dakai ni Viti** 'Fijian gun' or **dakai t°t°** 'gun of mangrove root'. 'Gunpowder' was called **nuku** (sand), 'ramrod' **ivutu** (pounder), 'ammunition' **gasau** (reed arrow). There are many other examples of extension: 'cat-o-nine-tails' **kuita** (octopus), 'hat' **isala** (barkcloth turban), 'chain' **sinucodo** (garland of interlocking **sinu** flowers) – and compounding: 'ship' **waqavanua** (land canoe), 'button' **ibulukau** (wooden stopper), 'sword' **iseleiwau /iselewau** (clubbing knife), 'kind of felling axe' **tabumagimagi** (not bound with sinnet).

2. The Fijian Alphabet

In the early decades of the last century, it was only the trade for sandalwood and bêche-de-mer that attracted Europeans. They were followed in the 1830s and 1840s by the traders in souls. Unlike their predecessors, they were not content to get by with rough-and-ready 'foreigner talk', but were under strict instructions from their superiors at the Wesleyan Methodist Mission Society in London to learn the Fijian language well, devise an orthography, and eventually publish not only religious but also linguistic works.

The first and most important of these early missionaries was David Cargill, a Scot with a solid background in classical languages who arrived in Fiji in 1835 with co-worker William Cross, having acquired fluency in Tongan during two years' residence there. He had already started work on Fijian among the many Fijians living in Tonga, as well as Tongans who spoke Fijian, and had begun devising an orthography.[3] Cargill based

---

[3] Even this, the first and least controversial decision regarding Pacific orthographies,

the orthography on the one that was already well established for Tongan, which in turn was based on Tahitian. It was the Tahitian missionary John Davies who had recommended as early as 1805 that vowels be represented as in the classical and Continental languages rather than as in English, and this system was generally accepted by subsequent devisers of Pacific orthographies. Excellent though it was, it had a defect which is still with us today – the failure to distinguish between long and short vowels. In Tonga, it was probably Nathaniel Turner (L~tìkefu 1977: 122) who had made the insightful observation that /þ/, though represented by the two letters **ng** in English (as in 'si<u>ng</u>er'), is in fact one sound, and might therefore be represented by a single letter, **g** being both apt and available (the present Tongan spelling **ng** is a mid-twentieth century reform). This convention was followed for Fijian.

Cargill then had to tackle the Fijian sounds that were not found in Tongan. Four – **r, s, w** and **y** – were relatively straightforward, being familiar in European languages. But six more presented problems: the voiced apical fricative /ð/ (as in English '<u>th</u>is') and a set of five prenasalized stops. The voiced apical fricative was indeed a sound of English, but a single sound customarily represented by the digraph **th** (which also represents the voiceless q, as in '<u>th</u>ick'). Cargill at first wanted to use the Greek theta, but on the advice of the printer, who had neither thetas nor means to cast them, decided on using **c** (Schütz 1985: 21) – apparently uninfluenced by Castillian Spanish.

The realization that /ð/ represented a single sound would have come easily to the linguistically-trained Cargill. The prenasalized stops, however, are phonetically perceived as a sequence of two sounds, a nasal and a corresponding stop, and in the days before the discovery of the phoneme, it was inevitable that they would be written initially with two symbols. So they were, but the system did not meet with native speaker approval, as Cargill observed:

---

was strenuously opposed by the majority of missionaries in Tahiti. According to Davies' account, on March 11th, 1805 "Another meeting was held to consider the Tahitian Alphabet... Much dispute took place, and it appeared that several were but little acquainted with the subject they debated about, having never paid much attention to it, their chief and only argument against what was proposed last meeting [which included the 'continental' five-vowel system] was that they had been used to a different way of spelling and could not master this new way". The reactionaries were a majority and won that particular battle, so that epsilon was used for /e/ and **e** for /i/ until the publication of a Tahitian spelling book in 1810 (Newbury 1961: 77-78).

> We at first wrote two consonants where these compound sounds occur, but the natives could not pronounce the two consonants without inserting a vowel between them. We therefore substituted one consonant for the two & the natives were quite delighted with the improvement, and joyfully exclaimed, "You have just now known the nature of our language; we are just now able to read the books which you have written". (*ibid*.: 21)

Thus, [mb] was written **b**, [nd] **d**, and [ŋg] **q**. Note that complete parallelism with European spelling conventions – the symbol for voiced stop representing prenasalized voiced stop – was not possible, because **g** was already being used for [ŋ]. Had Fijian orthography not been based on Tongan, **g** probably would have been used for [ŋg], and a different symbol sought for [ŋ].

The remaining two prenasalized stops were not so satisfactorily handled. The prenasalized form of **r** has an excrescent **d** – [ndr] – and was perceived as a sequence of **d** and **r**, so written **dr**. This remains the only Fijian digraph to this day. The other was [ndž] (as in 'e<u>n</u>gine'), the prenasalized form of [t°] (as in 'chur<u>ch</u>'), palatalized allophones of **d** and **t**, respectively, before the vowel **i**. The latter, /t°/, was written as **j**, following the orthographic practice of Tonga; and, whether because of the value of **j** in English, or because the distinction was considered unimportant, its voiced prenasalized counterpart was written with the same symbol. This deficiency became less important when 'Bauan', which has no palatalized /d/, was chosen as the standard language in 1843, but has been the subject of the latest orthographic reforms, as will be recounted below.

3. Introducing Vocabulary

While establishing the alphabet, the missionaries were also considering more spiritual aspects of their work. The main purpose of teaching Fijians was for them to read the Scriptures and other religious works, and this entailed introducing religious and educational terms. To a certain extent they had been pre-empted by the Tongans, who had been practicing Christianity in Fiji before the missionaries' arrival, though not proselytizing. Moreover, much of the early work of the mission was carried out by Tongan catechists. So many early borrowings connected with religion and education are from Tongan, or from English via Tongan; **lotu** 'Christianity, worship' is originally Tongan (defined in William Mariner's dictionary, compiled in 1806-1810 (Martin 1817), as 'adoration, invocation, to invoke, to pray'), and the Tongan for 'Wednesday', **pulelulu** (originally from Tahitian) is the source for the Fijian forms **burelulu, purelulu**, and Standard Fijian **vulelulu**, which later became **vukelulu**. Most, however, are ultimately of English origin: **papitaiso** < **baptize**, **t—voro** < **devil** (T. **t—volo**),[4] **mÐnite** 'Monday', **tìsite** 'Tuesday', **laione** < **lion**, **pepa** < **paper**, **peni** < **pen**, **fika** 'arithmetic' < **figure**.

One suspects though that the missionaries had some misgivings about the Tongan linguistic influence in Fiji, as indeed they frequently had about the general behaviour of the nominally Christian Tongans in Fiji. Thus Tongan **h—vani** < **heaven** they soon replaced with the Fijian **lagi** or **lom~lagi** 'sky', **p~sova** < **Passover** with **lakos°via** 'go past', and **toci** 'writing, book', a calque on Tongan **tohi**, soon became **ivola** 'line, mark'. In some cases, however, the Tongan prevailed in spite of the missionaries' efforts – the **profiti** < **prophet** of the early printed works gave way to **parÐfita** (T. **palÐfita**), **aposila** < **apostle** to **apositolo** (T. **'aposetolo**), **koliti** < **gold** to **koula**. Note, incidentally, that certain consonant clusters were introduced (Fijian had none naturally) – **Kraisiti** < **Christ**, **profiti** < **prophet**, **prasi** < **brass** – as was the letter **h** in loanwords, but neither innovation appears to have been accepted, and they are not found in the first printed Bible. The introduced **p** and **f**, which occur naturally in Lauan (where Cargill was first based) but not in Bauan, were however retained. Though probably originally both pronounced as **v** by most non-Lauans, they have now become an accepted part of the Standard Fijian sound system.

Since Lauans were active as missionaries and teachers in the rest of Fiji – as Tongans had been in Lau – a number of Lauan words for introduced concepts became generally accepted: **m~cawa** 'week', from Lauan **m~cawa** 'space', **vavaloaloa** 'blackboard' from Lauan **papaloaloa**, and the way of compounding tens with units using Lauan **ka** rather than Bauan **mani**, e.g. **ruasagavulukarua** '22' rather than **ruasagavulumanirua** (**ruasagavulu** 'twenty', **rua** 'two').

In cases where the question had not yet been settled in favour of Tongan or Lauan, the missionaries apparently preferred extension or compounding of native elements to borrowing (or rather bestowing, cf. Schütz 1976) from English. Extended meanings, many of which have parallels in other

---

[4] Note that Tongan /l/ has an intervocalic allophone that is closer to Fijian /r/ than to /l/ (Churchward 1953: 1).

Pacific languages, include **wili** 'count, read', **masu** 'beg, pray', **ivola** 'mark, writing, book', **italatala** 'messenger, religious minister', and **gauna** 'section, time'; compounds include **Sigatabu** 'sacred day, Sunday', **sigavakarau** 'preparing day, Saturday', **vakaotiwilivola** 'finish school, Friday' and **iVolatabu** 'sacred writing, Bible'. Loans were many: **same** < **psalm, cosite** < **Thursday** (soon replaced by **lotulevu** 'big church service'), **asa** < **ass, koti** < goat (later replaced by the onomatopoeic **m—**).

An interesting difference between the work of the missionary wordsmiths in Hawaii, Tahiti, and Samoa as opposed to Tonga and Fiji is that the former introduced a large number of terms derived from the classical languages, especially Greek. This is apparently because the relative lack of consonant clusters in Greek meant the word could be more readily adapted to the phonology of Polynesian languages without "losing its identity" (John Williams 1842:137). Very few words in Fijian are of Greek origin, the best known being **KarisitÐ** 'Christ' and **agelosi** 'angel'. Certainly the larger consonant inventory of Fijian (and Tongan to a lesser extent) allowed more faithful replication of English words; but maybe the missionaries were also more aware that it was of little consequence to those who were to use the words what the original identity was!

4. Introducing Old High Fijian

The history of the linguistic work of the missions in Fiji is, sadly, one of genius giving way to mediocrity and ultimately to ignorance and dogmatism. David Cargill was not only a fine linguist, but also a sensitive observer. The alphabet he devised has stood the test of time. Inevitably his early work in Fiji was affected by his prior knowledge of Tongan (Schütz and Geraghty 1980), but most of the early errors were soon erased. His only big mistake was that he had landed on the wrong island – Lakeba rather than Bau.

Lakeba, the chiefly island of the Lau (eastern) group, was in constant touch with Tonga, so it was quite natural that it would be the first step from Tonga for the missions. But it was only a stepping-stone. As the extent and political situation of the Fiji group gradually became known, it became clear that Lau was on the periphery. It paid tribute to the ruler of Bau, a tiny island just off the south-east coast of Vitilevu, Fiji's largest island, and its language was hardly known beyond Lau. Bau was described (Thomas Williams 1858: 257) as "at once the Athens and the Rome of Fiji". Bauan, or something similar, had long been used as a lingua franca of at least Eastern Fiji, and was known by chiefs and well-travelled commoners throughout the group (Schütz 1985: 63). In 1843, the decision was taken that Bauan would be the standard and that publication in all other Fijian languages would cease.

This was an inevitable and reasonable decision, in view of the economics of printing, but it had unexpected consequences. Cargill had left Fiji three years earlier never to return, and his missionary-linguist successors John Hunt and David Hazlewood were of not quite the same calibre. Moreover, they were under pressure to produce translations of the Scriptures quickly. Inevitably, they relied heavily on Cargill's manuscript grammar and dictionary of Lauan, which was all that was then available, so that their translations had a strong Lauan flavour. And we begin to see too in their work the influence of 'foreigner talk' and eurocentric notions of 'correctness'. The language this small band of well-intentioned amateur language-planners thus forged was far from native, it even verged on the pidgin in some respects, yet the Bible was written in it, and, wholly or partially, most Fijian literature since. It became a norm, but an externally imposed one, not based on the speech of native speakers but on that of foreigners – a kind of standard for which I have coined the term 'exonorm'. Though traditionally known as 'Bauan', I prefer to refer to it as 'Old High Fijian' (OHF), reserving 'Bauan' for the language actually spoken on Bau.

4.1 Lauan Influence in Old High Fijian

A number of Lauan words occur in OHF for no apparent reason: **sabogibogi** 'morning' (Bau **mataka**), **lekutu** 'wilderness' (from Lauan **lekutu** 'forest' – an odd choice!), and **lako**, a postverbal particle meaning approximately 'around' (Bau **voli**). But the greatest area of Lauan influence is where the authors of OHF apparently considered Lauan more regular or etymologically correct. The verb **vak~** 'like, resemble', for instance, which is morphologically **vaka+a**, behaves in Lauan like all other verbs by appearing as **vakai** (**vaka+i**) before proper noun objects; but in Bauan, the form before proper noun objects is the irregular **vak~taki**. Similarly, **vaka** is a regular adverb-forming prefix in Bauan and Lauan. The adverb derived from Lauan **zina** 'true' is **vakaizina** 'truly'; but Bauan has **dina** for both functions. In both of these cases, the regular Lauan form was used in OHF in preference to the irregular Bauan. Evidence for this policy is found in the first Fijian Dictionary (Hazlewood 1850) under the combined entry for **virikoto-ra**, **virinD**, **viritoka**, and **viritì**, where the author states: "These ought, according to analogy, form their tr[ansitives] thus, virinoca, viritokara, viritura, but these terminations are not used in B[auan] though they are in some dia[lects]. In these the B[auan] is irreg[ular] and perhaps ought not to be followed".

Even more pervasive than justification by regularity was justification by ancestry – some Lauan words were preferred for OHF because they appeared to be historically conservative. Thus the Lauan **ko** 'you (sing.)', **ko** proper article, **ki** 'to' and **tawa** 'not' were generally used rather than the Bauan **o**, **o**, **i**, and **sega ni**, respectively, because their Tongan cognates **ke**, **ko**, **ki** and **ta'e** suggested that the Lauan forms had a longer pedigree. Again, indications of this policy are found in Hazlewood's dictionary – e.g. "Ualuvu [flood], pronounced, and therefore perhaps more properly spelt, Waluvu; but ualuvu shows its derivation". Other Lauan words were apparently admitted to OHF because they marked contrasts found in European languages, but not in Bauan. Thus Lauan **ka** survived as a relative clause marker (Bauan has none); Lauan **kivei** directional preposition before proper nouns survived because the Bauan **vei** does not distinguish directional from locational; and **ilevu** 'size' remained, because the Bauan **levu** is not distinct from the adjective **levu** 'big'.

4.2 'Foreigner Talk' in Old High Fijian

As noted above, the use of Fijian 'foreigner talk' was extended in the early nineteenth century from Tongans to European traders. The early missionaries may also have begun speaking it, but they did manage to avoid many of its features in their translations, such as **vosa** 'speak' to mean 'say', **sarasara** 'look at' to mean 'see', use of the intransitive verb in transitive clauses, meaningless reduplication, and the use of simple independent pronouns instead of preverbal subject markers and possessive pronouns (Geraghty 1978: 59-61).

At least two elements, however, remained. One was the use of **kitaka**, a mildly derogatory term meaning 'play around with, interfere with' to mean 'do'. The second, the meaningless use of **s~**. All Fijian languages have two optional preverbal particles marking an aspectual contrast between continuing and new. In Bauan, the particles are **se** and **s~**, respectively: **era se yali** 'they are still missing', **era s~ yali** 'they've gone missing, they're now missing'; **se bula** 'is still alive', **s~ bula** 'has recovered, has escaped death'. Had the missionaries begun their studies in Bauan, they might have grasped the distinction, since it is marked by vowel quality. But in Lau, the difference is only one of quantity – **sa/s~** – which is relatively difficult for an English speaker to perceive, and not distinguished in the orthography. Moreover, it is the custom in Fijian foreigner talk to ignore the aspectual contrast and simply prefix **s~** to every verb (*ibid.*: 59-60), so in OHF **s~** was used frequently, and without meaning, e.g., **rau sa gonedau** 'they had now become fishermen' for **erau gonedau** 'they were fishermen', **era sa kalougata** 'they are now blessed' for **era kalougata** 'they are blessed'.

4.3 Eurocentrism in Old High Fijian

The native language of the early missionaries – all English – and the classical languages some of them had acquired inevitably interfered with their learning Fijian. They thus failed to notice that in Fijian all verb phrases must include a preverbal marker indicating the person and number of the subject (third person singular being unmarked under certain conditions). An example is **sa kalougata ko ira** 'they are blessed', for the Bauan **era kalougata**, **era** marking third person plural. Similarly ungrammatical sentences such as **ra lako me voli kakana** 'they go to buy food' (for **ra lako mera voli kakana** or, more idiomatically, **ra lai voli kakana**) and **kau sa lako mai me vakaotia nai vunau** 'I have come to abolish the law' (for **meu vakaotia**) may also have been accepted initially by Cargill because elision in such circumstances is grammatical in Tongan (Churchward 1953: 53).

Conversely, distinctions not found in Fijian were imposed. Tense marking, for instance, is optional, and, though the grammarian Hazlewood did note this (1850: 46), a tediously large proportion of verb phrases in the Bible begin with **a sa**, which the translator thought was a past tense marker, but is in fact a rarely used pluperfect. Fijian locative prepositions do not indicate source (English to/from), but relative distance: **e/mai** (Geraghty 1976). The authors of OHF, however, consistently used **mai** to translate 'from'. Other functions which are zero-marked in Fijian but not in English, such as clause conjunction and duration phrases, were given marking: **keitou na tucake ka lako** 'we will stand up and go' for **keitou na tucake lako**; **kania na madrai ka bogi vitu** 'ate the bread for seven days' for **kania bogi vitu na madrai**.

Other faults in OHF were due to misanalysis or overgeneralization. Somehow – perhaps because one of its English equivalents is the suffix -**er** – the preverbal particle **dau** 'always, usually' was misconstrued as a prefix, resulting in such ungrammatical phrases as **ena qai mai dau veivoli** 'he will then come to trade' rather than **ena qai dau mai veivoli**. The **e**, which precedes numerals, was seen as obligatory, whereas it does not appear in certain contexts, so that OHF has **sega e dua** 'not one' for **sega ni dua**. And the possessive construction for pronominal possessors was extended to noun phrases by just tacking on the noun phrase, rather than using the portmanteau possessive particles available, thus: **na luvena tagane ko Sera** 'Sera's son' (this actually means 'Sera is his/her son') for **na luvei Sera tagane**.

Even punctuation was affected by eurocentrism and misanalysis. For the former, the postverbal politeness particle **saka** was frequently flanked with commas in imitation of the English 'sir', although there is no pause in speech. For the latter, the **u** allomorph of the first person singular subject marker – in fact historically prior to the **au** allomorph – was preceded by an apostrophe, on the assumption that it was an abbreviated form of **au**.

Old High Fijian became, to varying degrees, the standard for all writing, for speech in the church and classroom, and subsequently in government. It became a superimposed foreigner talk which was imitated because it was the language of the masters. In the minds of its users, if it differed from the way they spoke, it was because their speech was wrong. While the devising of the alphabet was undoubtedly a boon, the creation of OHF was not; indeed, it could be argued that it hindered the development of real literacy for Fijians in the twentieth century.

4.4 Variation on a Theme: Catholic OHF

The French missionaries who established Catholicism in Fiji in the 1840s found that the standard literary language as laid down by the Methodists had been accepted by the Fijians, so they adopted the same medium. Nevertheless, there are minor features which serve to distinguish a Catholic variety of OHF.

Some are features that were originally shared with the Methodists, but subsequently rejected – for instance **daulato** 'virgin', a Lauan word, now replaced by **goneyalewa** 'girl' in Methodist OHF, and **s~ yaga**, literally 'it is now useful', for 'should, must' replaced by **s~ dodonu**, 'it is now right'. The most distinctive aspect of Catholic OHF is its religious terms and proper nouns – many of which are not part of Methodism. In a few instances, Fijian words were selected for extension or compounding: **bete** 'priest of traditional religion, Catholic priest', **matuatabu** 'sacred elder, religious (noun)'; **Tui Tabu** 'sacred king, Pope'. But the great majority were loanwords. Whereas the Methodists had generally used English as a base, the Catholics used Latin or Italian (more rarely French) – some probably by way of East Uvean, the home of Catholicism in the Western Pacific at that time. In addition, they chose to Fijianize simple voiced stops, which do not exist in Fijian, as prenasalized voiced stops (voiced nasal in velar position), whereas the Methodists had preferred simple voiceless stops (sometimes voiced fricatives in bilabial position). Examples of Catholic terms derived from Latin or Italian are: **misa** 'Mass', **pane** 'host', **vino** 'wine', **gar~sia** 'grace', **santo** 'male saint', **santa** 'female saint',[5] from French: **papitema** 'baptize' (F. **baptême**, cf. Methodist **papitaiso** from E. **baptize**), **viole** 'purple' (F. **violet**). The following proper names also illustrate the same contrasts: 'Adam' – Catholic **Adama**, Methodist **Atama**; 'Abel' – C. **Abele**, M. **Epeli, Eveli**; 'Jesus' – C. **Iesu**, M. **J°sì**; 'John' – C. **Ioane**, M. **Jone, Joni**; 'Peter' – C. **PeterÐ**, M. **Pita**; 'Mary' – C. **Maria**, M. **Mere, Meri**; 'Judea' – C. **Iudea**, M. **Jutia**.

4.5 Government Old High Fijian

A number of attempts at western-style government were made in the 1860s and early 70s, and in 1874 Fiji became a British colony after an offer of cession by some of the leading chiefs. During this period a new generation of users of OHF came in the form of government administrators. They coined words related to the new form of government, again using both native and English sources. Extended meanings and compounds included **yasana** 'a side of it, province', **tikina** 'a piece of it, district', and **tìraganilew~** 'lord of judgement, judge' (the biblical term had been **dauveilewai** 'people-judger'). Loans, all from English, included: **sitaba** < stamp, **lawa** < law (via Tongan **lao**; the biblical term had been **vìnau** 'admonishment'), **laiseni** < licence (the compound **ivolatara** 'writing + permitted' was also coined and is still in use) and **kÐvana** < **governor**.

In general, these administrators were keen to create a truly Fijian nation or colony, with administration based on traditional government, and using the Fijian language as far as possible. In the OHF which the missionaries had created they found a variety of Fijian which – and this may well be its most salient characteristic – was easy for English-speakers to

---

[5] These last two are the only Fijian words which appear to have always included a consonant cluster, both written and pronounced.

learn, and acceptable to Fijians because it was the talk of the masters. Fijian preachers and teachers until quite recently affected the anglicized intonation and even the aspirated stops and diphthongized vowels of the Fijian of their models. But because it was so easy for anglophones to learn, it perpetuated the notion that Fijian is a simple and therefore primitive language – a notion that would become an important rationalization for the denigration of Fijian that was to begin around 1930. A fine example of OHF is the motto of the colonial government, a translation of 'Fear God and honour the King', as **Rerevaka na Kalou ka doka na Tui**, which includes the OHF conjunction **ka** and the ungrammatical – as indeed it is in contemporary English – imperativization of **rere** 'fear'.

Throughout the earlier colonial period, Government OHF was maintained by the monthly publication **'Na Mata'**, which was practically the only Fijian literature apart from school texts and religious works. It was probably through this medium that many new terms were introduced, e.g., **livaliva** 'lightning, electricity', **waqavuka** 'boat+fly; aeroplane', **w~lesi** 'wireless', **motok~** 'motorcar'. Although it came to include many contributions by Fijians, they were written in OHF, which had become the only written norm.

5. Old High Fijian and the Deed of Cession

Historians differ as to the relative importance of the various factors that led to a number of powerful Fijian chiefs offering sovereignty of the islands to Great Britain in 1874. Certainly one major consideration was the fact that, despite Cakobau, the Vunivalu (war-chief) of Bau, being acknowledged as the most important of the chiefs, there was no single authority in the land, and local wars were still being fought. Cakobau himself was heavily in debt to the government of the United States, which had threatened military action if the debt was not paid. The Tongan prince Ma'afu also had a significant following and had been threatening to make much of Fiji into a colony of Tonga. Moreover, Fijians had seen and acknowledged the material benefits of western civilization, the Pax Britannica and the Christian faith, and were keen to obtain them. After much debate and vacillation, the chiefs made a conditional offer of cession in March 1874. The British were initially reluctant to accept, particularly in view of the recent Maori wars in New Zealand. Their eventual acceptance of the offer seems to have been motivated by three considerations: to protect the lives and interests of citizens of Britain and its Empire resident in Fiji, to acquire territory in a strategic mid-Pacific location, and to halt blackbirding – the kidnapping of Pacific Islanders to work on plantations in Queensland and Fiji.

At the time of Cession in 1874, there were, as we have seen, significant differences in the linguistic repertoires of the two major races in Fiji – Fijians and Europeans. The Fijians were largely monolingual Fijian speakers, though some knew Tongan. Fijian Christians, now by far the majority, had also become or were becoming literate in OHF. A very small number of Fijians could also communicate in Melanesian Pidgin English, which was used primarily on the plantations by imported labourers (Siegel 1987: 88-90).

Among the Europeans, on the other hand, there was a good deal of bilingualism. Most could speak some Fijian, especially those whose work required it, such as missionaries and planters (*ibid.*: 44, 69, 76). Some gained a reputation as being experts in the Fijian language, for example the planter and politician David Wilkinson, who was to translate the Deed of Cession.

It is very difficult now to assess the competence of Europeans in spoken Fijian, since the only extant records are written, but it is certain that all written translations were in OHF, which had become the norm for Europeans in authority. I would suspect that, while some Europeans who lived in a Fijian environment may well have spoken native Fijian, all other oral communication between Fijians and English speakers, and all written communication, was in the OHF exonorm.

It is very clear, both from contemporary accounts and from a comparison of the language of the English and Fijian versions, that the Deed of Cession was not composed in Fijian. Sir Hercules Robinson, the Governor of New South Wales who had been empowered by Queen Victoria to accept Cession on her behalf, explained on the 25th of September 1874 that the conditional offer of Cession made in March that year was unacceptable to Her Majesty. Cakobau replied with his much-quoted speech to the effect that it was not chief-like to attach conditions, and that he had only done so against his better judgement and under pressure from some other chiefs (De Ricci 1875: 121-2). Sir Hercules then offered an alternative Deed of Cession without conditions which would be acceptable to Her Majesty, and which had been composed, in English, by the Attorney-General of New South Wales (Scarr 1984: 74-5).

For the next two days, Cakobau continued discussions with Sir Hercules on the proffered Deed of Cession, during which "whatever Sir Hercules

Robinson said was interpreted sentence by sentence to the King [Cakobau], who before the next clause was entered on, always signified that he had quite understood the gist of His Excellency's previous observations" (De Ricci 1875: 123). At the same time, Cakobau's most trusted advisor, the planter John Bates Thurston, was studying the document and explaining it in detail to Epeli Nailatikau and Savenaca Naulivou, Cakobau's heir and half-brother respectively, who were also his senior ministers (Scarr 1984: 75).

On the 28th of September, Cakobau presented and explained the Deed of Cession to the Council of Chiefs meeting on Bau and it was approved by the major chiefs present – Epeli Nailatikau, Savenaca Naulivou (both of Bau), Tui Bua, and Ratu Isikeli (of Viwa). On the 30th of September, the resolution of the Council of Chiefs offering to cede Fiji was handed to Sir Hercules. Although this resolution appears in the Gazette as a Fijian text with an English translation, its wording makes it clear that it was composed in English and translated into Fijian, and the first paragraph follows closely the wording of the Deed of Cession and its Fijian translation.

The Deed of Cession was then taken to Vanuabalavu, Ma'afu's headquarters in northern Lau, where it was fully interpreted to both Ma'afu and Tui Cakau, the chief of Cakaudrove, before they signed (de Ricci 1875: 124). Again, on the day of Cession, the 10th of October, Wilkinson not only interpreted but also explained the document so that all the signatories fully understood its contents (Derrick 1950: III).

Although the Fijian translation was written in OHF rather than native Fijian, it would have been readily understood by the chiefs, since they were familiar with OHF. There are only three minor discrepancies in the published translation:

1. Where the English version mentions Cakobau "and other high chiefs", the Fijian version translates as "and the other high chiefs"; that is, the English version implies (correctly) that some high chiefs of Fiji are not signatories, but the Fijian implies (incorrectly) that all are. This discrepancy occurs at least three times. While it is possible that this mistranslation was deliberate, it is far more likely that the translator was simply not skilled enough to translate accurately, or (which amounts to the same thing) that the means to distinguish between these two meanings did not exist in OHF as then spoken.

2. In clause 1, the English word 'foreshores' is translated as **baravi se**

matasawa, which means 'shores or landing beaches'; but other parts of the same paragraph make it clear that all land and sea is included.

3. In clause 7, "the rights and interests [of the ceding chiefs] shall be recognized" is translated rather vaguely as "their chiefly status shall be acknowledged, and their things shall be preserved".

It should also be noted that some of the words used in the Fijian version to convey western concepts were probably unfamiliar to the signatories. Such words are **sivilaisesoni** 'civilization', **latitute** 'latitude', **meritiani** 'meridian', and possibly **sili** 'seal'. Unfamiliarity with these particular words would however not have affected overall comprehension of the document.

Another apparent example of mistranslation occurs at the beginning of the Instrument of Cession, where the Council of Chiefs resolves that: **"Keimami soli Viti walega vua na Marama ... ni keimami sa vakararavi ni na lewai Viti vakadodonu ena veilomani, me yaco tu ga mai kina na tiko vinaka"**. The English version reads thus: "we give our country unreservedly ... and we trust ... that she will rule Fiji justly and affectionately, that we may continue to live in peace and prosperity".

It has been argued by some that a more accurate rendering of the Fijian would have been: "we give our country only because we will depend on her to rule Fiji justly and kindly..." – in other words, that Cession was not unconditional, but conditional upon Her Majesty (and her heirs) ruling justly and kindly.

However, as already noted, the Deed of Cession was composed in English and then translated into Fijian; and, although the passage cited here is from the Resolution of the Council of Chiefs, that part of the resolution was based on the wording of the Deed of Cession. This objection presumes that the Resolution was composed in Fijian, which was not the case.

It is of course possible that later generations of chiefs would have referred back to the Fijian translation, and formed their own impressions there from. Even so, they would have understood the deed in terms of the OHF in which it was patently written, and so interpreted **walega** to mean 'unconditionally' (cf. Hazlewood's dictionary (Hazlewood 1850): **wale, walega**, ad[verb], uselessly; idle; only; for nothing, gratis [my emphasis]). It is true that **walega** does not mean this in native Fijian (**wale** does), and that the conditional meaning is one of the meanings that the sentence might have had, were it read as a sentence of native Fijian. But the whole text is clearly composed in OHF, and it is therefore very unlikely that any Fijian would have, on that basis, understood cession to be conditional.

The full text of the Deed of Cession is reproduced in an Appendix to this paper.

6. Old High Fijian 'Improved'

A revised translation of the Fijian Bible was produced during the 1890s by the Rev Frederick Langham (Wood 1978: 210-211). A comparison with the earlier version reveals that modifications were minor. Had it been the intention to translate the Bible into Fijian as spoken by Fijians, a completely new translation would have been in order. Some of the modifications were in fact improvements, e.g. the removal of the Lauan **tawa** 'not', **sabogibogi** 'morning', **vakai** 'like', and **lako** post-verbal particle; and the substitution of **kau** 'brought' for the ungrammatical **kauti**, **m~liwa lala** 'open space' for **m~liwa** 'space between', **lumulumu** 'fallow' for **vakacegu** 'rest', and **iv~q~** 'provisions for journey' for **oco** 'food given to house builders'.[6]

These, however, are minor lexical matters. All of the major non-Fijian features of OHF were retained in this new translation, and some removed even further from true Fijian. It has been noted that the Lauan proper article **ko** was frequently used in preference to **o**, apparently because it was considered purer. Hazlewood, in his 1850 grammar, suggested a rationalization – that **o** was sometimes used "for the sake of euphony, chiefly at the beginning of a sentence". Langham's revision incorporated this suggestion, all occurrences of **o** being replaced by **ko** except for the odd one in sentence-initial position. In a bout of linguistic eurocentrism, Langham decided that Fijian should have an obligatory plural marker, and so commissioned the prefix **vei**, which usually means 'group, clump'.[7] Thus **e na valenisoro kei na gaunisala** 'in the temples and the streets' was changed to **e na veivalenisoro kei na veigaunisala**.

The already grotesque possessive system of OHF was even further

---

[6] The error in the last example can be traced to Tongan influence. Cargill had assumed that Fijian **oco**, which means only 'food given to house builders', had the full range of meaning of its Tongan cognate **oho**, which includes 'provisions for a journey', and this error was transferred from Lauan into OHF.

[7] See Schütz 1985: 365 for an illustration of how early grammarians, unhampered by OHF, had a clearer idea of the function of this prefix than their successors.

distorted by the gratuitous insertion of **kena** 'its'. For example, the correct **a isau ni mata na mata** 'an eye for an eye' (literally, 'the price of an eye is an eye') became the ungrammatical **me kena isau ni mata na mata**. Most interesting, from the point of view of the study of Fijian grammar, is that it appears to have been Langham who fixed the order of sentence elements so that the subject noun-phrase always came after the verb and object noun-phrase, e.g. **a sa sega ni curuma rawa ko Mosese na vale** 'Moses was not able to enter the house' became **a sa sega ni curuma rawa na vale ko Mosese**, and **a sa kaya na gata vua na yalewa** 'the snake said to the woman' became **a sa kaya vua na yalewa na gata**. Thus apparently originated the grammarians' myth that Fijian is strictly VOS, when in fact almost every order is permissible.

In most respects, therefore, the revised translation of the Bible was even further removed from true Fijian than its predecessor. This is hardly surprising, since Langham did most of the work in Britain during his retirement, without the assistance of a single Fijian. One might even question the motives behind the revision, since Langham then used it to solicit an honorary D.D. from Glasgow University. The Wesleyan Mission Board lent their support, reporting that it was considered "a classic; missionaries and natives speak in the highest terms of the accuracy of rendering, the purity of diction and beauty of style" (Wood 1978: 211) – presumably Fijians added their hosannas because it read even more like the Fijian of the European ministers than the previous translation. The D.D. was awarded.

7. Fijian in Decline

In the 1920s the use of Fijian was at its peak. It was the major medium of communication between government and people, and used almost exclusively in education. But in the 1930s there was a sudden reverse (Geraghty 1984: 41-42), the main reason being that education, hitherto in the benevolent but impecunious hands of the missions, was entrusted to the New Zealand education authorities, with their tradition of the promotion of English to the detriment of Maori, the language of the native population of New Zealand. The teachers of this new generation were unwilling or unable to learn Fijian, and introduced punishment for use of Fijian at any time in schools. They justified their actions by claiming that Fijians must learn English to survive in the modern world and also to communicate with the Indians, descendants of indentured labourers who then comprised over 40% of the total population. The real reasons though were that the new authorities did not have the trust in Fijians to allow them to converse freely in their own language; and that they considered Fijian a poor longwinded language unsuitable for the modern world – a prejudice transplanted from New Zealand, and reinforced by the presence of the pidgin-like OHF exonorm.

Within a short time, this prejudice had made its way into the colonial parliament, the Legislative Council, in the form of a debate on spelling reform (for a blow-by-blow account see Schütz 1985: 29-33). The proposal was that the Fijian spelling system be changed to make it 'phonetic' – which meant simply more like English – by spelling **b**, **c**, **d**, **g** and **q** as **mb**, **th**, **nd**, **ng** and **ngg**, respectively. The debate was long, heated, and punctuated with ignorance and ethnocentrism reminiscent of the early debate on the spelling of Tahitian vowels. In the end, it was decided that the anglicized spelling would only be used in maps and other publications likely to be read mostly by persons unfamiliar with Fijian spelling.

A minor bout of official neologizing occurred during the Second World War, in which Fiji served as a training ground for American and New Zealand troops, and a Fijian battalion fought with distinction in the Solomons campaign. There was an enhanced need – as always in wartime – for public relations, and since Fijians were still obstinately speaking Fijian, the government set up a small unit to publish and broadcast in Fijian.

After the war, official antipathy towards Fijian continued, the former Principal of the Teacher Training College and Director of the Educational Research Institute for Fiji and the Western Pacific declaring:

> The whole community must understand that any improvement in living standards depends on improved technology, and that this requires English. The government should give a lead by using English on all possible occasions. Its instructions, advice and news bulletins should be published in simple English instead of Fijian and Hindi. English should be programmed in early stages for firm foundations. Time for teaching vernacular in schools should be transferred to English. The government should study the present use of English with a view to a wide extension of opportunities for learning, reading and speaking English, especially in villages... The aim of education is the spread of English. (Adam 1959 cited in Geraghty 1989: 391)

This extreme sentiment is indicative of the tenor of official language policy in the last two decades of colonial rule. In the 1950s and 1960s, there were virtually no publications in Fijian; and when a government-subsidized broadcasting service was introduced in 1954, Fijian, the language of about 45% of the population, was allotted less than 15% of the broadcasting time.

Interesting light is shed on the status of OHF during the 1950s by the following extract from the autobiography of the English historian, author and television presenter Peter France, who began his career in the colonial service in Fiji. In it, he tells how he committed the sin of learning to speak native Fijian rather than OHF:

> I had an ear for the sounds of language .. [and] being taught by a Fijian instructor, the first sounds I heard in the language were the sounds which he made and which I imitated. This was to cause disquiet in the local European population. My boss, the District Commissioner, was approached one day in Morris Hedstrom's store by the manager, an Australian who had spent twenty years in the colony, who said, 'You should keep an eye on young France. I heard him in the store the other day trying to speak Fijian *like the Fijians*'. When the DC told me the story, without comment, I realized that there were two ways of speaking Fijian: the native way and the way of the Europeans, who, after all, learnt it from each other. To attempt to speak like a Fijian was to 'go native', and this was not acceptable. (France 1998: 55)

8. Language Use in Independent Fiji

Fiji became an independent member of the Commonwealth in 1970. Unlike many newly-independent nations, Fiji did not immediately throw out the colonial and install the indigenous as the national language. For one thing, Fiji was never a reluctant colony, and most citizens of Fiji still retain much affection and admiration for Britain. In addition, the Fijian themselves had come to accept the colonial credo of Fijian being an impoverished and longwinded language belonging to another era. Moreover, there was the question of the Indians, now over 50% of the population, few of whom spoke Fijian. So there were no significant official moves to adapt Fijian for use beyond the domains of community and church.

Nevertheless, Fijian expanded naturally. With localization, Fijian came to be used increasingly in domains which had been the exclusive preserve of English – offices, classrooms, government departments. The fact that

Fijians still insisted on speaking their own language meant that it could not be ignored by commercial media. Books, newspapers, audio cassettes, and broadcasting in Fijian all increased considerably.

The first official body to acknowledge the existence – or rather persistence – of Fijian was the Ministry of Education, which has gradually extended the teaching of Fijian to the highest secondary level, albeit with little regard for quality. The University of the South Pacific also now offers courses in Fijian Language Studies. In another development, the government took over the **iVolavosa Vakaviti** (Fijian Dictionary Project), initially sponsored by the American actor Raymond Burr, a unit set up to compile a monolingual (Fijian-Fijian) dictionary. This became the de facto centre for the study of Fijian language and culture in the 1980s and 1990s, and was accordingly re-named the 'Institute of Fijian Language and Culture' in 1987. It is this Institute, of which the writer was for many years the acting Director, which was the main initiator of language development after Independence.

The broad aim of the Institute's policy was to bring about true vernacular literacy with a literary standard based on spoken Standard Fijian rather than the OHF exonorm, while also encouraging the use of non-standard varieties of Fijian. Although it was never given statutory powers, its findings and proposals were disseminated in a weekly radio programme, a weekly television programme (from 1998 to 2000), through publications of its own and articles in newspapers, and through liaising with the Ministry of Education and the University of the South Pacific in training teachers. Generally speaking, the media have been quick to accept the reforms, as have most religious denominations (who are the major Fijian-language publishers), while acceptance within the educational system has taken longer.

Spelling and word division were an important area of its work (for a more detailed discussion, see Schütz 1985: 35-46). To accommodate sounds of non-standard dialects and borrowings, all letters of the Roman alphabet were pressed into service, plus a number of digraphs and one new symbol. The most important was **z** for [ndʒ], which features in many loans, e.g. **ziza** < **ginger**, **izini** < **engine**. The velar fricative **x**, glottal stop **ʔ**,[8] and labiovelars **gw**, **kw**, **qw**, and **xw** were introduced mainly for

---

[8] Most Pacific languages have used an apostrophe for the glottal stop, or an accent on the following vowel in some areas of French influence. The problem with the apostrophe is that it has no capital form, and reinforces the idea that the glottal stop is a

use in non-standard varieties of Fijian. Following the widespread practice in Pacific languages and among Fijian grammarians and lexicographers, it was decided to indicate vowel length with a macron in the Institute's publications. It is very unlikely that such length marking will gain popular acceptance in the immediate future, and it is perhaps best that length be marked in non-linguistic publications only where confusion would otherwise arise. Meaningless punctuation, such as the apostrophe in supposed contractions and the comma where there is no pause, was removed.

Word division has long been an area of disagreement, mainly because of unsound decisions made by the early missionaries and rendered sacrosanct by their application in the Bible. A case in point is the writing of the nominalizing prefix **i-** in OHF as a separate word, or even as a suffix to the preceding word, whereas all twentieth century analysts are agreed that it is a prefix, and should be written as such. An example is **na idola** 'the opener', derived from the verb **dola** 'open', which was previously written as either **nai dola** or **na i dola**.

There is even one common word the spelling of which the Institute changed, for the simple reason that it had been spelt wrongly for over 150 years – the first person singular independent pronoun **yau**, which had previously been spelt **i au**. This misspelling can be traced right back to the pioneer linguist Cargill, who was misled by both its Tongan cognate **au** and the Fijian first person singular preverbal subject-marker, also **au**.

Some vocabulary was introduced by the Institute, almost exclusively in the area of language study, again with a preponderance of extension and compounding over, but not to the exclusion of, borrowing. Examples include: **ivosavosa** 'book + language, dictionary', **vosanivanua** 'language of land, dialect, communalect', **nauni** 'noun', **vì** 'source, origin, verb', **matanauni** 'group + noun, noun-phrase'. However, the Institute recognized the futility of attempting to coin words in other domains. The public quickly assimilates words from the English-language media, using closed syllables and certain consonant clusters which have become standard for loanwords in contemporary Fijian, e.g. **plestik** 'plastic bag', **teks** 'tax' (this is now far more common in speech than the nineteenth century government coining **vakacavacava**). The media, especially radio, have occasionally coined with some success. An example is the word for 'coup',

---

'missing letter'. With the advent of the computer age alleviating the difficulties of creating new letters, the Institute chose a symbol based on that used in the International Phonetic Alphabet: ʔ.

for which Fijians use either **kì** (or the eye borrowing **kup**) or **vuaviri**, which was first broadcast on the radio and then taken up by the newspapers, derived from an obsolescent word defined in early dictionaries as "a round of musket shot".

In the areas of syntax and style, the Institute strove in all its broadcasting and publications to stress the importance of moving away from the OHF exonorm as a literary standard and using instead the spoken language, which is virtually free of influence from OHF. Unless this happens, Fijians will never achieve, or even see the value of complete literacy in their own language. As it is, those who know even a little English prefer to read the English translation of the Bible because it is so much clearer than the Fijian. Fijian newspapers are still to some extent influenced by OHF, though they have visibly moved away from it in recent years (25 years ago the proper article was the OHF **ko** – rather than Standard Fijian **o** – 90% of the time, now the figure is more like 10%). Fijians who would talk to each other in Fijian frequently correspond in English, and, though all their thoughts be in Fijian, they would most commonly be written in English in personal diaries. The three main interconnected reasons are: the lesser prestige of Fijian, the fact that it is of little importance in schools and taught very poorly, and the continuing influence of OHF. The Institute of Fijian Language and Culture saw it as its mission to tackle the problem on all three fronts: to raise the prestige of Fijian, to work with the Ministry of Education and the University of the South Pacific in improving the quality of Fijian teaching in schools, and to counter the negative influence of OHF. It must be borne in mind that most of the 'reforms' were merely changes to bring written Fijian, which unlike most literary languages was not based on an older form of the spoken language, into line with Fijian as spoken.

9. Conclusion

In 1997 the constitution took an important step forward when it finally raised the status of the languages of the people in two simple sentences: "The English, Fijian and Hindustani languages have equal status in the State; and: Every person who transacts business with a department, an office in a state service, or a local authority, has the right to do so in English, Fijian or Hindustani, either directly or through a competent interpreter" (Constitution (Amendment) Act 1997: 61). This is a promising start, though in a country with no tradition of translation, it will be extremely difficult to implement. The government has been accustomed to operating solely in English, and enormous changes will be required to make it sensitive to local languages. There will need to be coordinated language development along with training for a cadre of professional interpreters and translators, and none of this is in place at the moment. While many civil servants are fluent speakers of Fijian and Hindi, they are not necessarily literate in those languages, and in most cases far from being 'competent interpreters', as required by the constitution. It is unfortunately not generally realized in Fiji that competent interpretation and translation require not only a rare aptitude but also arduous professional training. The few translators that do exist in the civil service are poorly paid and totally untrained – a situation which could have serious consequences, particularly in courts of law.

Even if all government documents were to be translated into Fijian, this would not lead to the Fijian-speaking public becoming instantly active and equal participants in government. They have not been educated to use literacy as a tool in the same way as, for example, English-speakers in New Zealand. As noted above, most Fijians are accustomed to using Fijian language literacy for reading the Bible and the hymn book, and for writing the occasional personal letter, but very little else. For complete and effective literacy, the Fijian language will need to be developed for all domains and integrated fully into the education system.

Nevertheless, the 1997 constitution has pointed to the direction that must be followed in order to make the government truly one of the people. All citizens of Fiji can now look forward to a time when they will not be forced to beg for help from an English speaker before they can fill in an application form, or read the instructions on their prescribed medication, and when their letters in Fijian or Hindi to the servants of the people will be actually read and acted on, and not consigned to the rubbish bin, as has so often been the case in the past.

References

Adam, R. S. (1959) 'Social Factors in Second Language Learning, with Special Reference to the Fiji Islands', Unpublished doctoral dissertation, University of London.
Ai vola-tukutuku ni vei ka e ra sa cakava mai Levuka ko ira na TUI VITI vata kei ira kece na turaga lelevu kei VITI ni ra sa soli Viti ki vua na marama dauloloma na Ra Nadi kai Tui ni Piritania e na vula ko Okotova nai ka tini ni siga ni yabaki *oqo ko 1874* (1874) Levuka [Fiji]: Government Printer.
Churchward, C. M. (1953) *Tongan Grammar*, Oxford: Oxford University Press.
Constitution (Amendment) Act 1997 of the Republic of the Fiji Islands, 25 July, 1997 (1997) Suva: Government Printer.
De Ricci, J. H. (1875) *Fiji: Our new Province in the South Seas,* London: Edward Stanford.
Derrick, R. A. (1950) *A History of Fiji,* voume one, second edition, Suva, Fiji: Printing and Stationery Department.
France, Peter (1998) *Journey: A Spiritual Odyssey*, London: Chatto & Windus.
Geraghty, Paul (1976) 'Fijian Prepositions', *Journal of the Polynesian Society* 85(4): 507-20.
------ (1978) 'Fijian Dialect Diversity and Foreigner Talk: The Evidence of Pre-missionary Manuscripts', in Albert J. Schütz (ed) *Fijian Language Studies: Borrowing and Pidginization*, Bulletin of the Fiji Museum No. 4, Suva: Fiji Museum.
------ (1984) 'Language Policy in Fiji and Rotuma', in George B. Milner, David G.Arms and Paul Geraghty *Duivosavosa: Fiji's Languages: Their use and their Future*, Bulletin of the Fiji Museum No. 8, Suva: Fiji Museum.
------ (1989) 'Language Reform: History and Future of Fijian', in Istvan Fodor and Claude Hagège (eds) *Language Reform: History and Future*, Volume IV, Hamburg: Helmut Buske.
------ (1994) 'Linguistic Evidence for the Tongan Empire', in Tom Dutton and Darrell T. Tryon (eds) *Language Contact and Change in the Austronesian World*, Trends in Linguistics Studies & Monographs 77, Berlin: Mouton de Gruyter.
Geraghty, Paul and Jan Tent (1997a), 'Early Dutch Loanwords in Polynesia', *Journal of the Polynesian Society* 106(2): 131-60.
------ (1997b) 'More Early Dutch Loanwords in Polynesia', *Journal of the Polynesian Society* 106(4): 395-408.
Hazlewood, David (1850) *A Feejeean and English Dictionary*, Vewa, Feejee [Viwa, Fiji]: Wesleyan Mission Press.
L~tikefu, S (1977) 'The Wesleyan Mission' in Noel Rutherford (ed) *Friendly Islands: A History of Tonga*, Melbourne: Oxford University Press.
Martin, John (1817) *An Account of the Natives of the Tongan Islands*, London: John Murray.

Newbury, C[olin] W. (ed) (1961) *The History of the Tahitian Mission, 1799-1830, written by John Davies ... Hakluyt Society, Series* 2 No 116, Cambridge: Cambridge University Press.
Scarr, Deryck (1984) *Fiji: A Short History,* Sydney: George Allen and Unwin.
Schütz, Albert J. (1985) *The Fijian Language,* Honolulu: University of Hawaii Press.
------ (1976) 'Take *my* Word for it: Missionary Influence on English Borrowings in Hawaiian', Oceanic Linguistics 14(1): 75-92.
------ and Paul Geraghty (eds) (1980) *David Cargill's Fijian Grammar,* Bulletin of the Fiji Museum No. 6, Suva: Fiji Museum.
Siegel, Jeff (1987) *Language Contact in a Plantation Environment: A Sociolinguistic History of Fiji,* Studies in the Social and Cultural Foundations of Language 15, Cambridge: Cambridge University Press.
Tent, Jan and Paul Geraghty (2001) 'Broken Sky or Shattered Myth?: The Origin of *Papalagi*', *Journal of the Polynesian Society* 110(2): 171-214.
Williams, John (1842) *A Narrative of Missionary Enterprises in the South Sea Islands,* London: John Snow.
Williams, Thomas (1858) *Fiji and the Fijians: The Islands and their Inhabitants,* London: Alexander Heylin.
Wood, A. Harold (1978) *Overseas Missions of the Australian Methodist Church, Volume II, Fiji,* Melbourne: Aldersgate Press.

APPENDIX: Documents of Cession

The following English text of the Deed of Cession of Fiji to Great Britain is taken from the original as reproduced in Derrick 1950: I-III. Note that an anglicized form of spelling is used for Fijian names, e.g. Thakombau for Cakobau.

Instrument of Cession of the Islands of Fiji by Thakombau, styled Tui Viti and Vuni Valu, and by the other high chiefs of the said islands to Her Most gracious Majesty Victoria, by the grace of God, of the United Kingdom of Great Britain and Ireland Queen, Defender of the Faith, &c &c &c:-

Whereas divers of the subjects of Her Majesty the Queen of Great Britain and Ireland have from time to time settled in the Fijian group of islands and have acquired property or certain pecuniary interests therein; **And Whereas** the Fijian Chief Thakombau styled Tui Viti and Vuni Valu and the other high native chiefs of the said islands are desirious [sic] of securing the promotion of civilization and Christianity and of increasing trade and industry within the said islands; **And Whereas** it is obviously desirable, in the interests as well of the native as of the white population, that order and good government should established therein; **And Whereas** the said Tui Viti and other high chiefs have conjointly and severally requested Her Majesty the Queen of Great Britain and Ireland aforesaid to undertake the government of the said islands henceforth; **And Whereas** in order to [sic] the establishment of British government within the said islands the said Tui Viti and other the [sic] several high chiefs thereof for themselves and their respective tribes have agreed to cede the possession of and the dominion and sovereignty over the whole of the said islands and over the inhabitants thereof and have requested Her said Majesty to accept such cession, – which cession the said Tui Viti and other high chiefs, relying on the justice and generosity of Her said Majesty, have determined to tender unconditionally, – and which cession on the part of the said Tui Viti and other high chiefs is witnessed by their execution of these presents and by the formal surrender of the said territory to Her said Majesty; **And Whereas** His Excellency Sir Hercules George Robert Robinson, Knight Commander of the most distinguished order of Saint Michael and Saint George, Governor Commander in Chief and Vice Admiral of the British Colony of New South Wales and its dependencies, and

Governor of Norfolk Island, hath been authorised and deputed by Her said Majesty to accept on Her behalf the said Cession:-

Now These Presents Witness,

1. **That** the possession of and full sovereignty and dominion over the whole of the group of islands in the South Pacific Ocean known as the Fijis (and lying between the parallels of latitude of fifteen degrees South and twenty two degrees South of the Equator and between the Meridians of longitude of one hundred and seventy seven degrees West and one hundred and seventy five degrees East of the meridian of Greenwich) and over the inhabitants thereof, together with the possession of and sovereignty over the waters adjacent thereto and of and over all ports and harbours havens roadsteads rivers estuaries and other waters and all reefs and foreshores within or adjacent thereto, are hereby ceded to and accepted on behalf of Her said Majesty the Queen of Great Britain and Ireland her heirs and successors, to the intent that from this time forth the said islands and the waters reefs and other places as aforesaid lying within or adjacent thereto may be annexed to and be a possession and dependency of the British Crown.

2. **That** the form or constitution of government, the means of the maintenance thereof, and the laws and regulations to be administered within the said islands shall be such as Her Majesty shall prescribe and determine.

3. **That** pending the making by Her Majesty as aforesaid of some more permanent provision for the government of the said islands His Excellency Sir Hercules George Robert Robinson, in pursuance of the powers in him vested and with the consent and at the request of the said Tui Viti and other high Chiefs the ceding parties hereto, shall establish such temporary or provisional government as to him may seem meet.

4. **That** the absolute proprietorship of all lands not shown to be now alienated so as to have become bona fide the property of Europeans or other foreigners or not now in the actual use or occupation of some Chief or tribe or not actually required for the probable future support and maintenance of some chief or tribe shall be and is hereby declared to be vested in Her said Majesty her heirs and successors.

5. **That** Her Majesty shall have power, whenever it shall be deemed necessary for public purposes, to take any lands upon payment to the proprietor of a reasonable sum by way of compensation for deprivation thereof.

6. **That** all now existing public buildings houses and offices, all enclosures and other pieces or parcels of land now set apart or being used for public purposes, and all stores fittings and other articles now being used in connection with such purposes are hereby assigned transferred and made over to Her said Majesty.

7. **That** on behalf of Her Majesty His Excellency Sir Hercules George Robert Robinson promises (1) that the rights and interests of the said Tui Viti and other high chiefs the ceding parties hereto shall be recognised so far as is and shall be consistent with British Sovereignty and Colonial form of government, (2) that all questions of financial liabilities and engagements shall be carefully scrutinized and dealt with upon principles of justice and sound public policy, (3) that all claims to title to land by whomsoever preferred and all claims to pensions or allowances whether on the part of the said Tui Viti and other high chiefs or of persons now holding office under them or any of them shall in due course be fully investigated and equitably adjusted.

In Witness whereof the whole of the contents of this instrument of Cession having been, previously to the execution of the same, interpreted and explained to the ceding parties hereto by David Wilkinson Esquire, the interpreter nominated by the said Tui Viti and the other high chiefs and accepted as such interpreter by the said Sir Hercules George Robert Robinson, the respective parties hereto have hereunto set their hands and seals.

Done at Levuka this tenth day of October, in the year of Our Lord one thousand eight hundred and seventy four.—

	Cakobau R. Tui Viti and Vunivalu	(Seal)
	Maafu	(Seal)
Hercules Robinson (Seal)	Tui Cakau	(Seal)
	Ratu Epeli	(Seal)
	Vakawalitabua Tui Bua	(Seal)
	Savenaca	(Seal)
	Esekele	(Seal)
	B.V. Tui Dreketi	(Seal)
	Ritova	(Seal)
	Kato-nivere	(Seal)
	Ratu Kini	(Seal)
	Matanitobua	(Seal)
	Nacagilevu	(Seal)

I hereby certify that, prior to the execution of the above Instrument of Cession – which execution I do hereby attest – I fully and faithfully interpreted and explained to the ceding parties the whole of the contents of the said document, the interlineations appearing on line 33 of page 1 and on line 30 of page 2 having been first made, and that such contents were fully understood and assented to by the said ceding parties. Prior to the execution of the said instrument of Cession I wrote out an interpretation of the same in the Fijian language, which interpretation I read to the Tui Viti and other high chiefs the ceding parties, who one and all approved thereof. A copy of such interpretation is hereto annexed marked A. Dated this tenth day of October, A.D. 1874.

D. Wilkinson
Chief Interpreter
The interpreter named in the foregoing instrument of Cession

Although Derrick (1950) did not reprint the Fijian translation referred to above, it is found in a Government publication (Ai Vola-tukutuku... 1874) and is reprinted below, preceded by Cakobau's brief letter offering Cession. While showing the usual features of Old High Fijian, this translation is notable for a number of idiosyncrasies, the most remarkable of which is the substitution of the – a transitive ending for the expected –i suffix, e.g. **solia** for **soli** 'give', **rauta** for **rauti** 'sufficient for', **kunea** for **kunei** 'find', and **veitarotaroga** for **veitarotarogi** 'enquire, enquiry'. Other idiosyncratic forms include **devaki** for **deivaki** 'firm', **gouna** for **gauna** 'time', and occasionally **kai** for **ka** 'and'. Confusion of final –i and –e, as in **veivole** for **veivoli** 'trade', **mataqale** for **mataqali** 'tribe', and **lavi** for **lave** 'copy, translate' is probably due to the typical English-speaker's inability to distinguish between those two vowels in final position. Wilkinson also consistently uses **e ya** for the expected OHF **o ya** or **ko ya**, which may reflect the influence of the language of Bua, where he lived, where 'ea has a similar function. Square brackets enclose corrections of typographical errors.

KI VUA NA MARAMA NA TUI PIRITANIA-

Keimami na Tui Viti, vata kei ira na Turaga lelevu kei Viti, keimami sa solia Viti walega vua na Marama levu ka dau loloma na Ra Nadi kai Tui Piritania Levu kei Airaldi [Airaladi] ni keimami sa vakararavi sara ni na lewai Viti vaka dodonu, e na veilomani, me yaco tu ga mai kina na tiko vinaka.

Io keitou kerea vua na Kovana ko Sir Hercules Robinson, na nona Talai na Marama me rogoci ira na neitou veivuke e na ka eso era na tukuna vua, ni keimami sa vakararavi vei ira, ka qara me tinia vinaka na veivosaki oqo.

(Sa Tabaki)   CAKOBAU R.

A I VOLA-VEIVOSAKI NI SOLIA na vei yanuyanu ko Viti, Ko ira na vunivalu ko Cakobau, ko na Tui Viti vata kei ira na kena Turaga Lelevu era sa soli Viti, ki vua na Marama levu ka dau-loloma, ko Vikitoria e na loloma ni Kalon [Kalou] sa Tui, ka dau maroroya na Lotu dina ni Piritania levu kei Airaladi.

Me vaka:- Ni sa so na kai Papalagi na nona tamata na Tui Piritania levu kei Airaladi, era sa mai tiko e na veiyanuyanu ko Viti, e na vei gouna e so, ka ra sa rawata mai kina na vanua e so kei na yau talega. Ia ko ira na Vunivalu ko Cakobau na Tui Viti, vata kei ira na kena Turaga Lelevu, kai taukei ni vei yanuyanu oqo, era sa gadreva ka qara me yaco rawa vakavinaka na vaka Sivilaisesoni, kei na Lotu, ka me tubu cake devaki na tiko vinaka, na veivole, na qumatua [gumatua] ni rawa yau, e na vei yanuyanu qori. Ka ni sa macala vaka sigalevu ni sa ka yaga vei ira na lewenivanua taukei kei ira na kai Papalagi me yaco tu ga mai kina, na lewa vinaka vaka Matanitu, kei na tiko vinaka.

Ia ni sa lomadra dina kina, era sa taroga ka kerea ko ira na Tui Viti kei ira yadua na kena Turaga lelevu, vua na Marama dauloloma na Tui ni Piritania levu kei Airaladi, me mai taura na lewa vaka Matanitu mai an [na] gouna oqo, ka me vakatura kina ni [na] lewa vaka Piritania e na vei yanuyanu oqo era sa solia ko na Tui Viti vata kei ira na kena Turaga Lelevu ni ra sa loma vata kina me ra solia, era sa roqota, ka musuka oqo, vakai ira ga, ia e na vukudra tale ga na vei mataqale, na nodra tamata na lewenivanua i Viti, era sa solia ka roqota ka musuka vua na Marama, ka kerea me vakadonuya na nodra soli oqo, ka me taura ko koya, ni ra sa qai solia Viti walega vua na Marama, ko ira na Tui Viti kei ira na kena Turaga Lelevu, ni ra sa vakararavi ki na nona lewa dodonu kei na nona dau veilomani.

Ia sa caka nai vola oqo me kenai vakatakila, ka me macala kina ni sa nodra cakacaka vakai ira ga, ko na Tui Viti, kei na kena Turaga Lelevu, ka sa kenai solisoli, kai kaukau, me musuka kina vua na Marama.

Ia ni sa lesi na Turaga vinaka ko Sir Hercules George Robert Robinson, Knight Commander of the Most Honorable Order of Saint Michael and Saint George, Kovana, ka nodra Turaga na Turaga ni valu mai na Yasana vaka Piritania, ko Welesi Vou mai na Ceva (e ya ko Siteni), kei na kena vei vanua, ka, Kovana ni yanuyanu ko Novoka. Ia ni sa lesia ko na Marama ka talai koya mai, me mai cakava na kena cakacaka e na yacana, ka me taura ka vakadonuya nai vola oqo, e ka [ya] sa solia kina na vanua, na vei yanuyanu ko Viti.

Ia sai koya oqo na ka sa vakatakilai e nai vola oqo, sa vaka.

Ai matai.- Ia sa na taura tiko na vei yanuyanu oqo ko Viti vakai taukei sara ko na Marama, vata kei na kena lewa vaka turaga vaka Tui, me yacova na kena vei yalayala, me vaka sa volai tu oqo. Ia ko Viti sa tiko mai na tikini vuravura e na wasawasa na yacana ko Pesivika Osani ki na ceva; ia na kena vei yalayala me vaka sa vola tu e na kena Mapi, ena yasai vuravura ki na ceva nai ka 15° ni Latitute i ceva, kei nai ka 22° ni Latitute i ceva ga, ni wilika mai na vei mama kei vuravura. Ia na vei yalayala mai na Ra mai nai ka 177° ni Ra, ki nai ka 175° ni Tokalau (se na tui cake,) ko ya ruarua ni wili mai na meritiani ni koro ko Kirinesi, qori na kena vei Yalayala kei Viti; ka sa solia vata, ko ira na Lewenivanua kecega sa tiko mai kina, kei na kena Waitui sa vakavolevolita [vakavolivolita], kei na kena vei Toba, se Daveta, se Kelekele ni Waqa, se Uciwai, se Drakaniwai, e ya na Wai kecega, kei na Cakau kece, kei na Baravi, se Matasawa kece, kei na kena ka kece tale me vaka sa tu kina, se voleka kina, sa yalataki ka solia sara oqo, ka sa vakadonuya talega me taura tiko ko na Marama na Tui ni Piritania levu kei Airaladi kei ira sa na tarava e na nonai tutu vaka Tui, me vaka oqo e ya mai na gouna oqo ka yaco va na vei gouna mai muri ka tawa mudu, me sa vanua vaka Piritania na vei yanuyanu oqo ko Viti, na kena wai, na kena cakau kece talega sa tu kina, se voleka kina, se sa volita, me nona vakai Taukei dina sara, ka me vakaroroga [vakarorogo] ki na Lewa vaka Tui ni Piritania.

Ai ka rua.- Ia sa na lewa ga na Marama na kenai valavala, se ai tovo, ni lewa vaka Matanitu sa yaga me vakaturi mai kina e ya me rauti Viti vinaka, kei na vei ka me rawa kina na kena gacagaca, ka me sauma rawa kina na kena cakacaka vaka Matanitu, Kei na vei Lawa, se Lewa me vakatura, ka vakayacora kina e na vei Yanuyanu oqo ko Viti.

Ai ka tolu.- Ia ni sa bera mai na nona lewa na Marama me vaka sa tukuna e cake, e ya nai tutu dina ni lewa vaka Matanitu, e na vei yanuyanu oqo ko Viti. Era sa kerea, ko na Tui Viti kei na kena Turaga Lelevu e ya ko ira sa kitaka ka vakayacora na soli vanua oqo, ki vua na Turaga na nona Talai mai na Marama, ko Sir Hercules George Robert Robinson, me vaka na nonai lesilesi sa taura tu oqo ko koya, e ra sa kerea vua me lewa ka vakatura na lewa vaka Matanitu, e na gouna ga edaidai e na veiyanuyanu oqo ko Viti, ia me vaka e nanuma ko koya sa na yaga kina.

Ai ka va.- E na vuku ni vanua i Viti ko ya sa volitaki oti vei ira na kai Papalagi e so, ni ra na tukuna ni sa nodra, ka sa macala mai na kena veitarotaroga [veitarotarogi] ni sa dina ni nodra vaka dodonu se ko ya e ra sa taura tiko ko ira na turaga e so, se mataqale, se ko ira na lewenivanua taukei; e ya ni sa vakayagataka tiko oqo, se ni na qai vota vei ira na Turaga, se mataqale se lewenivanua me rauta ira vinaka na tamata yadua, e na gouna oqo, ka me na rauta ira vinaka e na vei gouna mai muri. Ia na vanua sa vo ni sa votai oti vaka, sa yalataki ka sa solia sara oqo ki vua na Marama, me nona dina sara vakai taukei vaka turaga, vata kei ira sa na tarava e na nonai tutu vakatui.

Ai ka lima.- Ia kevaka sa na yaga e dua na tikinivanua ki na Matanitu se kena cakacaka, e na dua na gouna mai muri, ka sa vanua vakai taukei, sa na qai rawarawa ka tara vua na Marama me taura na tikinivanua ko ya ka vakayagataka kina. Ia ke sa na sauma vaka dodonu vua nai taukei, ni sa kauta tani mai vua na kena vauna [vanua].

Ai ka ono.- E na vuku ni ka ni Matanitu oqo i Viti, e ya na vei vale kece na vei tikini vanua sa taura tu se vakayagataka tiko e na ka vaka Matanitu na kena yau, se yaya, se gacagaca se dua tale na ka, sa tauri ka vakayagataki tiko se vakatokai me ka vaka Matauitu [Matanitu] ni Viti sa qai solia vata talega vua na Marama me nona dina, ka me kenai Taukei, ka me vaka yagataka, ko koya.

Ai ka vitu.- Sa tolu na ka sa yalataka oqo ko na Kovona [Kovana] ko Sir Hercules George Robert Robinson, ena yacana na Marama, me na vakabau mai muri. (Ai matai). E na vukudra na Tui Viti kei ira na kena Turaga Lelevu era sa cakava, ka solia oqo, sa na vakabau tiko, ka vakadinadinataka na nodra tutu vaka turaga, ka maroroya na nodra ka yadua, ia me vaka ga e rawa ka kilikili kei na Lewa vakatui ni Piritania vaka Matanitu sa dau vakatura e na kenai vei vanua kisau, e ya vaka sa na qai vakaturi i Viti mai na gouna oqo (Ai ka rua.) E na vuku ni dinau ni Matanitu kevaka sa tu e dua nai vola-veivosaki ka sa kunea ni sa caka dodonu ni sa veitarotaroga vakalalai vakavinaka ka na qai lewa kina me vakadonuya vaka ga, sa dodonu, ka yaga kei na Lewa vakavuku ka devaki. (Ai ka tolu.) E na vuku ni vanua sa voletaki [volitaki], se soli oti ni ra na qai tukuna, se taroga ko ira na tamata ni ra sai taukei ni tikinivanua e so ka vaka me vakadinadinataki vei ira sa na qai vakataroga sara me kila na dina. Ia ena vukudra talega, na Turaga sa vakai tavi e na cakacaka ni Matanitu ka vaka me dua na kedrai sau, se vakavakacequ [vakacegu] mai na nodrai tavi, se ko ira na Tui Viti, kei ira na kena Turaga Lelevu kece, se so vei ira sa na vaka taroga talega ka me lewa dodonu kina e na kena gouna.

SAI VAKATAKILAI nai vola oqo ni ra sa vakadinadinataka ko ira na Turaga sa cakava, ni sa laveta oti mada ki na vosavakaviti ko Tevita Wilikisoni ko koya era sa lesia ko na Tui Viti kei ira na Turaga Lelevu, ka sa vakabauta talega ko Sir Hercules George Robert Robinson, na Kovona [Kovana]; me kena dau lavi [lave] vosa kina; ka sa wilika, ka vakamacalataka oti, ko koya ki vei ira kece e na vosavakaviti ni sa bera ni ra tabaka. Era saqai vakadinadinataka ko ira yadua na Turaga e na Ligadra dina, kei na nodra Sili, ni ra lomadina ki na ka era sa cakava oqo.

Sa caka ka vakayacori mai Levuka, e nai ka tini ni siga ni vula ko Okotova ni yabaki ni nodra [noda] Turagi [Turaga] e dua na udolu ka walu na drau ka vitusagavulu ka va.

(Sd)	Cakobau R.	(L.S.)
Tui Viti kai Vunivalu		
Maafu		(L.S.)
Tui Cakau		(L.S.)
Ratu Epeli		(L.S.)
Vakawaletabua, Tui Bua		(L.S.)
Savenaca		(L.S.)
Isikeli		(L.S.)
Roko Tui Dreketi		(L.S.)
Nacagilevu		(L.S.)
Ratu Kini		(L.S.)
Ritova		(L.S.)
Katunivere [Katonivere]		(L.S.)
Matanitobua		(L.S.)
(Sd) Hercules Robinson		(L.S.)

Oqo nai vola sa tukuni e cake e ya kau sa vakadinadina kina ni kau sa laveta oti ki na vosa vaka Viti me vaka sa tukuni.

Koi au ko T. WILIKISONI

Na Dau Lavevosa.

Tokelau

Background: Originally Tokelau was settled by Polynesian emigrants from surrounding island groups. The Tokelau Islands were made a British protectorate in 1889. They were transferred to New Zealand administration in 1925.
Land Area: 10 sq km
Capital: None, each atoll has its own administrative centre.
Population: 1 431; Polynesian
Languages: Tokelauan, English

Decolonization by Missionaries of Government
The Tokelau Case

TONY ANGELO
Victoria University of Wellington

AND TIONI VULU

> Abstract. *When three small and separate atoll communities of the tropical Pacific are required by international standards to develop a joint system of national government which can take over the central role of the colonial power, the task for translators is huge. It is demanding in terms of both vocabulary and culture. This paper concerns the translation endeavours of the people of Tokelau in the context of their decolonization. The paper uses a number of key Government documents written since 1980 to provide evidence that Tokelauan translators have been slow to adopt a consistent terminology for the new legal and political ideas, and that they have preferred to source the words of translation in the existing language. A consequence of the use of traditional words for the alien ideas of Western European style government has created some resistance to the social acceptance of the ideas because they are not understood or because the cultural resonance of the ideas in the Tokelauan words of translation is often at odds with the political concepts of the English source text.*

> We recognise that new language will result from the use of these law making powers. Put another way, the political and constitutional development of Tokelau is enriching the language.
> General Fono Law Making Powers Preamble,
> Letter of Ulu of Tokelau to the Administrator
> of Tokelau, 14 May 1996.

Tokelau is a traditional South Pacific atoll society, which is having to deal with the introduction of Western European ideas of law and government. Tokelau is not an unwilling recipient of these ideas, but many of them are alien to Tokelau, obviously or apparently contradictory of its culture, and expressed in a foreign language. The political and economic transformation of Tokelau has been particularly noticeable since 1970. It has been promoted externally as part of the achievement of the United Nations' goals of decolonization and conditioned by external budgetary support.

The purpose of this paper is to trace the development of the translation into Tokelauan of English words and phrases that deal with governance and law, and to try to relate that development to the development of Western European style government in Tokelau.

This paper is in particular concerned with translations and the Tokelauan language from 1980 to 2002, which has been a period of active political development. It considers briefly the extent to which the available dictionaries and word lists can assist translators. It also records the translation usage at key points as it is recorded in selected documents for which Tokelauan texts are available.

An analysis of the words and concepts used in the translations gives some insight into how alien political concepts from a distant culture, expressed in a foreign language, are finding their way into the target language. The analysis also indicates the extent to which target language words or new words are used and to what effect.

The evidence from the documents appears to show a very slow change in the relationship of language and culture and that the vocabulary is stabilizing in use in political circles. Words for political and legal ideas may have been accepted, but the concepts and their content appear not to have been. The culture change is much slower than the language change. There is also evidence of a preference, in translation of English ideas, for Tokelau derived words. Those words are more likely than imported words to have some resonance for Tokelauans not involved in government affairs. Nevertheless, they are still descriptive of an alien phenomenon, not of a local reality.

A slow rate of change is consistent with the fact that there has never been a national government center in Tokelau: each village is run independently on traditional lines. To the extent that there was in the past a national government center outside of New Zealand, it was at Apia in Samoa, the chief port of entry for Tokelau. Equally there has been no colonial presence in Tokelau and no national government has been visible locally to provide a model for the development internally of national self-government distinct from the villages.

1. Tokelau Political Development and the Law – an Overview

Tokelau is a Polynesian community of 1500 people situated north of Samoa and just south of the Equator. The territory is made up of three small coral atolls – Atafu, Nukunonu, Fakaofo – where life for many is still basically that of a subsistence economy.

The islands became a British protectorate in 1889 and since then have been, in turn, a part of the Gilbert and Ellice Islands Colony, and a British territory administered by the New Zealand government out of Western Samoa. Since 1 January 1949 Tokelau has been part of New Zealand, and administered by New Zealand from Wellington and through a Tokelau office in Apia the capital of Samoa.

Tokelau is listed by the United Nations as a non-self-governing territory with a right to self-determination according to the rules of the United Nations. It is currently developing internal self-government in preparation for exercising its right to self-determination. Because of the co-operative engagement of New Zealand (the administering power) and Tokelau (the non-self governing territory) with the United Nations, and because of Tokelau's unique approach to the development, Tokelau is described as a model for decolonization in small island territories (of which 16 remain).

Other than in connection with the development of a Tokelau Public Service in 1969, the interaction of Tokelau with Western European style government processes was very limited until 1993 when a new and more intense phase of development of self-government began. The first move came with the appointment of local people to have control of the Tokelau Public Service. This was followed soon after by the delegation by the Administrator of Tokelau of executive powers held by New Zealand. This grant was made to the national representative body of Tokelau – the *General Fono* – and to the senior elected officials of Tokelau, the three *Faipule*.

The political features of Tokelau are (1) a local government which is based in the village of each atoll and which runs independently in each village, and (2) a nascent national government made up of representatives of each of the three villages. The national government has legislative and executive powers and meets as the *General Fono* two or three times each year on each atoll in turn. The chief elected officer in each village is the *Faipule*, and the three *Faipule* together perform a ministerial role in the national government. The Chief Minister is the *Ulu*. The *Faipule* are elected for a 3 year term and take the role of *Ulu* for one year each in rotation. There is no recognized capital or chief island of Tokelau; all islands take their turn at being the center of national government activity.

In international law terms Tokelau is a territory of which New Zealand is the administering power. The equivalent of a colonial governor is the Administrator of Tokelau who is an employee of the Ministry of Foreign Affairs and Trade in Wellington, New Zealand. Public services in Tokelau are provided at the national level by the employees of the Tokelau

Public Service. The Tokelau Public Service was established by the Tokelau Amendment Act 1968 which came into force on 1 January 1969. The service grew rapidly and by 1975 it had more than 240 Tokelauan employees. Between 1969 and 2001, this public service was controlled by the State Services Commission of New Zealand. Since mid-2001, the Tokelau Public Service has been controlled by Tokelau itself.

From the time of the introduction of the Tokelau Public Service in 1969 the cash economy began to have a clear impact on Tokelau. As that service grew, more and more members of the community had a cash income, which distinguished them from their compatriots in the villages who still lived within a subsistence economy. The questions raised by the public service phenomenon concerned both this cash flow and also the existence of an authority separate from the elders in each village.

Following the United Nations Visiting Mission to Tokelau in 1981, there was an increasing emphasis on matters of law within the community but changes in local administration and a series of natural disasters at the end of the 1980s slowed the development of law thinking and legal institutions.

The current phase of heightened activity in terms of the government structures began in 1993. It was given a substantial boost by the impending visit of the United Nations Special Mission in 1994, and after that by the focus in the United Nations and in Wellington on the first International Decade for the Eradication of Colonialism. The Special Visiting Mission of the United Nations to Tokelau in August 2002 reinforced the governmental development profile and placed the current Tokelau activities clearly in the context of the UN Committee of 24 work plans and of the Second International Decade for the Eradication of Colonialism.

Much of this political and international activity is reflected, in an accessible form, in the reports from the United Nations Decolonization Committee beginning with its visit in 1976. There are also annual reports to the New Zealand Parliament on the administration of Tokelau. The format of the government reports through till 1993 was rather formal and reflected the slow change of things within Tokelau itself. The reports after 1993 however are clearly different and reflect the current political activity in Tokelau, Wellington, and New York. They also reflect the fact that from 1993 to 2003 the office of the Administrator of Tokelau has been a full-time position within the Ministry of Foreign Affairs and Trade of New Zealand.

2. The Translator's Challenge

The translators confronted by the task of presenting the new ideas of the government in Tokelauan had little beyond their oral language knowledge to help them. There was no established set of words and phrases in the dictionaries and wordlists. In fact the main assistance was often found in English descriptive dictionaries.

2.1 Dictionaries and Word Lists

There are three general dictionaries for the Tokelau language.

The first was the *Vocabulary Tokelau-English* by DW Boardman published in 1969 by the Department of Education, Wellington, New Zealand. This has about 1200 items in a Tokelau-English section and then repeats the material in an English-Tokelau section. The *Vocabulary* was compiled as part of a sociology research endeavour and therefore does not include much legal or political terminology.

The Boardman list includes 'election', 'government', 'vote', and 'country'. These are the only items of any relevance to the topic under discussion. From that small selection two points may be made. The first is that *nuku* (typically translated as 'village') is the word given for 'country' (that usage is also indicated in 1986 in the *Tokelau Dictionary*). The second point is that the word *tulafono* does not appear in the Boardman vocabulary. This is interesting given the general role of *tulafono* to designate a rule of any kind, that is, not just a rule of law.

The second dictionary is the *Tokelau English Dictionary* compiled by Hosea Kirifi and JH Webster; it was published in mimeographed form in 1975. In this collection of just over 3000 words there is again a very limited number relating to legal or political matters. There are 10 entries, which in a very general way could be of legal significance, such as *folafolaga* (announcement; proclamation) and *molimau* (witness). Only two of the ten (*pule* and *tulafono*) are specifically in the field of the present enquiry and even they are given only a general meaning. Again this is not surprising given the year: there was little concern in 1975 with government or Tokelau-wide political issues.

Following the Kirifi Webster dictionary there was an *English Tokelau word list* compiled by Maselino Patelesio. It built on the Kirifi Webster dictionary and provided the preliminary work for the *Tokelau Dictionary*. Specifically, 11 entries are relevant to the present topic. The word list includes under the entry 'Cabinet', '*tofiga fakamalo* (political position); *kapineta*'. This entry is also in Kirifi and Webster but without description and spelt as *kapeneta*.

'Government' is given as *faiga o malo; itukaiga malo; malo o he nuku*, 'Minister' is given as *minihita*, 'political' as *(mea) e tau ki te malo*, and 'politics' as *mea e tau ki te malo*. And, interestingly and unheralded, there are five terms relating to international political developments of the kind that from the 1990s have been of particular importance for Tokelau. These are 'equality' *(tutuha)*; 'freedom' *(haolotoga)*; 'independent' *(haoloto)*; 'republic' *(itukaiga malo)*; 'self-government' *(malo tutokatahi)*.

The *Tokelau Dictionary* (Office of Tokelau Affairs, Apia, Samoa, 1986) is a substantial work and the first publication to move very much beyond a simple word list. The *Tokelau Dictionary* includes approximately 11,000 entries in a Tokelau-English section. This is supported by an English-Tokelau word list at the back of the book. This text gives examples of usage and, more than the Boardman or Kirifi Webster texts, also reflects New Zealand based usage. The words and examples given reflect not only the Tokelau environment but also the environment of metropolitan New Zealand and of Auckland in particular. This is natural given that by 1986 the bulk of the native speakers of Tokelauan were resident in New Zealand. The *Tokelau Dictionary* shows that there are at least two Tokelaus: the Tokelau of telephones, the mixing of cakes, game hunting, and cars – metropolitan New Zealand, and the very different Tokelau of fishermen – the atoll homeland.

The *Tokelau Dictionary* speaks of the influence of Samoan on vocabulary items not only because of the geographical closeness and the fact that Samoa is the port of entry for Tokelau but also because religious knowledge in Tokelau depends to a very great extent on the use of the Samoan Bible.

The influence of English on the language is perhaps just beginning. Given the number of Tokelauans (mostly those born outside Tokelau) who have a good knowledge of Tokelauan from their parents but who are not themselves fluent speakers, it may be that English structural patterns as well as vocabulary will come to influence the language. To date the English language influence does not appear to be strong, at least not in the subject area under review here.

In the *Tokelau Dictionary* there are fewer than 40 entries that are relevant for this paper. Most of those are general words, which would have application in a law context as well as the general community one – words such a *tautoga* (oath) or *tukutukuga* (conditions). There are fewer than 20 words in the Dictionary, which have a specific legal or political connotation, and it does not include all of the specific words that were used in the government prepared guidebook of 1980 that is discussed later in this paper. The specific words and phrases included in the Dictionary as entries or as examples are:

Faiga	method, way
faiga o te Malo	running of government
Fakaikuga	policies
Fakalapotopotoga a tagata e galulue i te Malo	Tokelau Public Service Association
Fakapolitika	Politics
Fono a te Malo	Legislative Assembly
Feagaiga	agreement, treaty
Haolotoga	Independence
Kapeneta	Cabinet
Kaufaigaluega	workers, employees
Komihi	Commission (as in State Services Commission)
Lafoga	Taxation
Malo Kaufakatahi (team; united by common goals)	⎫
Malo Tukufakatahi (put together; contributing)	⎬ United Nations
Malo Hokofakatahi (linked; coming together)	⎭
Matakupu tau fafo	foreign policy
Minihita	Minister (of government)
Pulega	administration, controlling, governing
tagata lautele	the public

This is not an extensive list. It includes proper names, is clearly influenced in a number of cases by the experience of New Zealand speakers of Tokelauan, and includes general words which have been attributed a specific meaning in the political context.

The words for 'Legislative Assembly', 'Cabinet', 'Minister' and 'taxation' are clearly influenced by the New Zealand experience. Taxation was known in a limited form in Tokelau from 1983 but would have been part of the daily experience of Tokelau workers in New Zealand from an earlier date. There is no 'Legislative Assembly' as such in Tokelau. The reference therefore to the *Fono a te Malo* is clearly to the Legislative Assembly of New Zealand (or perhaps to that of Samoa where there is a sizeable Tokelauan community). The words for the 'United Nations' with the nuances of meaning indicated in parentheses, show an unsettled terminology.

In 1993, seven years after the appearance of the *Tokelau Dictionary*, when Tokelau began to take over national government from the New Zealand authorities in Wellington, the standing committee of government was for a period of a year or two often described as the 'Cabinet' and the three members of that group as 'Ministers'. Since about 1996 however the preference has been for words already within Tokelauan usage. The equivalent of the 'Cabinet' in the New Zealand government is in Tokelau the 'Council of Faipule' (*Fono a Faipule*) and the members of that Council are the *Faipule*. They are each responsible for a number of departments of government. The Chief Minister is described as the *Ulu* and all of the *Faipule* are now described as *Aliki* to distinguish their national role from their village role. The Chief Minister is therefore now described as the *Aliki Faipule* (his name), *Ulu o Tokelau*.

In order to see how the translators have proceeded, it is therefore appropriate to consider a series of official documents that are available in English and Tokelauan. These documents are identified and described in the next part.

2.2 The Documents

Tokelauan is a living language and used almost exclusively in Tokelau by Tokelauans in the management of their daily affairs. There are, however, relatively few documents in Tokelauan, which deal with government and legal matters and most are translations from an English text into Tokelauan. The paucity of documentation flows from two main factors. The first is that concern with government in an internationalist sense is recent in Tokelau, and the second is that within the tradition of an oral culture the use of documents as a medium of communication has developed relatively slowly.

In the case of all but village generated documents, it is fair to say that the documents are English language based in the sense that English language thinking had an influence on the product e.g. United Nations generated requests for information, New Zealand Government related reports, budgets, economic planning documents.

Over the last twenty or so years there has been a small group of native speakers (perhaps a maximum of 10 persons) involved in translating. Most of them were bilingual in English and Tokelauan, and most had a good knowledge of Samoan. Mostly the translations were done by people who worked independently. All were senior members of the Tokelau Public Service. Primarily the documents were translated from English by Tokelauans who were not lawyers or political scientists. Increasingly since 1994 internal documents are being generated in Tokelauan and subsequently translated into English for the use of the Government in Wellington.

The usages appear to change with the experience of the translator and in response to context. Sometimes the differences in the texts arise from different translators or from professional as distinct from lay translations. Many of the documents have been translated by the same people but without consistency of terminology. To the extent that the variations reflect the situation, that is much, one might speculate, as the words of an orator might change in response to the topic and audience of the moment.

The main audience has been the Elders of Tokelau. Twenty years ago this group was literate in Samoan because of the Church use of the Samoan language Bible. Tokelauan was the spoken and first language, but reading and writing was done with difficulty. Few of this group had English. In 2002 the Elders are mostly literate in Tokelauan and about half of them would also be literate in English.

Though it is not apparent in the sampling done for this paper, it should also be noted that between the three islands there are some small differences of language of a very subtle nature. This is primarily a matter of different vocabulary and is most noticeable as between Atafu and the other two islands.

2.3 Tokelau (1980)

The first document surveyed is the booklet entitled *Tokelau*, which was published by the New Zealand Ministry of Foreign Affairs in 1980. It is in two parts: a Tokelau language text and an English language text. The booklet had the specific purpose of relating the government processes of New Zealand to the Tokelau context, and attempted to bridge the gap between the colonial power's culture and the traditions of Tokelau. The analogy of a Tokelau canoe with an outrigger, sail and other fittings was used as a way to describe the operation of Tokelau government from a Western European point of view. The hull was depicted as the people of Tokelau, the sail as the Tokelau Public Service (standing above but not touching the hull), the three outrigger stays each represented the Council of Elders of an atoll, and the outrigger float was depicted as the General Fono.

The booklet was produced as a guide to explain to the people in Tokelau the relationship of their traditional systems to the national external government. The booklet identified clearly the differentiation of roles of the village and the nation, and spoke also about the separation of powers and the independence of the national public service. It is significant that many of questions, which it was written to answer, have arisen in precisely the same context in 2002 with particular reference to the Tokelau Employment Rules of 2001. In 1980 some of the questions concerned the independence of public servants from political and other social pressures; after the making of the Employment Rules in 2001 questions were again asked about whether politicians and others could be consulted about the appointment of senior public officers. The abiding cultural pattern would be for substantial community discussion of matters of such importance. The time lapse is 22 years. The answers from a Western European governance perspective have not changed. What is clearly indicated therefore is a significant cultural divide.

2.4 Treaty of Tokehega (1980)

The second document is also of 1980. It is very short; it is the Treaty of Tokehega, a treaty between the United States of America and New Zealand. The subject matter is the exclusive economic zone, which surrounds the islands of Tokelau. The treaty was signed on behalf of New Zealand by the three Faipule of Tokelau and for that purpose was translated into Tokelauan.

2.5 Fakaofo Rules, and Commissioner's Handbook (1983)

The interaction of lawyers with Tokelau began in a serious way in 1983. On the occasion of the first visit of the lawyer who was appointed to advise the elders of Tokelau on constitutional and other legal matters, two documents were presented and discussed. The first was a statement prepared by the Elders of Fakaofo which set out rules of Fakaofo and which the Elders said identified what, for them, was law. The other document was the translation into Tokelauan of a handbook prepared by the advisor for the lay magistrates of Tokelau – the Law Commissioners' Handbook. That handbook dealt briefly with the formal relationship of New Zealand and Tokelau by way of background and presented guidelines for the prosecution of criminal offences and the holding of criminal trials.

2.6 Law Lexicon (1986)

In 1986 the law advisor together with the chief translator and interpreter of Tokelau prepared a draft *Lexicon of law terms*. This was to assist with translation as more and more documents on the law were prepared in Tokelauan; it also sought to provide a basis for consistency of usage in the future.

2.7 Matagi Tokelau (1990)

Matagi Tokelau was published in 1990 as a statement by Tokelau of its history and culture. It is a two-volume work of which one volume is in English and the other in Tokelauan. In *Matagi Tokelau* the people of Tokelau provide a brief description of the law and administration in their country.

The Tokelauan language volume of *Matagi Tokelau* is closer to oral Tokelauan than the official documents surveyed. A feature of the oral language is that it leaves nuances to be captured by the listener: an aspect of the ancient stories, chants, and formal speeches was to make the audience guess the meaning *(fakatupua)*. The development of written Tokelauan since the 1970s has, in the hands of able speakers enriched the oral language by giving it an added discipline. It allows discourse to be organized where appropriate to good effect, by spelling things out in a way that leaves nothing to the imagination of the listener.

2.8 Human Rights (1990)

Also in 1990 a booklet was produced containing all the main international human rights documents that applied to Tokelau, translated into Tokelauan. This translation exercise produced an array of terms with new usages in the human rights area and in the field of international law.

2.9 Tokelau Amendment Act 1996

The New Zealand Parliament spoke in Tokelauan for the first time in the Tokelau Amendment Act 1996. At Select Committee stage the Members of Parliament enquired whether the people of Tokelau understood clearly what was in the Amendment and whether they agreed to the changes that were being made to the law that affected them. The answer from Tokelau was affirmative. By way of confirmation of that agreement a two page preamble was provided for the Amendment Act and that preamble now appears in the law of New Zealand: first in Tokelauan and then in English.

2.10 Modern House of Tokelau (2000)

As part of the preparation for self-determination, a major effort was made in 2000 to strengthen internal self-government. The project involved was the Modern House of Tokelau project (*Te fale fou o Tokelau*); it developed from Tokelau initiatives with strong support from the New Zealand government. The approval document provides a modern statement relating to matters of government in Tokelau. It is therefore a useful source of vocabulary and a check on contemporary translation usage.

2.11 Political Documents 2001 and 2002

The most recent documents surveyed were the notes for the government-to-government talks held between the leaders of Tokelau and New Zealand Government officials in 2001, the Tokelau Public Service Rules of 2001, and a statement for the United Nations. In August 2002, there was a Visiting Mission to Tokelau from the Special Committee of the United Nations for Decolonization. The Mission visited the three islands of Tokelau and in the course of that visit the officials' speeches in Nukunonu (the atoll of the Chief Minister for 2002) were provided both in English and Tokelauan. The Nukunonu village statement to the Visiting Mission is the last of the documents considered for this survey.

3. Summary

With one exception, all of the documents are 1,000 or so words long. *Matagi Tokelau* is the clear exception because it is a book. Even in the longest documents the relevant portions, those that deal with law and government, form a very small part of the whole. The documents surveyed are not the sum total of the documents available but have been chosen as being among the more readily available in that all, except the notes for the government-to-government talks, are either published or in the public domain. There is also a large number of documents, particularly of the last decade, which relate to law and government but which appear only in Tokelauan.

The focus in this paper is on those documents, which are accompanied by an English language text. That English language text is usually the base for a translation into Tokelauan, and it would be possible to follow the translation against the original if produced in dual language format. The exceptions are *Matagi Tokelau* and the Nukunonu speech to the United Nations Visiting Mission. Both of these were community generated documents and sometimes there is no exact correspondence between the text on a given point in Tokelauan and the text in English. In these two cases, what the translation presents is another language presentation of the same sentiments. They are, at many points, translations of the sense and ideas rather than of the specific words.

4. Concepts and Words Translated

The key text is a booklet of 1980. Its full title is *Tokelau – ana faiga faka-te-malo ma na kuikuiga fakaofiha – its system of government and administration*. It was written in early 1980 and published by the Ministry of Foreign Affairs late in 1980. It is 40 A5 pages in typewritten format. There is a Foreword of approximately 300 words in both English and Tokelauan, followed by 16 pages of Tokelauan text (approximately 4500 words), and then the 11 page English text (approximately 3000 words). The balance of the booklet is made up of pictures and diagrams.

No mention is made in the booklet of translation. It is however clear that the source text was the English text. It is also known that the translation of the main text was made in Apia. The Foreword was written last and translated later – almost certainly in Wellington – apparently by a different translator, and without reference to the main text.

Taking *Tokelau 1980* as the base, and noting frequencies of occurrence over the twelve documents surveyed, the following are the key Tokelau words used in the translations:

> *Faigamalo, fakatonu, fakatonutonu, fono, malo, pule, pulea, pulega, tonu* and *vaega*.

The key English words translated are:

> Administration, Administrator, Charter, constitutional, General Fono, independence, non-self-governing, public, self-determination, self-governing, State Services Commission, Tokelau Public Service, United Nations.

Closer analysis identifies *fono, malo, pule, tonu,* and *vae* as key base words in Tokelauan. Therefore, in what follows, each of those words will be considered in terms of its use in the law and government context in Tokelau as shown by the documents surveyed.

These base words are subject to multiple variations by use of prefixes, suffixes, reduplication and use in compounds. The variation on the base is in some cases for purely grammatical reasons (e.g. a verb to a noun), but in other cases there is a shift in meaning along with the variation. These are all words of traditional Tokelauan and also, as Tregear *The Maori Polynesian Comparative Dictionary* shows, of longstanding Polynesian use.

The words are now considered one by one to see how they have been used by translators in the context of the political developments in Tokelau in the late twentieth century (A general view is provided by the Table at the end of this paper).

4.1 The Tokelauan Words

4.1.1 *Fono*

'General Fono': It is remarkable that none of the dictionaries or word lists have an entry for the General Fono which is the leading national political body and which fulfils both executive and legislative functions in Tokelau. All of the dictionaries and word lists have an entry for *fono* which includes 'meetings' or 'gatherings' within its meaning. The dictionaries and word lists also have a number of adjectives, which are often linked with *fono* to describe the General Fono. These words are:

aoao	supreme
aofia	inclusive
fakamua	doing something as a village group
lahi	big

Fono lautele is also in common use – *lautele* means 'broad', 'general', 'covering everyone'. *Lautele* is not in the *Tokelau Dictionary*; it is a word of Samoan origin. It is from the translation of this expression in the 1970s that the English name 'General Fono' is derived. *Fono tele* is also heard in reference to a 'big meeting', but usually with reference to a village rather than a national gathering.

When *aoao, aofia, fakamua,* and *lahi* are described in any of the lexical texts they are not given a specific reference to the General Fono. They refer in various ways to large meetings of the whole community, or meetings that include women and youth in a way that would distinguish that type of *fono* from the usual meeting of the *Taupulega*, the elders of the village.

It is clearly not a problem to describe accurately the General Fono, the national gathering of representatives of the three islands of Tokelau which meets two or three times a year. Context makes clear which meeting is being referred to. The existence of the General Fono is something that is known to all in Tokelau and it is frequently spoken about.

The usage appears to have settled to the extent that there is a specific descriptor for this body. It is the *Fono Fakamua*. Other titles are still heard and sporadically also the newer title *Fono Fakaatunuku*. This later expression appears, in the written documents, to go in and out of favour. The more standard reference is to the *Fono Fakamua*. When *fono fakaatunuku* is used in translation there is implicit a promotion of the idea of an institution which is separate from and to a degree above the three islands. It represents a sense of nationalism and an appeal for the political unity, which is generally agreed but which also runs somewhat at odds with the traditional cultural principle that the Elders of a particular island hold the ultimate authority in Tokelau. This principle is currently in the process of being refashioned to take account of the fact that Tokelau politics are no longer purely island based. That is to say, with the development of self-government in Tokelau there is a substantial shift to accommodate a national body alongside the Elders of each village.

There is a tension and also a potential clash of cultures because there is in 2003 no consensus in Tokelau on the way forward. It remains to be seen whether in the future the General Fono will become clearly the agent of the three villages to attend to national matters, or whether (as in many other South Pacific countries) the newly established national body with its elected members will gradually take on a significant role in village management as well.

In *Matagi Tokelau* the 'General Fono' is referred to in two different ways: *Fono faka atunuku (Fono Lahi)*, and as *fono a te atunuku*. In the Human Rights documents of 1990 *fono aoao* is used to translate "General Assembly" of the United Nations.

Fono also appears in the compound *tulafono*, which is the generic word for a 'rule'. Tokelau law (much of which is in English only) uses a vast array of different words for 'law'. The Tokelauan language has only *tulafono* (custom of the elders). Since 1984 the usage has been as shown in the following table.

Tokelau has no entrenched constitutional document. For that reason a word for 'constitution' is at present rarely needed. When it is, *tulafono fakavae* is used. This usage covers not only the existing basic laws of Tokelau but also any entrenched constitution of the future.

Tulafono is as much a heavy-duty word in Tokelauan as 'law' is in English. It is used to translate all of 'rule', 'law', 'regulation', 'Act', 'Or-

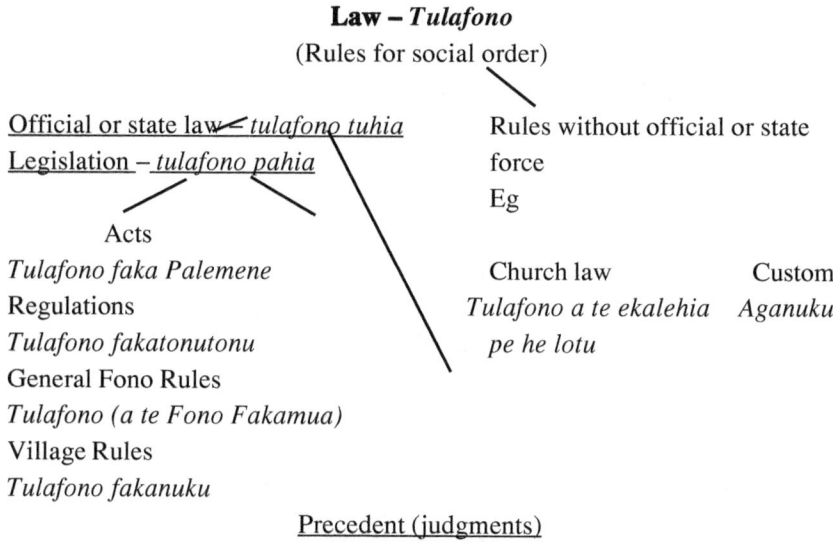

Te tulafono o te tulafono tuhia translates the technical legal phrase 'rule of law'.

dinance', 'legislation', 'statute'. Unlike English there is no established pattern of specialized words for special types of law with the exception of 'regulation' and 'Act', both of which have some currency as *Tulafono fakatonutonu* and *Tulafono fakapalemene*. Here it is to be noted that the jargon is being developed by way of adjectival phrases rather than independent words.

4.1.2 Malo

Malo means 'government', 'administration', 'politics', 'the state', a 'nation', 'the administration', and by synecdoche the 'Administrator of Tokelau'. It serves to distinguish national and other government from the traditional village based government of the *Taupulega*. *Malo o te nuku* is therefore village based non-traditional authority.

Malo appears as a translation for 'nation' in the 'United Nations', and is used as a translation of 'state' in some translations of 'State Services Commission', and also in the treaty context in references to 'States parties' (*Malo auai*). On this basis the United Nations and the United States of America might come through with a similar translation. However the standard usage for the United States of America is *Amelika;* South America is *Amelika i Haute.* Exceptionally *Unaite Hitete o Amerika* was used in the Treaty of Tokehega. The reason is not known but perhaps the formal use of 'United States of America' in the English language version rather than simply 'America' militated in favour of the atypical usage. When in the Treaty the shortened form 'United States' is used the translator made the adjustment to *Unaite Hitete.*

In the *Lexicon, malo* is used also to translate the 'Crown' in its reference to the government or state of New Zealand. 'Tupu' is 'King' or 'ruler': It was regularly used in pre-Christian Tokelau to describe the *aliki* (village chief) to foreigners.

In compound form *faigamalo* translated in *Tokelau (1980)* both 'system of government' and 'politics'. In *Matagi Tokelau* (1990) the question was discussed:

> I lototonu o te tauhaga 1976 na fakaatunuku ai te ahiahiga a te Komiti Fakapitoa a Malo Kaufakatahi ki Tokelau; e fia iloa e kilatou te tulaga e fofou ki ei ia Tokelau mo hona malo.
>
> Ko te tali a Tokelau ki tenei faigamalaga, e fia pipiki pea lava ia Tokelau ki Niu Hila. Ko heki mafaufau ia Tokelau mo hona malo i te lumanaki.
>
> I te taimi nei, kua tau i ei he ata e kikila ki ei ia Tokelau; kae koi tokalahi pea lava ia tagata koi fia malamalama i na mea e lua ienei:
>
> 1.   Malo – Administration
> 2.   Malo – Politics
>
> E veia ona takau i luga, e fokotahi te kupu faka-Tokelau 'Malo' mo na kupu e lua fakapapalagi e kehekehe o la uiga. Ko te fehili la e veia: "Ko ai te fai ki ei na galuega a te malo (administration), kae ko ai te fai ki ei na galuega a te malo (politics)?" Ko te tahi fehili: "Ko ai na tino o te malo o Tokelau, kae ko ai na tino o te atunuku ko Tokelau?" Ko he tahi fehili: "Ko na galuega e fakatonu e te Malo i loto o te nuku, e mo te lelei o te nuku; ko na galuega foki e fakatonu e te taupulega o te nuku, e mo te lelei o te nuku tena, kae tulaga mai, ko ietahi tino (malo) e maua to latou taui, kae ko ietahi tino (nuku) e he totogia; kae ko na tino uma ienei, e galulue mo te lelei o te nuku". [*Matagi Tokelau*, p160].

In mid-1976 a visiting mission from the United Nations came to Tokelau to find out what kind of government and political status the people sought for themselves, but Tokelau's answer was that it still wished to remain as part of New Zealand and had no thought of future self-government or independence.

At the present time, while some things are becoming clearer for Tokelau, there are still many people who seek clarification of the two related concepts of 'Administration' and 'Politics', both of which are covered by the same Tokelau word *malo*. The relevant questions are these. "Who does the work of 'administration' and who is it who is involved in 'politics'?" Another question is, "Who are the people who run the government of Tokelau, as distinct from the people of Tokelau?" Again, "The work which the government decides should be done in the villages is for the good of the villages. But in practice it is only the government workers who get paid, while village workers receive nothing. Yet all of them work for the common good!" Matagi *Tokelau*, p174

In the human rights documents (for instance the International Covenant on Civil and Political Rights) *fakafaigamalo* is used to translate 'political'. Most recently the expression comes through in relation to the decolonisation process in the government-to-government talks paper of 2001 ('self-government' is referred to both as *te faigamalo fakalotoifale* and as *malo fakalotoifale*) and in the Nukunonu presentation to the United Nations Visiting Mission the 'act of self-determination' is rendered as *filifiliga faigamalo fakalotoifale*.

4.1.3 Pule
Pule refers basically to 'authority', 'power', to 'the authorities', to 'the council' (meaning the Council of Elders – the *Taupulega* of a village). It appears with the meaning of 'power' or 'authority' both in the Fakaofo statement of 1983 and in the Commissioner's Handbook; in *Matagi Tokelau* and in the Nukunonu statement of 2002 it has the meaning of 'authority' (of the Elders).

It is a word with many common emanations. For instance the village council, the power holding group of the village, is the *Taupulega*. The two chief officers of the *Taupulega* are the *Faipule* (the one who makes the decisions) and the *Pulenuku* (the power in village matters). The word *Faipule* is not grammatical (*fai* + *pule*) in Tokelauan; it is a British import from Samoa or through Tuvalu during Tokelau's period as a British Colony.

Pule seems a perfectly good translation for 'power' or 'authority' within the governmental or law context. However in the late 1990s there is evidence of some ambivalence in the translation of 'power' or 'authority', particularly in regard to the use of *pule* in relation to newly established power holders as distinct from the traditional. *Pule* is readily used in relation to the Elders and traditional sources of power or traditional holders of power. The ambivalence is obvious when, as has happened, an interpreter enquires whether it is legitimate to translate 'power' by the word *pule* or whether *paoa* (from English 'power') should be used. The expressions *paoa o te pulega fakatonutonu* (the authority of the administering power) and *paoa faitulafono* (law-making power) should be noted.

The most obvious example is seen in the preamble to the Tokelau Amendment Act 1996 where *pule* and its derivatives *(pulea, pulega, pulepulea)* are each used more than once for a total of twelve times and *paoa*, is used twelve times. Since 1996 there is some evidence in oral usage that *pule* is being used more extensively as the newly created institutions of national government become more integrated into the local context. *Pule* suggests continuity of authority and an understood and accepted authority which gives considered decisions. *Paoa* in Tokelauan is more than 'power'; it is absolute, raw power; it need not be an accepted authority and need not be exercised after due consideration.

In the 1996 Amendment Act *mafai* appears along with *paoa* and *pule* to translate power. The use of *mafai* focuses on a capacity given by law or agreement, which runs between the traditional authority which must be obeyed *(pule)* and the unchallengeable *paoa*. The use of the verb *mafai* to translate 'power' has the merit of requiring the translator to rethink the structure of the sentence in Tokelauan as a verbal one relating to 'ability to do'.

In the Tokelau Amendment Act 1996:

Tokelauan	English
Malo pulea failotoifale	self-governing
filemu, pulea ma te malo lelei	peace, order and good government
pule faifakamahinoga	jurisdiction (of court)
pulega faigamalo fakateatunuku	government at a national level
pulega mahani	traditional (usual) authority
pulega o taupulega	Administration of the Elders
paoa o na nofonofoga pule a Tokelau	power of Tokelau's own political institutions
paoa ...	... of the Administrator
paoa ...	... of the State Services Commission
paoa faitulafono	lawmaking power
paoa o te pulega fakatonutonu	Administrative power (delegated by the Administrator)

paoa ke fakamautu	power to enforce
ko ho he paoa	any power (given by Parliament)
te paoa ke fakamautu ai ana tonu fakafaigamalo	The power to enforce its governmental decisions
Ko te Kovana Hili e mafai i ...	The Governor-General has the power [ie may] in ...
tiute ke atiake te mafai e Tokelau ona pulepulea	The duty to develop the power for Tokelau's own governance

All these usages are consistent with the view that *paoa* is of the *malo* and the *pule* is of the *taupulega*. The only exception to the pattern is in respect of the courts – an alien, externally imposed system – where *pule* is used. Whether this was an aberration or whether it was intentional is unknown. If intentional, it may reflect the fact that the judge (a century old institution) is a villager, and the power of the judge is restricted to the village: this authority or jurisdiction is *pule* because it is village not nation based.

Te pule a te malo in the human rights documents translates as 'authority of the government'.

Pulega is a derivative with meanings similar to the base. It is used in the documents to refer to 'authorities', 'power', and 'administering'. *Pulega fakatonutonu* is 'administrative authority', and *pulega fakakolone* is 'colonization' in the phrase *komiti fakapooa mo te holoia o na pulega fakakolone* (the Special Committee for Decolonization).

Pulepule translates as 'governance', 'administering' or 'governing'. The duplication indicates the process of doing something. It appears in the statement about the Modern House of Tokelau, in the notes for the government-to-government talks of 2001, and on many occasions in the Nukunonu statement of 2002.

In the Nukunonu statement it appears as *malo pulepule* with the meaning 'administering power' and also in the phrase *tulaga pulepule o te malo*, with the meaning of 'governing institutions', and alone meaning 'governs' (the use of *tulaga* (role, position, status, standing) does not fit well in this phrase in isolation, however it does fit in the context from which it is taken.) Finally, it is used with reference to the government of New Zealand as *malo pulepule ko Niu Hila*. Of interest in this village document is the shift on the one hand to the objective political language of *pulepule* with reference to New Zealand but also in the same context a reference to the more traditional and emotive expression for 'administering power' which is *malo tauhi*. *Malo tauhi* suggests a relationship of dependence and a caring or nurturing role on the part of the administering power.

Pulea (order) carries the connotation of a society that is well governed according to *pule*. *Pulea* translates sovereignty and is so used in the Treaty of Tohekega, in *Matagi Tokelau* and in the preamble to the 1996 Amendment Act.

4.1.4 Tonu
Tonu has a basic meaning of 'command', 'decree'. *Tonu* indicates a decision that has flowed from agreement, or that has been agreed to, or that has been negotiated or is correct by way of the procedure followed. It is not dictated; it suggests the involvement of more than one person in the decision-making.

Tonu is used in the expression *fai mea tonu* to translate 'justice' (literally 'the correct way').

It appears alone in the phrases *na tonu mo na fuafuaga* translated as 'policy decisions' (literally 'commands in respect of proposals'). *Fuafuaga* is regularly used to translate 'objects' (in the sense of purposes or objectives) and 'proposals'. *Fuafuaga* implies a balancing, a giving of due consideration to alternatives. *Ko tonu o tona malo* (decision of its government) is translated as 'political and administrative decisions'.

More frequently in the documents surveyed *tonu* appears in compounds. *Fakatonu* is used to translate 'executive' and appears as such in the title 'Administrator of Tokelau' – *Ulu fakatonu o Tokelau*. It also appears in the compound *fakatonutonu* with the usual sense of 'administrative'. Therefore *tulafono fakatonutonu* (literally 'administrative rules') is the standard translation for 'regulations'. In the human rights documents *pulega fakatonutonu* translates 'administration'.

By adding the prefix *faka* the meaning of 'direct' is obtained. *Fakatonu* may or may not have involved consultation. Reduplication produces *fakatonutonu* and the sense of a step by step process, or a series of decisions leading to the final one.

4.1.5 Vae
The last of the key Tokelauan words is *vae*. Its basic meaning is a 'part' or a 'leg'. It has very general connotations and occurs in the *Tokelau 1980* document with the meaning of 'institutions'. It is to be compared with the usage in the Nukunonu 2002 document where *tulaga pulepule o te malo* translates 'governing institutions'.

Vaega is not only 'institutions' but it can refer to bodies (e.g. corporate bodies), to 'teams' and to the groups within the *inati* sharing system of the villages.

Other expressions available to deal with groups of people or entities include *fakalapotopoga* ('incorporated body'); the same usage appears in *Matagi Tokelau* as *fakapotopotoga*. *Tino tukufakatahi* was used in the Tokelau Village Incorporation Regulations 1987 to translate the English expression 'body corporate'.

Till 1987, when the villages of Tokelau were incorporated by the Tokelau Village Incorporation Regulations, there were no bodies corporate in Tokelau. The need to translate words such as societies, associations, corporations, unions, companies, cooperatives and partnerships has therefore not been great. When that need arises in the law there is an array of Tokelauan words from which a choice could be made. Examples are:

Fakalapotopotoga	an organisation, association or community (e.g. the United Nations, the *aumaga*, the Women's Committee of the village, Tokelauans in Porirua)
Felagolagomaki	Cooperative; mutually supporting eg *falekoloa felagolagomaki*, cooperative store
kaiga	extended family group
Kau	Team
Kalapu	Club
Kamupani	company (business)
Komiti	Committee
Pihinihi	business venture
pihinihi fakatahi	joint venture
Hohaiete	society; club
Fakatahi hokotaga	⎫ All indicate
Felagolagomaki	⎪ relationships that
Hokofakatahiga	⎬ might translate as
Hokotaga fakataugahoa	⎪ 'partnership'; *hokotaga fakatagahoa*
Hokotaga tuku	⎭ suggests that two groups are involved
Vaega	a group of persons (e.g. a team, a Tokelau delegation)
Vahega	a group of persons (less specific in focus than *vaega*) not exceeding 30 – 40 people; the focus is here on the members rather than on the group e.g. a school class; in Nukunonu, a group devoted to a particular patron saint

Kauhaga is used in *Tokelau 1980* (in the Foreword only) to translate 'institutions'. *Kauhaga* is an ancient Tokelauan usage to describe a group of people combining for a purpose such as a fishing expedition or turtle catching. This word is current in the oral language. It is not in any of the dictionaries and, apart from the once in *Tokelau 1980* is not used (at least not for 'institutions') in the translations surveyed here.

5. The English Words

Working from English covers some of the same ground as is dealt with under the Tokelau base words but also provides new insights as to the development of the political and legal vocabulary.

The documents show 'public' being translated regularly and without confusion either by the expression *fakamua* or the expression *o te malo*. *Fakamua* suggests the village and *Taupulega* control; *o te malo* suggests the nation. Thus a 'public building' is *fale fakamua* or *fale o te malo*. 'Public facilities' and 'public works' are both rendered as *galuega fakamua*, 'public servants' as *tino faigaluega o te malo,* or in another document as *tagata faigaluega fakamua* (the person or people who are doing the work of the government or the public work). The village co-operative store is the *falekoloa fakamua*.

'Constitutional' is rendered as *mea tau fakavae o faigamalo* (matters concerning the basis of the system of government). *Te tulaga e iei te tulafono fakavae* (literally, 'the positions which are in the basic law').

'Self-determination', in addition to the expressions listed under *malo*, has been translated by the descriptive *te faia o a latou tonu e ki latou lava* (The making of their own commands /decisions for themselves).

'Charter' (the Charter of the United Nations) was translated in the Treaty of Tokehega by *fuafuaga*. Elsewhere it is referred to as *Feagaiga fakavae*, meaning the 'foundation treaty'. *Feagaiga* is the standard translation for 'treaty'. *Feagaiga* is a borrowing from Biblical Samoan to translate 'an agreement of a formal kind'. Tokelauan *maliega* is an agreement, often informal and oral. *Feagaiga* has the meaning of 'Covenant', and of 'Testament' (as in the *New Testament*).

'Declaration' as in the name Universal Declaration of Human Rights, is translated in the 1990 Human Rights documents as *Takutinoga*. Literally, *takutinoga* is 'oath' but in context the extended use is meaningful.

'The Administrator': for at least a quarter of a century the key national governmental figure for Tokelau has been the Administrator. The Administrator is a New Zealand based public official whose role is analogous to that of a Governor. While the role was a significant one constitutionally it was of little practical significance in Tokelau itself because the government administration had no presence in the islands of Tokelau. The Administrator was always based in Wellington and traveled to Tokelau rarely. The main office for the administration of the general affairs of Tokelau was the Office for Tokelau Affairs in Apia, Samoa. The heart of the colonial government was therefore always offshore as far as the three islands of Tokelau were concerned. Nevertheless the post was known and respected and the Administrator looked up to as something of a father figure. It is remarkable therefore that there is no entry in the *Tokelau Dictionary* in relation to the Administrator. The documents show there has been some ambivalence in respect of the title, but the current usage is quite clear – it is *Ulu Fakatonu*.

The 'Tokelau Public Service' began as *kaufaigaluega fakamua a Tokelau* (communal workforce of Tokelau). In *Matagi Tokelau* there is reference to *kaufaigaluega a te malo* (the government workforce). Then in the 1996 Amendment Act the shift is made to *kaufaigaluega Tautua a Tokelau* and that translation is also used in the 2001 Rules. The shift is significant for at least two reasons: *fakamua* suggests communal in the sense of controlled by the villages and *tautua* focuses on 'service' rather than control. *Fakamua* was rejected because the Elders had no authority in respect of the public servants. They were national not village employees, and their employer was the New Zealand government (the State Services Commission).

'Lawyer': there was no cultural experience of lawyers in Tokelau until very recently and the *Tokelau Dictionary* lists *fautua* as a word which includes among its meanings 'lawyer'. *Fautua* is used for biblical translations where for instance 'advocate' has had to be translated. *Fautua* has the general meaning of 'advisor' or 'counselor'. A specific professional to deal with advice or counselling on matters of the law has come to be referred to as *loia*, borrowed directly from English or indirectly from English through Samoan. Elsewhere in the *Tokelau Dictionary* the word *loia* is used and that is given as the translation in the English Tokelauan word list that appears at the back of the Dictionary. This therefore is a case of a local general word being displaced by an imported word for the specific legal context.

6. Conclusion

The word for 'law' in the Western European cultural sense in Tokelau needed both translation and explanation because of the absence of any equivalent. The rate of absorption of ideas through language has broadly reflected the rate of political and economic transformation. Tokelau is not a case of dramatic forced transformation or of a neo-colonialism, which resulted from internal economic crisis.

It is apparent that in the written language, political usage, even among experts, is still far from settled and this is so even in respect of proper names. The development of a specific law and politics vocabulary can be seen but that vocabulary is not yet settled. There are still instances of concepts being described rather than named. It is equally clear that this flexibility is not hindering communication. The latent ambiguities of the process are dealt with in practice by the context. If for instance it is said that "I was elected a village representative to the *Fono Lahi*" it is clear that the reference is to the General Fono because at village level the *Fono Lahi* includes everybody and there is therefore no possibility of being a village representative to that gathering. Equally, if it is said that "I will meet with the Elders of the other islands at the *Fono Lautele*", the reference can only be to the General Fono.

The conversion of Tokelau to Christianity took place in the 1860s. It was not an unchallenged acceptance by the locals but, given that it happened over a very few years, it was rapid and, according to all the evidence, thorough going. The destruction of the local supreme god Tui Tokelau happened at the end of the 1850s. Christianity soon became an integral part of the Tokelau culture to the extent that the missionaries' prescriptions for family relationships are now identified as the customary law and have superseded what preceded them.

By comparison the agents of European style government have been less successful. There is at least a century of contact with British style government and from 1969 a clear interaction at a community level between the members of the local community and their public service. Yet there is still no complete acceptance of the foreign ideas.

What might account for this difference in acceptance or absorption is the obvious fact that Tokelau and the international community of the mid nineteenth century were very different from what they were in the latter part of the 20th century. The material and social conditions of Tokelauans in the late twentieth century probably made them less vulnerable to outside influence and also more questioning of the changes being proposed. Another factor of some importance is that the arrival of Christianity coincided, for Atafu and Nukunonu, with a local political agenda to break the feudal hegemony of Fakaofo.

Christianity displaced the traditional Tokelau deities and Fakaofo kingship but seems not to have displaced the traditional government systems of the villages. By contrast the governmental systems of external origin, which are now being introduced to the Tokelau leaders have on occasion been seen, and perhaps are still being seen, as a threat to local village governance. That is to say the imported institutions are viewed as a possible substitute for the traditional leadership structure. More importantly however the new systems provide for the division of governmental powers (by comparison with the monopoly of authority held by the Council of Elders of each village). The new governmental systems tend to be individualizing of power, and that tendency is contrary to the communal and consensual tradition of governance in Tokelau. Also, and related to the other aspects, the new systems provide for the establishing of a national government running in parallel to the traditional governments of each of the villages and this suggests subordination of village authority to an authority external to itself – this also is anathema to the culture.

Christianity was for everyone, and the ideas were widely disseminated. Government is for the few, and its ideas have limited circulation. The arrival of local radio in Tokelau in 2002 has the potential to change this factor. At the cultural level therefore the ideas, and indeed the demands, of the modern globalized world are contending with the need for a transformation of culture or at least for an acceptance by the local culture. There has been no rejection of the external ideas of government. On the contrary there has been a cautious acceptance of them, but the process of working out how these new ideas fit into the existing cultural setting is still being worked out. This is evidenced by significant projects such as the Modern House of Tokelau project, which is concerned precisely with managing the interface between the traditional systems and the new national systems. The Modern House of Tokelau project seeks to confirm the authority of the traditional leaders within the local government structure, and in turn to have them confirm the appropriateness of new structures at a national level in order to deal both with the outside world and with those matters that properly have to be dealt with by the three islands working together rather than by each island individually.

The Tokelauan words of the translations resonate in tradition with reference to authority, commands, and community. This is not the vocabulary of democracy, rights (*aia*), and duties (*tiute*), but of the monopoly of power in communal authority. The missionaries of government and their translators have therefore much still to do to achieve the desired conversions.

Using the terminology of Jacquemond as presented in *Translation and Empire – Post Colonial Theories Explained* by Douglas Robinson (1997: 36), the 'colonizing moment' for Tokelau was probably when Britain became the protecting power or at the latest by 1912 as is evidenced by the 1912 Rules and the 1917 Native Laws for the Gilbert and Ellice Islands Colony. Unlike colonial laws of the New Zealand period of administration these rules seem to have been well received and were still in the public consciousness fifty or sixty years later and have left as a legacy elections for the offices of *Faipule* and *Pulenuku* and also the titles that are given to those offices. The pattern of voting for village officials seems not to have been disruptive. The tension (if it exists) with democracy is probably much more recent because of its effect of equalizing the status of individuals, because Government authority is no longer the preserve of elderly males and in its individualization of authority – in the national government a single elected individual may alone exercise extensive political power. The transformation will be complete in Western European terms when such individuals also have authority, the *pule* that tradition requires. When the 'decolonizing moment' began is a more difficult question to answer. The resistance to the colonial values was clear by 1970 as is evidenced by the reaction to the introduction of the colonial style Public Service and by the need for the explanatory booklet *Tokelau 1980*.

In 1980 it was probably a case of the translator requiring that the reader come to the author. More recently the attempt has been clear, both in the preparing of the scripts in English for translation and in the translating of them, to bring the author to the reader. This has not yet borne fruit. The continuing development of suitable local vocabulary is not the only feature that makes a translation of the English texts appear foreign in Tokelauan. Those texts dominate through their English structure and Tokelauan translators are constrained by the sentence by sentence pattern of translating those texts.

What the Elders have said about government applies equally well to the related translations:

Ko te Ofiha o Pulepulega ma na politiki ni vaega fou e o te olaga

i Tokelau koi taumafai lava ke ati ake ma fakamalohia atili.
Matagi Tokelau, p148

Administration and politics are much more recent features of Tokelau life and are still being built up, developed and strengthened.
Matagi Tokelau, p163

TABLE OF TRANSLATIONS

The following table is indicative only. It has a single dimension based on the words and phrases used in the documents of 1980.

It provides a glimpse of the development of Tokelauan in the late twentieth century for the translations of English expressions related to politics and government. The English expressions in the left hand column are from the 1980 English texts. The right hand columns indicate the translations used in the documents described in the text, from 1980 to 2002. E.g. 'United Nations' was translated in the Tokelau booklet (T) 1980, in the Lexicon (L), in the Tokelau Amendment Act 1996, and in the Nukunuku speech 2002, by the phrase *Malo kaufakatahi*.

The Table shows what has changed, what has not changed, what is settled, and what remains unsettled. The Table also shows the prevalence of key Tokelauan words in different English language situations.

1980	T	TT	FR	CH	L	MT	HR	Act	MH	GT	TPS	N
Administration												
Kuikuiga fakaofiha	✓											
Pulega fakatonutonu	✓						✓					
Fakatonutonugia				✓								
Malo						✓						
Te pulega (administration of custom)								✓	✓			
Pulepulega						✓						
Taukikilaga (a Niu Hila)												
Administrative												
Kuikuiga fakaofiha fakatonutonu	✓											
na gaoioiga faka pulega fakatonutonu (administrative acts)	✓											
matakupu tau pulega fakatonutonu (administrative matters)	✓							✓				
paoa o te pulega fakatonutonu (administrative power)												
galuega fakatonutonu (administrative services)	✓											
pulepulega										✓		
Administrator (of Tokelau)												
Ulufakatonu matakupu tau Tokelau	✓											
Tino Ulu Fakatonu	✓											
Ulu Fakatonu o Tokelau				✓	✓	✓		✓				✓
te malo						✓						
Ulu Fakatonu hili o Tokelau						✓						
administer												
tauia		✓										
Malo pulepule; malo tauhi (administering power)												✓

1980	T	TT	FR	CH	L	MT	HR	Act	MH	GT	TPS	N
authorities												
te pulega (a Niu Hila)	✓											
pule (village/Elders)			✓	✓	✓							✓
te pule a te malo (authority of the govt)							✓					
Bodies												
vaega	✓											
body												
Fakalapotopotoga	✓											
tino tuku fakatahi (corporate body)		✓										
constitutional												
mea tau fakavae a faigamalo	✓											
Crown [the State]												
Tupu	✓											
Malo					✓							
executive												
fakatonu	✓											
General Fono												
Fono Lahi	✓				✓	✓						
Fono Aofia	✓	✓			✓							
Fono fakamua					✓			✓		✓		✓
Fono Faka atunuku						✓			✓		✓	
Fono Aoao				✓								
government												
Faigamalo	✓											
malo	✓					✓		✓				
faiga faka te malo (system of government)	✓											
Tulafono faka te malo (government law)			✓									
Government												
Malo	✓					✓		✓				
Malo pulepule (Ko Niu Hila)												✓
governance												
pulepule												✓
independence												
tutokatahi	✓					✓						
institutions												
vaega	✓											
kauhaga	✓											
na nofonofoga pule a Tokelau (Tokelau's own political institutions)								✓				
law and order												
tulafono ma te nofo lelei	✓											
pulea (order)								✓				
legal												
faka te tulafono	✓											

1980	T	TT	FR	CH	L	MT	HR	Act	MH	GT	TPS	N
legislative power												
paoa faitulafono								✓				
local laws												
tulafono faka te nuku	✓											
tulafono fakanuku (village rules)		✓			✓							
meeting												
fono lahi			✓									
peace, order and good govt												
te filemu te nofo lelei ma he malo lelei o tagata	✓											
policy												
na tonu mo na fuafuaga (policy decisions)	✓										✓	
fuafuaga o na mea fai				✓								
policies												
fuafuaga	✓											
political												
tau faigamalo	✓											
faiga fakafaigamalo (political system)	✓											
Ko tonu o tona malo (political and administrative decisions)						✓						
faka faigamalo							✓					
politics												
faigamalo	✓											
mea tau faigamalo	✓											
malo						✓						
power												
pule					✓							
pulega						✓						
paoa								✓				
public												
o te malo	✓											
fakamua	✓						✓	✓				
Regulations												
Tulafono fakatonutonu	✓											
Self-determination												
Te faia o a latou tonu e ki latou lava		✓										
filifiliga totino							✓					
pulepulega o te lumanaki										✓		
filifiliga faiga malo fakalotoifale												✓
sovereignty												
pulea		✓										
pulega							✓					

1980	T	TT	FR	CH	L	MT	HR	Act	MH	GT	TPS	N
State Services Commission												
Ofiha o Pulega o Kaufaigaluega fakamua	✓											
Komihi e pulea ia tagata faigaluega	✓											
Komihi o Galuega a te Malo				✓								
Komihi o tautuaga a te Malo								✓				
team												
vaega	✓											
Tokelau Public Service												
Kaufaigaluega fakamua a Tokelau	✓			✓								
Kaufaigaluega tautua a Tokelau								✓	✓	✓	✓	
United Nations												
Malo kaufakatahi		✓			✓			✓				✓
written laws												
tulafono	✓											
tulafono tuhia	✓											

References

Primary Sources

Administrator of Tokelau (1970-2002) *Annual Report*, Wellington: Government Printer.
No Author (1986) *Tokelau Dictionary*, Samoa: Office of Tokelau Affairs.
United Nations (1976, 1986, 1991, 1994, 2002) *Report on the Visiting Missions to Tokelau*, New York: United Nations.

Secondary Sources

Angelo, Tony (2001) 'Establishing a Nation – A Second Look', *Revue Juridique Polynesienne 1* (Hors series): 235-250.
------ (1999) 'Establishing a Nation – Kikilaga nenefu' – 30 VUWLR: 75-89.
------ (1988) 'Tokelau – The Village Rules of 1988' 4 QUTLJ 209 [Queensland University of Technology Law Journal: 209-223].
------ (1987) 'Tokelau – Its Legal System and Recent Legislation', *6 Otago Law Review:* 477-498.
------ 'Translating "bank"' – 21 VUWLR [Victoria University of Wellington Law Review]: 35-39.
------ and Hosea Kirifi (1975) *'Treaty of Tokehega'*, 17 VUWLR 125 [Victoria University of Wellington Law Review]: 122-134.
No Author (1990*) Matagi Tokelau,* Suva, Fiji: Institute of Pacific Studies, University of the South Pacific Press.
Robinson, Douglas (1997) *Translation and Empire – Post Colonial Theories Explained*, Manchester: St Jerome.

Kingdom of Tonga

Background: The archipelago of 'The Friendly Islands' was united into a Polynesian Kingdom in 1845. It became a constitutional monarchy in 1875 and a British protectorate in 1900. Tonga acquired its independence in 1970 and became a member of the Commonwealth of Nations. It remains the only monarchy in the Pacific.
Land Area: 748 sq km
Capital: Nuku'alofa
Population: 106 137; Polynesian, about 300 European
Languages: Tongan, English

The Translation of Queen Sälote's Poetry

MELENAITE TAUMOEFOLAU
The University of Auckland

> Abstract. *In this article I will be concerned with explaining some of the difficulties of translating the poetry of Queen Sälote (QS) from Tongan into English. Tongan belongs to the Polynesian branch of the Austronesian language family. Along with Niuean, it is a daughter language of Proto-Tongic, one of the two major subgroups of Polynesian. The other subgroup is Proto-Nuclear Polynesian, to which belong all other Polynesian languages, including the Outlier Polynesian languages in Micronesia and Melanesia. Whenever difficulties in translation arose, I found it was mainly for either of two reasons: structural differences between Tongan and English – examples of these will be given in section 2 – and cultural differences or differences in cultural knowledge between the Tongan-speaking audience for whom the Tongan original was composed and the non-Tongan-speaking audiences for whom the translation was produced – examples of these will be given in section 3. In section 4 I present two translated poems and their commentary.*

The 150 or so islands of Tonga (about 30 are inhabited) are part of Polynesia and lie in the southwest Pacific near where the international Dateline intersects the Tropic of Capricorn. They are scattered between latitudes 15 and 24 degrees south and between longitudes 173 and 175 degrees west. The total land area is 700 square kilometres. The four island groups in Tonga are the southern Tongatapu group (where the capital, Nuku'alofa, is situated), the central Ha'apai group, the northern Vava'u group, and the far northern Niua group. The Tongatapu group is some 650-800 kilometres from Fiji to the northwest and Samoa to the north northeast, 1,770 kilometres from Auckland and 3,220 kilometres from Sydney. Tonga and Samoa are the main island groups of West Polynesia.

Politically, Tonga is the only surviving kingdom in the Pacific and is unique in the Pacific in that it was never formally colonized. Although it has been much changed by European contact, it has retained its political independence and distinctive culture. Tongan society is highly stratified with the royal family at the top, the chiefly classes next, and commoners at the base of the hierarchy. A modern elitist middle class based on educational success and the possession of material wealth has also been formed.

1. Queen Sālote

Queen Sālote is the 21st *Tu'i Kanokupolu*, the last of Tonga's three royal dynasties, and mother of the present monarch, His Majesty King Tāufa'āhau Tupou IV. She lived from 1900-1965. She is probably most famous for her riding in the rain in the parade of carriages conveying monarchs from all over the world during the coronation of Queen Elizabeth II in 1953. When the rain fell, she refused to have the roof of her carriage pulled up to shelter her from the rain. In that act, she was conforming to the Tongan custom of lowering oneself (by not sheltering from the rain) if more high-ranking chiefs are present. This was her way of honouring the Queen of Britain whom she considered to be of higher rank than herself. The first paragraph of the blurb on the cover of Elizabeth Wood-Ellem's biography of Queen Sālote reads: "When Queen Sālote of Tonga attended the coronation of Queen Elizabeth II in London 1953, she was greeted as the tallest queen of the smallest kingdom and gained universal admiration by her natural dignity and the warmth of her personality. This event reinforced Queen Sālote's reputation as a universally beloved monarch" (Wood-Ellem 1999).

Queen Sālote had a special concern to maintain and consolidate the Tongan language and culture. She was instrumental in setting up the Tonga Traditions Committee to collect and document Tongan traditions. This included the employment of an anthropologist, Elizabeth Bott Spillius, who researched and produced the history book *Tongan Society at the Time of Captain Cook's Visits: Discussions with Her Majesty Queen Sālote Tupou* (1982). Many scholars of Polynesia have written about Queen Sālote as a remarkable ruler, but her work as an orator and poet is much less known. This is probably because her compositions were all in Tongan, making the work inaccessible and unknown to non-Tongan-speaking audiences. Many people have translated some of her poems, but these were translations of individual poems only. For the first time a book is being produced about the Queen's poetry. In that book (forthcoming) I translate 114 of her poems. This article focuses on my translation of Queen Sālote's poems.

QS wrote different categories of poems during the period of 1920 to 1960: **hiva kakala** or love songs, literally 'flower songs', **ūpē** 'lullabies', **laulau** 'chants', **tutulu** 'laments', **mā'ulu'ulu** 'songs for seated dances', and **lakalaka** 'songs for standing dances'. Many of her love songs were written for her consort, Tungï Mailefihi. The lullabies were written for some of her children and grandchildren when they were very young. Her chants were written in praise of people and places that she loved. Her laments mourned the deaths of some of her close relatives. Her choreographed poetry was composed for dances to be performed on special occasions, such as state or church celebrations.

In QS's poetry, there are copious references to Tongan traditional culture, many of whose features are uniquely Tongan and different from Western cultures. Most importantly, the poetry brings out the importance of rank, which is based on a variety of factors, the most important of which are gender, seniority and descent from high-ranking ancestors. Most of the poems are sung and therefore have such sound devices as rhyme and metre.

1.1 Translating Queen Sälote's Poetry

My translation of QS's poetry from Tongan into English may be said to fall under the kind of translation that Casagrande (in Grace 1981: 63), classifies as 'aesthetic-poetic'. In this kind of translation, "while content obviously is not ignored, express consideration is given to the literary or aesthetic form of the message in both languages". The single most important factor that influenced my translation was the fact that some cultural information, presumed to be available to the Tongan-speaking audience, was not explicitly expressed in the original. To explain this information for the sake of reader understanding would mean longer lines and a sacrifice of the aim and attempt to render the translation 'aesthetic' and 'poetic'. Furthermore, to explain it would mean that the translation would be obliged to include content that is not present in the original. Thus, my translation approach has tended to be on the literal side and therefore the translations may at times be somewhat enigmatic.

When I translated QS's poetry I came across many of the issues of poetic translation often discussed in the literature (e.g. Lefevere 1992) such as how to deal with the use of foreign words, metaphors, proverbs, and other devices. In this paper, however, I shall be confined to a discussion of a few issues only, chief among which is the extensive use of cultural allusions and the Tongan poetic device **heliaki** (see below). These are particularly difficult to translate because much of the cultural knowledge necessary to understand them is not given in the original.

An issue that concerned me was that of cultural values. Some Tongan values relating to the chiefly society may not have corresponding values in Western cultures. In Tongan culture, there are certain perceptions of chiefs as brave and benevolent leaders who love the common people rather than as privileged individuals. Among commoners, there are values of wanting to serve the aristocracy, values of being **mateaki** 'to be loyal even unto death', and of being humble and respectful. The Tongan language has ways of expressing the social status of chiefs, such as the sociolect of honorific language. QS's poetry is about consolidating the chiefly classes and perpetuating these chiefly and commoner values. These values are praised in aesthetically pleasing ways. In English these sentiments may not sound as pleasing as in Tongan, and the democratic values and sometimes anti-royal feelings of a western audience may not help make them sympathetic towards such messages of the poetry.

In the process of translating QS's work, I have been made aware of the very wide cultural gap between the target language and the source language and the impossibility of faithfully rendering the source language meanings in the target language. I have been made aware of the vast information gap that needs to be filled before the target language audience can really understand the meanings conveyed in the source language. I hope the discussion of the two poems in section 3 illustrate this need.

1.2 Translation and Change

Since the 1970s, a large number of Tongans have migrated overseas. There are now sizable Tongan communities in the United States, Australia and New Zealand. More and more Tongans are being born overseas, and increasingly young people are losing their Tongan language and their familiarity with Tongan culture. QS's poetry is difficult even for fluent Tongan speakers who do not know enough about Tongan culture to understand the meanings of the figures of speech used in the poetry. It is my hope that the translation will make QS's poetry accessible to non-Tongan-speaking Tongans and foreigners alike. The translation also speaks about those aspects of culture that may already be lost to overseas-born Tongans. It speaks about the importance of rank in the traditional culture, about the fact that Tongans in traditional Tongan society are far from equal, and that members of the family are ranked. It speaks about the traditional values of respect for and the desire to serve the aristocracy, how these values are celebrated and are the mark of Tongan cultural identity even though these values may be questioned in more democratic societies. My aim has been to make the translations of the poems as complete and as self-explanatory as possible for the sake of non-Tongan-speaking audiences.

2. Structural Differences

The structure of Tongan, the source language, is different from the structure of English, the target language, in several respects, thus preventing the smooth transfer of meaning from Tongan into English.

2.1 The Pronoun System

The Tongan pronominal system has three number categories – singular, dual and plural (e.g. **ma, kimaua** = we two; **mau, kimautolu** = we three or more) whereas English has only singular and plural (see the figure below). In those three number categories of the first person, Tongan distinguishes between inclusive and exclusive pronouns (e.g. **ma, kimaua** = we two excluding the addressee, but **ta, kitaua** = we two including addressee – you and I) whereas English does not. In the third person singular, there is no gender or animate/inanimate distinction in Tongan (**ne, *ia*** = he, she, it) whereas there are in English.

Person, Exclusive/Inclusive, Number	Preposed Pronouns (before verb)	English Gloss	Postposed Pronouns (after verb)	Possessive Pronouns
1st exc. singular.	ou, ku, u, kau	I	au	'eku/hoku
dual	Ma	we two*	kimaua	'ema/homa
plural	mau	we three or more*	kimautolu	'emau/homau
1st inc. singular	Te	one, I	kita	'ete/hoto
dual	Ta	we two**	kitaua	'eta/hota
plural	Tau	we three or more**	kitautolu	'etau/hotau
2nd singular	Ke	you (one)	koe	ho'o/ho
dual	Mo	you two	kimoua	ho'omo/homo
plural	mou	you three or more	kimoutolu	ho'omou/homou
3rd singular	Ne	he, she, it	ia	'ene/hono
dual	Na	they two	kinaua	'ena/hona
plural	nau	they three or more	kinautolu	'enau/honau

Figure: The cardinal pronouns with some corresponding possessive forms

* excluding you
** including you

2.1.1 The first person inclusive singular

Use of the first person inclusive singular is often more formal, more respectful, and more humble than the use of the more common first person exclusive singular pronouns. Consider these phrases: **'ete fiefia** 'my happiness', **hoto kahoa fakataukei** 'my garland as an indigene'. In these phrases, the possessive form of the first person inclusive singular is selected over the exclusive form (**'eku fiefia, hoku kahoa fakataukei**). The difference in meaning between the two kinds of 'my' is that the exclusive form is more formal and more indicative of humility on the part of the speaker. Because English does not make this distinction, it is not possible to bring about this subtle difference in tone in the translation.

2.1.2 The first person inclusive dual

In Tongan formal speech, it is more conventionalized to use the first person inclusive dual pronouns than the plural. For example, instead of saying 'Let us-*inclusive-plural* repent our-*inclusive-plural* sins', a preacher delivering a sermon in Tongan is more likely to say to the congregation, 'Let the two of us (you and me) repent our-*inclusive-dual* sins'. Many lines from QS's poetry make use of the first person inclusive dual forms. **To'o mai 'eta fala päongó** 'Give me our-*inclusive-dual* **päongo** mat'. Here the word **'eta** is the first person, inclusive dual possessive pronoun. So in the Tongan, 'our' refers to possession by two persons, the addresser and addressee. Because English does not make the dual/plural and inclusive/exclusive distinctions, this particularity in the Tongan is lost in the translation.

Another example:

> *Ne'ine'i fili ko e Nofo'a*
> 'O e Ha'a Tu'i hota fonuá
>
> No wonder it was culled for the Throne
> Of the Kings of our land

In the Tongan, the possessive pronoun **hota** 'our-inclusive-dual' is used, but because English does not make this distinction, the translation is an approximation only. Sometimes I would translate lines containing the inclusive, dual 'us' as 'you and I' as in 'Let us go down to Fakala'ä, you and I' or as 'we two...' in order to retain the dual meaning of the pronoun.

2.1.3 The first person exclusive plural
In the second of the following lines, the first person exclusive plural possessive pronoun **homau** is used, so the addressee is excluded from the possession.

> *Pe'i nonga ho'o fifilí ka te u fakamatala*
> *Ko homau ve'eve'e tui ki he pötatala*

> Then cease your wondering while I explain
> It is our garland strung for the night of conversations

Because English does not make the inclusive/exclusive distinction, the English possessive allows both possibilities of possession that includes the addressee and possession that does not.

2.1.4. The inclusive dual and exclusive dual pronouns
When both inclusive dual pronouns and exclusive dual pronouns are translated by the general English 'our', the translation is ambiguous. Consider the following lines:

> *Ko 'ete poaki atu ki he fä*
> *'Ana Fangaafa si'eta tamá*
> *Ke tuku ke fafa 'i hoku tu'á*
> *Ke ma ö ki homa käingá*

> The *fä*'s permission I solicited
> That our dear child, 'Ana Fangaafa
> Be carried on my back
> To go with me to visit our people

In the Tongan, the 'our' (*si'eta*) in the second line is the first person inclusive dual possessive pronoun (emotional and definite form), so that the child belongs to the persona and 'Ana Fangaafa (yours and mine), the addressee. Because English does not have this inclusive, dual category, English 'our' is ambiguous and may refer to people other than 'Ana Fangaafa as the possessors. This allows an interpretation of 'Ana Fangaafa as the name of the child. In the Tongan, the 'our' (*homa*) in the fourth line is the first person exclusive dual possessive pronoun and therefore refers to possession by the persona and the child.

Tongan has emotional and neutral forms of possessive pronouns as well as definite and indefinite forms. When emotional forms are used, then emotion is brought out through the use of adjectives in the translation. For example, **siʻeta tama** 'our-exclusive-dual-emotional child' is translated as 'our dear child'. English 'dear' brings out the sense of sympathy expressed in the Tongan by the emotional possessive pronoun.

2.1.5 O and A possession

Note that possessive pronouns in Tongan also come in two categories – what is known in the literature as *A* and *O* possession (see Taumoefolau 1996). When concrete nouns are possessed, *O* possession is 'partitive'. This means that the possessed is literally or figuratively part of the possessor. *A* possession is 'agentive' in that the possessor is seen as a literal or figurative agent of the possessed. The effect of *O*'s partitiveness is that the possessive relationship is closer or more intimate compared to *A* possession, which tends to stress a sense of practical agentivity in the possessive relationship. These connotations of more closeness in *O* possessions and more practicality in *A* possessions are not able to be brought out in the translation because English lacks the equivalent distinction. The connotations may be too subtle to be expressed in other ways, given the constraints of space in the aesthetic-poetic translation.

2.1.6 The third person singular pronouns

Because there is no gender distinction in Tongan in the third person singular pronouns, it is only the context of the poem that may inform the translator which of the English forms should be used. If the context does not tell whether the person is a 'he' or 'she', then there is no way of being certain whether the translation is accurate. In the following lines, I chose 'his' simply from working out from the context what may be the gender of the 'indigene'.

>   Pe ha taukei mei loto Bau
>   ʻOku navu tuʻui hono malumalu
>
>   Or an indigene from central Bau
>   Sporting his lime-treated up-standing hair

Below is part of a poem in which it was only my extra-linguistic knowledge that informed my selection of 'he' rather than 'she' (third line of translation).

>   Te ʻofa he mokopuna ʻo Fané
>   Mokopuna e Tu ʻipelehaké...

> Peheange mai ha 'ane pehë
> Ke ma mohe ki he Kaliopulé
> Ke ma 'eva he Hüfangalupé

> How I pity the descendant of Fane
> Descendant of Tu'ipelehake...
> How I wish he would tell me
> That we would spend the night at Kali'opule
> So we could stroll down Hüfangalupe

Throughout the 116 lines of this poem it is not possible to work out from the context whether the child referred to in the poem is male or female. The translation selects 'he' only because of the extralinguistic knowledge of the translator.

2.1.7 Demonstrative clitic pronoun na

Tongan has a demonstrative clitic pronoun **na** which means 'there near you (addressee)'. It points specifically to the direction of the addressee. It is so close to the addressee that it sometimes means 'your', as in **sino na** 'your body', literally that body there in your direction. This pronoun has no equivalent in English. It is used occasionally by QS in her poetry, e.g. **langi na** 'that langi there near you', **'alofi na** 'that 'alofi there in your direction', as in the lines below:

> *Tapu mo e takafalu 'o langi na*
> *He 'afio 'a Ha'a Moheofo*
> *Mo ha'a 'eiki 'o e 'alofi na*
> *Molofaha mo Mäliepö*

> My respects to the *takafalu* of the *langi* there
> The royal presence of Ha'a Moheofo
> And the chiefly lineages of the *'alofi* there
> Molofaha and Mäliepö

Because English lacks an exact equivalent giving this particular direction, the word 'there' is used as an approximation only. The word 'there' does not have the semantic element of 'near you (addressee)'. Occasionally, I use the word 'your' in the translation, when I judge it is appropriate, e.g.:

> *He fale hau na kuo täpuhä*
> *Hono fa'u 'e he kau tufungá*

> Your lordly house is sanctified
> Constructed by the originators

Another possible translation would have been 'The lordly house there is sanctified...'.

2.2 Aspects of Verbs

2.2.1 Derived words

Tongan verbs (and their nominalized uses) have executive and durational aspects. The executive aspect is indicated by the addition of the executive suffix **−'i**, and the durational aspect is indicated by the addition of the durational suffix **−a** or sometimes a mix of those suffixes, e.g. **−Cia** or **−Caki** (where C is any consonant). Often the resultant derived words form separate lexemes rather than inflected forms of the same basic verb. In an executive verb the action is more likely to be carried through to completion. For example, **toli** means to pick (flowers or fruits), but **toli'i** means that the picking is more likely to be carried through until no more flowers/ fruits are on the tree. These derived verbs do not readily translate into English. Durational verbs are often 'stative' verbs, sometimes designating processes or states. Sometimes the difference in meaning between the basic (unsuffixed) verb and the durational verb is merely that the durational verb is more 'poetic' and more formal. Many such forms are seldom ever used in conversational Tongan. Their English translations do not bring out their poeticness.

In QS's poetry there is very extensive use of verbs with aspects such as durationality. Examples in the same poem are **vakaia** instead of just **vakai** 'visit', **fotuaki** instead of just **fotu** 'to come into view', **tulikaki** instead of just **tuli** 'to chase', **ofongaki** instead of just **ofo** 'to wake', **tuia** instead of just **tui** 'to string', **takia** instead of just **taki** 'to guide', **kafia** instead of **kaka** 'to climb', **muia** instead of **mui** 'to follow', **le'eia** instead of just **le'ei** 'to move something aside', **talia** instead of **tali** 'to reply', **feliuekina** instead of **feliuaki** 'to change constantly', **falanaki** instead of **falala** 'to lean against', **fakahä'ia** instead of **fakahä** 'to reveal', **'avea** instead of *e* **'ave** 'to take'. The extensive use of these derived words by QS gives a distinctive poetic style in her poetry. When they are translated into English using just the meanings of the basic verbs, something of the poetic style and slightly more formal tone is lost.

2.2.2 Reduplications

Tongan verbs (with their nominalized uses) may also be reduplicated, partially or fully, resulting in variations in meaning, including a more poetic and formal use. A reduplication may have a moderative, intensificatory, frequentative or pluralistic effect on the basic unreduplicated meaning, but sometimes in addition to those meanings, a reduplication could simply be more poetic and formal than its unreduplicated form. When this is the case, it is often difficult to find satisfactory translations for such reduplications. Examples are **tātālolo**, reduplicated form of **tālolo** '(of people or birds) to settle, to sit or lie down to rest, **mämälele** instead of just **mälele** 'to sway in one direction', **'a'afu** instead of just **'afu** 'to be hot', **längä** instead of just **langa** 'to take off, to fly off', **maliuliu** instead of just **maliu** 'to move gently from one direction to another and back again', **hivehiva** instead of just **hiva** 'to sing'. As with derived words in 2.2.1 above, the extensive use of reduplicated forms by QS helps to mark the style as distinctively poetic.

3. Cultural Differences

Words and phrases expressing culture-specific knowledge do not always readily find equivalents in English. Often translations into English are vague, non-specific approximations only. Examples of these are given below.

3.1 Words for Cultural Items, Practices and Sentiments

Just as English has words that describe culture-specific items, Tongan has culture-specific words for practices and customs that are unique to Tongan or Polynesian culture. It is not always easy to find equivalents in English for such words. Sometimes an approximation is given, other times a short paraphrase is given, but often the word is left untranslated, with an explanation given in the glossary. Examples of such culture-specific words are: **palavalu**, **fatufä**, **'efinanga** – these are all kinds of bark-cloth or mats, each with their own patterns, sizes, uses and values; **falahola, fä, hingano, kukuvalu** – these are kinds of fragrant flowers or other plant parts, each with a particular rank or status, e.g. some flowers are high-ranking and symbolise chiefs and kings and other high-ranking people, while others are common, low-status flowers that symbolise people with no recognised rank. The phrase **fale fataki** refers to a house or carrier in which a chief is carried. Because Tongan society is a stratified society with chiefly classes and commoner classes, words/phrases like **fale fataki** would be parts of the culture of serving the higher classes. The phrase **teki faiva** refers to skilful use of head movements with accompanying facial expressions during particular dances. This is a cultural skill and is present only in cultures where particular dances involve head movements.

The following lines come from the poem ***Fanga-i-Lifuka***: Hurricane Song of **Vaea**: *Ke talia e angi na'a tö/ Ke me'ite Sia-ko-Veiongo* – these lines are a call for help. They ask the people to respond to the call for help and rescue the men from the sinking ship during the hurricane in case it be said that the call is given for no purpose, in order that the **Sia-ko-Veiongo** (hill beside the Palace) be pleased. This kind of request requires understanding of the spirit of wanting to serve the aristocracy, a cultural sentiment common among Tongans who are conditioned to think and feel in certain ways, given their unique hierarchical social structure. This sentiment is a product of the long rule of the **hou'eiki** 'chiefs'. Commoners would be happy to risk their lives to please the **hou'eiki**. Commoners have the spirit of **mateaki** 'loyalty even unto death'.

3.2 Conventionalized Poetic Usages

Particular usages that are common in the poetry have no idiomatic English equivalents. These include the use of the locative classifiers **funga** 'top of' and **loto Mu'a, loto Neifalu, loto Ha'angana**. Both **funga** and **loto** give a poetic meaning to the place name. **Funga** is used even if a place is not high or raised, and **loto** is used even if it is not the actual centre of the place that is being referred to. **Funga** is often left untranslated and **loto** is often translated with 'central'. The use of the emotional definite article **si'i** is often translated as 'dear' as in **si'i matangi** 'dear wind', **si'i mähina** 'dear moon', **si'i la'ä** 'dear sun'. This is an endearing, diminutive, personifying classifier, and although it is mostly translated with 'dear', it is translated by 'sweet' in some contexts. The use of **'ofa** 'love' at the beginning of sentences to express sympathy with or support for something is very common e.g. **'Ofa he matangi ni kuo funga 'Alaki** 'my sympathy lies with this wind that is blowing from **funga 'Alaki. 'Ofa he matangi kuo tokelau** 'how I love this wind that is from the north… Because things such as the wind are not usually sympathized with, it is hard to find translations that would not sound odd. So usually I use a translation like 'dear wind' to bring out the persona's sympathetic relationship with the wind. Sometimes the translation begins with 'how I love …'.

3.3 Chiefly and Regal Language

Tongan language has chiefly and regal vocabulary used only for chiefs and kings. These levels of vocabulary do not have direct equivalents in English. For example, the neutral word **hingoa** 'name' becomes **huafa** in the regal language. The complimentary effect of the use of regal and chiefly vocabulary is not achieved if neutral, everyday words are used. Because English lacks this distinction, other ways have to be sought to bring out the complimentary style. Examples are **ke fakahā'ele pea kauala**, escort and carry [him here]. The word **fakahā'ele** means to escort but it is used only of a king. The word **kauala** means to carry but the carrying is done by a number of people and the person being carried is a chief or king who is sitting or lying in a carriage. Because English does not have chiefly or regal words, the complimentary effect is lost in the translation. **Manumataongo si'ono huafa** – this line is translated as 'Manumataongo is his dear revered name'. The adjective 'revered' helps to give a closer translation for the word **huafa**. The word 'dear' brings out the emotion in the emotional pronoun **si'ono** 'his/her-emotional'. In another poem, QS says that a particular child is the **Fofonga 'o Ha'a Takalaua**, literally face-honorific of Ha'atakalaua (name of a royal dynasty). **Fofonga** is a chiefly word; I therefore use an approximation in English – the visage of Ha'atakalaua. The English word 'visage' at least captures the favourable atmosphere created by the chiefly word **fofonga**. In another poem, the Queen uses the chiefly word for child, which is **fale'alo**. The chiefly form is translated into 'child', and here again something of the complimentary tone is lost. Finally, these lines **Kuo malolo 'a Tonga ni 'o tatali/ Kia Tupouto'a ke ne me'a mai** are translated into 'Tonga has subsided, waiting for Tupouto'a to arrive'. Unfortunately, again the complimentarity is lost with the use of the normal word 'arrive' to translate the chiefly word **me'a**.

3.4 Culture-specific "Heliaki"

A major theme in QS's poetry is the celebration of her identity or her **'uhinga**. This is expressed through references to the chiefly kinship connections of herself and of her family. In Tongan this practice is called **laukāinga**, the reciting of kinship connections or, sometimes, **hohoko**. In QS's case, because these are high-ranking connections, the word **lau'eiki**, the reciting of chiefly connections, may be more appropriate. But instead of describing these kinship connections directly or explicitly, she refers to them using symbols. Two main kinds of symbols are used: flower (or other plant parts) symbols, in Tongan, **laukakala**, and symbols for places, in Tongan, **laumātanga**. **Heliaki** is the name of the Tongan poetic device used pervasively by QS in which she practises **laukakala** and **laumātanga**. **Heliaki** may be described as speaking or writing in symbols or riddles, or speaking/writing figuratively. **Heliaki** can be very difficult to translate because it assumes a lot of cultural knowledge that cannot all be explained in the translation.

We could say that there are two kinds of **heliaki** in QS's work: universal **heliaki** and culture- specific **heliaki**. Universal **heliaki** is readily understood by a general audience because the figures of speech used involve no isoteric knowledge restricted to speakers of Tongan language and members of Tongan culture. For instance, in many of QS's love songs (**hiva kakala**), there is universal **heliaki**:

> Oh, happy is the wind
> That blows wherever it pleases
> While I live a prisoner
> To love with its silver lock

And in other poems as well:

> Friday dawned
> And word came
> The war had begun
> At evening came the shock
> The army of death had won
> Disbanding the centre of my pitiful house

With universal **heliaki**, reference is made to common human experiences that are not specific to any particular culture. In the above verses, there is reference to the unhappy restrictions imposed by love and to death being described as a result of war.

The **heliaki** that I will explain here is culture-specific and consists of knowledge that may be shared by speakers of Tongan but not necessarily by others. It is therefore knowledge that is not easy to be acquired during a reading of the translation and needs to be explained. **Heliaki** comes in different kinds and levels of detail. It can be given as an explanation that is in the form of a riddle, but it can also be rendered simply in a single word – a place name or the name of a garland, but in that word are packed all the meanings and connotations associated with the kinship connection being alluded to.

4. Translation and Commentary

Below are translations of two poems by QS. The poems are the *Lullaby of Manumataongo* (born 1948) and *The Queen's Tears at the Passing of Ha'amea* (died 1960). Manumataongo is the name of the Queen's eldest grandchild, currently the Crown Prince of Tonga. Ha'amea was the holder of the **'Ulukālala** title, one of the most prominent chiefly titles in Tonga. When Ha'amea passed away in 1960, no one held the title for a long time, as Ha'amea had no heir. It was not until a few years ago that the title was bestowed on the king's youngest son, Prince 'Aho'eitu, **'Ulukālala Lavaka Ata**. It will be seen that the translations are somewhat enigmatic because they contain a lot of culture-specific **heliaki**. After each poem is a commentary explaining the cultural information that is assumed in the Tongan original but which cannot be brought out in the translations.

Lullaby of Manumataongo (born 1948)

1. My deference be to the tower
   While I render the appeasement
   Lullaby of Mu'a's row of *langi*
   The flower bushes serenading
   White bird, hush now
   Stroll with me on your home ground
   See your mound of *kakala*
   Strung by the women of Lapaha

2. *Faka'otusia* standing in pairs
   And the *ve'eve'e* of Tatakamotonga
   You will play at the *nusipalataha*
   And the profusion of *fakamatamoana*
   Your carpet is the *alamea*
   And the pandanus of Langi Taetaea
   Strung by the Paepae-o-Tele'a
   And 'Utulifuka still flourishing

3. Let Mala'ekula be exempt
   And the torch of Vuna Wharf
   Lest I be accused of presumption
   That you be carried on my back
   To the rejected island of Niua
   Tethering place of Takalaua

To reign over the high island
Refuge of the native birds

Chorus:
Lëlea and Veitatalo
Start up a *tauʻaʻalo*
Lea-ʻa-e-tohi, beach at Lifuka
Stand at the prow all night long
So our voyage will be pleasant
And Manumataongo stops crying

In the first verse, QS follows convention by acknowledging the Monarch of the land, who is really herself, but as a composer she steps out of herself to address the audience as an ordinary citizen. The 'tower' is the symbol for the Palace, residence of the Monarch. She tries to distract the royal infant from crying by singing a lullaby about the row of **langi** at Muʻa. The **langi** are the royal tombs of the Tuʻi Tonga kings situated at Lapaha, the eastern side of Muʻa, the old capital of Tonga.

There have been three royal dynasties in Tonga. The earliest was the Tuʻi Tonga dynasty (TT), literally King over Tonga. This was the sacred line of kings that began with ʻAhoʻeitu in about 950 AD and ended with TT Laufilitonga in 1865. The second was the Tuʻi Haʻatakalaua dynasty (THT), literally King over the Takalaua Lineage, which started with THT Moʻungamotuʻa, son of TT Kauʻulufonua Fekai, in about 1450 and ended with THT Mulikihaʻamea in about 1799. Both the TT and THT dynasties are now extinct. The third is the present dynasty of the Tuʻi Kanokupolu (TK), literally King of Kanokupolu, which started with Ngata, son of THT Moʻungätonga, in about 1610, and continues to the present day with H.M. King Täufaʻähau IV, QS's eldest son, now the 23rd TK. Although both the THT and TK lines were continuations by blood of the TT line and therefore may be thought of as equal in chiefliness to the TT, in fact the TT dynasty was by far the most chiefly and sacred of Tonga's three dynasties. According to QS, the degree of chiefliness of a person is derived from the closeness of their kinship relationship with the TT line (James 1995). This may be because of the divine origins of the TT line. Although the first TT ʻAhoʻeitu's mother was an earthly woman, his father was the generator god, Tangaloa ʻEitumatupuʻa.

There are four island groups in Tonga: the Tongatapu group consisting of the main island Tongatapu, ʻEua and the surrounding small islands; the Haʻapai group which includes the chiefly islands of ʻUiha, Häʻano and Tungua; the Vava'u group whose chief is the holder of the prominent 'Ulukälala title; and the Niua group consisting of Niuafo'ou, Niuatoputapu and surrounding small islands. The TT dynasty had residences in Lapaha, Mu'a, in the eastern side of Tongatapu. The THT was also from Lapaha but some THT kings resided in Niuafo'ou. The TK historically resided in Hihifo, the western side of Tongatapu, but now is based in Nuku'alofa, capital of Tonga.

QS's poetry contains many references to place names (**laumātanga**) and flowers (**laukakala**) associated with each of the dynasties. These place names and flowers are symbols of the Queen's kinship connections with the dynasties. Places and flowers (and garlands) are ranked – those associated with the TT rank highest. Thus, out of a vast array of Tongan poetic names for places and flowers, only the ones that are symbolic of the Queen's kinship connections with the dynasties are used in the poetry.

Mu'a, more specifically Lapaha, was the seat of the TT dynasty. Place names and flowers of Lapaha or Mu'a became symbols for the TT dynasty. Although QS is of the TK line, she is also descended on her mother's father's side, from the last TT, Laufilitonga. She also has an important link with the THT dynasty. Her mother's mother, Tōkanga, was a daughter of Fotofili, chief of Niuafo'ou. Fotofili is a direct descendant of the seventh THT Fotofili, who was sent from Lapaha to Niuafo'ou to look after that island. Since then, descendants of the THT line are the present chiefs of Niuafo'ou. We therefore find in the poetry a great number of references to Niuafo'ou because of that link. Another important link with the THT is through her consort, Tungï Mailefihi, who was the heir to the THT line. This means QS and Tungï Mailefihi's children had blood from all the three dynasties. Symbolism for the three dynasties in terms of place names and flower names are found throughout QS's poetry.

Thus, in the first verse, 'the flower bushes serenading' is reference to the poetic name of Lapaha, Kolo Kakala, literally town of fragrant flowers. Although the infant is the grandson of QS, then the current TK, she reminds the reader of the child's kinship connection with the sacred TT dynasty – 'stroll with me in your home ground' meaning Lapaha. There they will see a mound of **kakala** 'sweet-smelling flowers' of the highest kind because they have been strung by women of Lapaha – native women of the TT residences.

The second verse is dominated by **laukakala**, the reciting of high-ranking flower garlands and girdles – *faka'otusia, ve'eve'e, nusipalataha, fakamatamoana* and *alamea*. All these are symbolic of the boy's connections with the TT dynasty. Tatakamotonga, the name of the western side of Muʻa (Lapaha is the eastern side), was the estate of QS's consort, Tungï Mailefihi, heir to the THT title. In this context, Tatakamotonga is symbolic of the boy's THT connections. Langi Taetaea and the Paepae-o-Teleʻa are terraced tombs of TT kings. ʻUtulifuka is a tract of the TT dynasty. Their mention establishes the boy as being of TT stock.

In the third verse, the Queen asks that Malaʻekula and the torch of Vuna Wharf be exempt from the conversation in case they be insulted that QS wants to put the boy on her shoulder. Here QS as a composer acknowledges the high rank of the TK (herself), symbolized by Malaʻekula, the royal tombs of the TK, situated in Nukuʻalofa. She describes the TK Monarch as the 'torch of Vuna Wharf' shining from the wharf called Vuna, situated at the waterfront of Nukuʻalofa. She sits the boy on her shoulder and transports him to the 'rejected' island of Niuafoʻou, 'tethering place of Takalaua'. Niuafoʻou is a 'rejected' island because the people were taken off the island when the volcanic island erupted in 1946. Some of the people resettled on the island of ʻEua and others resettled in Tongatapu. Others, however, returned to their beloved island after some years. Takalaua is short for Haʻatakalaua, the lineage of THT. This is reference to the sending of Fotofili, the seventh THT, to Niuafoʻou, thus beginning the lineage of Fotofili. By taking the child to Niuafoʻou the Queen is celebrating her kinship connection with the THT line (through her maternal grandmother, Tökanga).

In the chorus, QS practises **laumätanga**, the reciting of scenic places. Lëlea and Veitatalo are places in Vavaʻu whose chief is QS's cousin ʻUlukälala. In these places are some of QS's relatives on her mother's father's side. She calls on them to sing a chant called *tauʻaʻalo*, a particular chant associated with the people of Holonga village in which reside QS's relatives on her mother's father's side, who are descendants of the TT dynasty. In the third line are places in Haʻapai – Lea-ʻa-e-tohi is the registered estate of QS's younger son, the late Prince Tuʻipelehake, and Lifuka is the main island of Haʻapai where QS's ancestors on her father's side (TK side) resided. She calls on them to steer the boat so that their voyage is a pleasant one, making the boy stop crying. The people of Haʻapai are well-known for their navigational skills, and metaphorically, QS is referring to her illustrious ancestor, Tupou I, whose skilled leadership and 'making of modern Tonga' is often described as skilful navigation of a boat.

Thus, ostensibly, this poem is a lullaby that sings about flowers and places and what may sound like ordinary events, but in fact they are significant cultural allusions to QS's kinship connections which are recited to celebrate her aristocratic origins and consolidate her ties with other chiefly lines in Tonga, ties that are not explicitly expressed and would not be clear from the translation. These references are culture-specific and need to be explained annotatively rather than within the translation.

The Queen's Tears at the Passing of Tangata 'o Ha'amea (died 1960)

1. Ha'amea, what strange behaviour is this
   Not getting up to greet me
   In Fïnau's house
   All would be astir when I enter

2. 'Ukalala, talk to me
   About your lost voyage
   Were you, perhaps, belittled
   By the old woman of Ha'a Havea
   For you to leave her in New Zealand
   To follow your grandchildren
   'Uluvalu and Täufa
   Siuilikutapu and Fusipala
   And the commoner, Ma'ulupekotofa

3. Ha'amea, I will speak out
   So the stranger may know
   And the next generation may understand
   About our meeting in the apex
   That is talked about so much
   We two being in Olotele and Lapaha
   You being in *tuitu'u* and I in *lavalava*
   And our exchange of named *kakala*
   In the garland-making of the Langi Kätoa
   Then we would visit the Siangahu
   With me in a *sisi fakavainiaku*
   While the *kau Lätü* would be clad in *kuta*

4. We will ascend the Funga-faa'i-mata
   Visit the *langi* called Siapua
   In case there are still *laufafa*
   Remnants of the Tungua mat
   The *ta'ovala* for you to wear to Parliament House
   Then we turn off at 'Uiha

Veimapu and Faime'alava
Go in front to the *tou'a*
While I follow to the *olovaha*

5. In Ha'apai I shall remain
While you complete the journey
Going ashore at Ha'afuluhao
And the tract called Pouono
And the *piu* house of Moheofo
Central Neiafu was struck silent
Shocked at the rain of bullets
And Veitatalo protests
Dear Veitatalo, dear Veitatalo
How I pity the tract that sleeps
When, oh when, will it awake

6. I will not speak of Vava'u
For it is no stranger to poets
The ace of Ha'a Ngata Tupu
Mele Siuilikutapu

7. I will speak only about Tonga
For Lëlea has been rejected
In your fondness for the Likutea
While we two sojourned in Nuku'alofa
Dear home of Niukäsä
Standing at the base of Sia
With the stream called Fotu'afinemä
Once trickling but now empty
Not a drop is left

8. Leave out also the Taungapeka
Lest our commoner side be discovered
Carriers of the rod
The old men who guard the *kava*

9. How I pity the weeping of Leafä
Dear daughter of Tu'isila
Arise and carry your son
And flee with him to Sämoa
To walk upon the forefront of 'Aleipata
There to tell our people
And tell the Tu'i Manu'a
To carry him ashore

On the fine mat Vä-‘o-Ofu-mo-Olosenga
To Manono and Apolima
Take the fog of the mountain
From it choose his *ta'ovala*
To wear before Tungï and Tu‘ifaleua
Fruit of the *kie hingoa*

10. How audacious of you, Fïnau
    To bring Tu‘ineau here
    To escort you in your voyage
    Then leave him here while you go

11. Grand-child of Matekitonga
    Lord of the two Niuas
    How precious is the son of Mïsini
    Younger brother to Mailefihi
    His was a sole presence
    Yet a thousand

This poem uses the Tongan custom of speaking to the dead as if they were alive. It is customary for people to talk to the dead during vigils in funerals. So in verse 1, QS reprimands Ha‘amea for forgetting his manners. Fïnau is part of the title ‘Ulukälala. Whenever the Queen visits the household of Fïnau ‘Ulukälala, there would be celebrations to welcome her. At this particular time, ‘Ulukälala is lying in state and not getting up.

She wonders in verse 2 whether the cause of ‘Ulukälala's departure was a quarrel with his wife, a woman from the chiefly lineage called Ha‘a Havea. Tonga has several chiefly lineages whose names are prefixed by the word **ha‘a** 'clan, tribe, lineage' and followed by the name of the founder of the lineage. These lineages consist of chiefly people, and ‘Ulukälala's wife, Tuna, was no exception. But rank in Tonga is relative. In some contexts, a chiefly woman can be referred to as a commoner woman, literally 'old woman'. In this particular context, QS is laying emphasis on the great chiefliness of the deceased, so that by comparison, his wife is an 'old woman', a commoner. This use of language (putting down someone in order that another is elevated) is known as 'self-derogatory language' because it is used only of oneself or of one's close relatives. Thus, when QS refers to the 'old woman of Ha‘a Havea' she is acknowledging that that woman is her close relative. Similarly, the boy Ma‘ulupekotofa is described by QS as a commoner, a **motu‘a**, literally old man, even though this boy is very chiefly, being the eldest son of Tuita, one of the most prominent noble/baron titles in Tonga. QS is here laying emphasis on the great chiefliness of the other children – 'Uluvalu, Täufa, Siuilikutapu and Fusipala, who are the sons and daughters of her own sons, (then) their Royal Highnesses Prince Tupouto'a Tungï (now king) and Prince Tu'ipelehake. By comparison to the royal grandchildren, Ma'ulupekotofa is a commoner. However, by calling him a commoner, QS acknowledges that the boy is her close relative.

In verse 3, she refers to Ha'amea as of equal standing with her in some lineages, such as the TT dynasty. Both Ha'amea and QS are descendants of the last TT, Laufilitonga, though through different wives of Laufilitonga. She thus mentions 'our meeting in the apex' which is reference to the most high-ranking of the dynasties, the TT dynasty. She says they are equal in that connection 'we two being in Olotele and Lapaha'. Olotele was the name of the main residence of the TT in Lapaha, Mu'a, and 'you being in **tuitu'u** and I in **lavalava**'. They both have access to the highest-ranking **kakala** – garlands traditionally worn only by the highest persons. They may exchange garlands in the garland-making of the Langi Kätoa. This is the name of one of the TT terraced tombs in Lapaha. In the next lines, QS uses **heliaki** to describe their kinship connections with the **Tamahä** of Tungua.

High-ranking though the TT was – the highest in the land – in accordance with Tongan custom in which sisters are ranked higher than brothers, even more high-ranking was his sister, the **Tu'i Tonga Fefine** (TTF), literally the Female Tu'i Tonga. So high-ranking was the TTF that she could marry only a foreigner, who was free of the **tapu** 'sacredness' of her person. Traditionally, the TTF could marry only a chief from the Falefisi, literally House of Fiji, a lineage of Fijian chiefs consisting principally of the Tu'i Ha'ateiho (THT), literally King of Ha'ateiho, and the Tu'i Lakepa (TL), literally King of Lakepa. Historically, these chiefs were brought from Fiji, but now their descendants reside in Tonga and hold the titles to the present day. Yet, most high-ranking of all, again in accordance with the Tongan custom of assigning the highest rank of all to the **tama-'a-mehekitanga** 'daughter of father's sister', was the TTF's daughter, the **Tamahä**, who was sired by either the THT or the TL.

Tungua is the island in Ha'apai that is associated with the **Tamahä**. It is said that Tungua was the home of some **Tamahä**, being an estate of the Tu'i Ha'ateiho. Thus, whenever mention is made of Tungua or places and flowers in Tungua, QS is making reference to this highest-ranking of her kinship connections. In Tongan culture, people who are descended from the **Tamahā** (and the TTF) are more chiefly than those descending from the TT (male) line. Other **Tamahā**, perhaps those sired by the TL, are said to have dwelt at Talasiu, the eastern side of Lapaha, where the TL has an estate. Note that although the institutions of TT and **Tamahā** are now extinct, descent from them is still the measure of chiefliness.

The Siangahu is the name of a hill in Tungua. In Tungua, QS refers to the **Kau Lätü**, literally 'the *Lätüs*' – this is reference to the children of **Tamahā** Lätüfuipeka (daughter of TTF Nanasipau'u and TL Lätünipulu) and Tuita, who lived in the eighteenth century. These extremely high-ranking children included Lätüniua, Lätü-'ala-i-fotuika, and Lätü'otusia. Because QS herself is descended from the male TT line (while the **Tamahā** is the female line of the TTF), she admits that she will wear only a **sisi fakavainiaku** 'girdle of leaves' whereas it is the descendants of the **Tamahā** who will wear **ta'ovala kuta** 'waist mat made of kuta'. Kuta mats are of Fijian origins, reflecting the Fijian origins of the Falefisi.

In verse 4, Funga-faa'i-mata and Siapua are places in Tungua where QS and Ha'amea will seek out remainders of the fine weaving of Tungua women. Because both 'Ulukälala and QS are descended from the (male, brother) TT line, they are considered to be subordinate in rank to the (female, sister) **Tamahā** line. Thus, in Tungua, it would be appropriate for Ha'amea to wear to Parliament only *remnants* of Tungua's weaving. And though the **Tamahā** line is supreme in rank, as sisters, they do provide, on important occasions, **ta'ovala** 'waist mats' for their male relatives. When they arrive in 'Uiha, Ha'apai, they would pause for some **kava**, the ceremonial drink of Polynesia. That they should relax with **kava** in 'Uiha is no accident. Both QS and Ha'amea are descended from 'Ulukilupetea, a chiefly woman from 'Uiha. QS's position in the royal **kava** circle is at the front – the most privileged position reserved for the Monarch – the **Olovaha**, while Ha'amea occupies the chiefly place of the **tou'a** (along with the title Tungï) where the **kava** drink is prepared. We can see that the Queen is talking about their positions or rank in various culturally significant places and occasions.

In verse 5, QS says she will remain in Ha'apai. This is because her ancestors on her father's side are from Ha'apai, specifically from 'Uiha, Hä'ano and Lifuka. In most places, they are more or less equal in rank, but in Vava'u QS lingers behind. In Vava'u Ha'amea will go to his estate. Ha'afuluhao is the poetic name of Vava'u. Pouono is a tract in Neiafu, the capital of Vava'u. Veitatalo is the name of the home of Ha'amea in Neiafu. QS speaks in **heliaki** (figurative language), bemoaning the fact that the title may not be held again for a long time as Haʻamea had no heir. 'Dear Veitatalo, dear Veitatalo, how I pity the tract that sleeps, When, oh when, will it awake?'

In verse 6, QS says that poets know Mele Siuilikutapu is the ace of Haʻa Ngata Tupu. Haʻa Ngata Tupu is the lineage of which ʻUlukälala is the head. Mele Siuilikutapu, the mother of Tungï Mailefihi, QS's consort, was the daughter of Fane Tupou Vavaʻu, sister of Matekitonga, grandfather of Haʻamea. In Tongan culture, because Mele Siuilikutapu is the daughter of the sister of the then ʻUlukälala, she and her descendants outranked the male line of ʻUlukälala. Part of QS's poetry is aimed at consolidating the chiefly kinship connections of her family. She deliberately clarifies the superior status of her consort Tungï Mailefihi to Haʻamea.

In verse 7, QS reveals how Haʻamea 'rejected' his estate in Vavaʻu, symbolized by the poetic name Lëlea, a pond located in Neiafu, capital of Vavaʻu, because he preferred the Likutea, the name of a beach at Hihifo, Tongatapu. Hihifo is the original residence of the TK. One of ʻUlukälala's ancestors, Tuituiohu, was a younger brother of the TK Maʻafuotuʻitonga. The lineage called Haʻa Ngata Tupu consists of the descendants of Tuituiohu, including the head of the lineage, ʻUlukälala. It is thus that ʻUlukälala is associated with Hihifo through his ancestor, Tuituiohu. QS tells how Haʻamea stayed in his Nukuʻalofa home, Niukäsä, located near the Palace. She gives a poignant **heliaki** about the fact that Haʻamea had no heir:

> Dear home of Niukäsä
> Standing at the base of Sia
> With the stream called Fotuʻafinemä
> Once trickling but now empty
> Not a drop is left

In verse 8, QS reveals that the Taungapeka, literally hanging place of the flying foxes, the poetic name for Kolovai, a major village at Hihifo, Tongatapu, is home to the chief Vahaʻi, who was Haʻamea's maternal uncle. In Tongan culture, one's mother's brother is one's lowest-ranking relative. Thus, Vahaʻi, though the chief of Kolovai, was Haʻamea's 'commoner side'. QS does not speak further about that connection except to say that Vahaʻi has the traditional role of 'guarding' the **kava** in the royal **kava** ceremony.

In verse 9, QS speaks about Haʻamea's Sämoan connection, which is linked to the Sämoan connection of the TK, since ʻUlukälala is descended from Tuituiohu, brother of TK Ma'afu-o-Tu'itonga. Many precious **kie hingoa** 'named fine mats' – the most high-ranking mats had their own names – were ceded to Tongan royalty by the Sämoans when the Sämoan woman, Limapö, was brought to the THT Mo'ungamotu'a. She gave birth to his son, Ngata, who became the first TK. Presumably these precious fine mats included the Vä-'o-Ofu-mo-Olosenga. Many of these fine mats were kept by Tongan royalty. It would be fitting that, as a descendant of Limapö (through Tuituiohu), Ha'amea would be provided with a **ta'ovala** 'mat worn round the waist to show respect' by the Samoans, which he would wear in the presence of the heirs of the TK line, themselves descendants of the named fine mat, Vä-'o-Ofu-mo-Olosenga, symbol for Limapö. Tungï and Tu'ifaleua were the sons of QS. Tungï is the current TK, HM King Täufa'ähau Tupou IV. In mourning the passing of Ha'amea, QS takes the opportunity to consolidate the kinship connections of herself and her family.

Verse 10 talks briefly about the Fijian connection of Ha'amea. In a trip to Fiji, he had brought the Fijian chief Tui Nayau (in Tongan Tu'ineau) to live in Vava'u with him.

Verse 11 describes Ha'amea as the 'Lord of the two Niuas', meaning Niuafo'ou and Niuatoputapu. Ha'amea had an ancestor, Siulolovao, who was a daughter of Fotofili, chief of Niuafo'ou. Siulolovao had a daughter with Fusitu'a, one of the two chiefs of Niuatoputapu. These links with the Niuas through female ancestresses establishes Ha'amea as higher-ranking than the chiefs of Niua because sisters outrank brothers. In Tongan custom, it does not matter that ancestors lived many generations ago – it is often the case that they become chieflier and more sacred for their chronological distance. QS also makes an important point about Ha'amea's rank with regard to her consort, Tungï Mailefihi. Ha'amea is the 'younger brother of Mailefihi'. In Tongan culture, the younger sibling is always less chiefly than the older. Seniority is very important in determining rank. Thus, she acknowledges Ha'amea's very high rank as a brother of Tungï Mailefihi. Yet, as a younger brother, he is subordinate to Mailefihi. In the last two lines, QS makes a pun about Ha'amea's nickname Taha-kae-afe, literally one-but-a-thousand.

5. Conclusion

In this article I have explained some of the difficulties in translating the Tongan poetry of QS into English. I have given examples of structural differences between the two languages and cultural differences between speakers of the two languages. Of particular interest has been the Tongan poetic device of **heliaki** – writing symbolically or in riddles. Understanding culture-specific **heliaki** depends on knowing the poetic names of places in Tonga and familiarity with Tongan history, oral traditions and the chiefly genealogies of the late Queen. Without adequate knowledge of these, culture-specific **heliaki** can be quite obscure. Translating **heliaki** is problematic because it raises the issue of finding a proper balance between adhering to and retaining the literary form of the original and explaining the cultural information behind the riddles so the reader can understand them.

References

Bott, E., with the assistance of Tavi (1982) *Tongan Society at the Time of Captain Cook's Visits: Discussions with Her Majesty Queen Sālote Tupou,* Wellington: Polynesian Society Memoir No. 44.

Curriculum Development Unit (1990) *Tala 'o Tonga: Ko e Tohi Tokoni Ma'a e Kau Faiako,* Tonga: Ministry of Education.

Churchward, C. M. (1946) *Tongan Grammar,* Oxford: Oxford University Press.

------ (1953) *Tongan Dictionary,* Oxford: Oxford University Press.

Collocott, E. E. V. (1928) *Tales and Poems of Tonga,* Honolulu: Bernice P. Bishop Museum Bulletin 46.

Gifford, E. W. (1924) *Tongan Myths and Tales,* Honolulu: Bernice P. Bishop Museum.

Grace, G. W. (1981) *An Essay on Language,* Columbia, South Carolina: Hornbeam.

James, K. E. (1995) 'Rank Overrules Everything: Hierarchy, Social Stratification and Gender in Tonga' in J. Huntsman (ed) *Tonga and Samoa,* Canterbury: MacMillan Brown Centre for Pacific Studies, University of Canterbury, pp. 59-83.

Ko e Tohi Hohoko 'o Tonga. Vol. I – 10. 800 – 1961. TS. n.d.

Lefevere, A. (1992) *Translating Literature: Practice and Theory in a Comparative Literature Context,* New York: The Modern Language Association of America.

Moala, M. (1994) *'Efinanga,* Nuku'alofa: Lali Publications.

Taumoefolau, M. (1996) 'Nominal Possessive Classification in Tongan' in John Lynch and Fa'afo Pat (eds) *Oceanics Studies: Proceedings of the First International Conference on Oceanic Linguistics, Pacific Linguistics,* C-133, pp. 293-304.

Velt, K. and L. Velt (1995) *Stars Over Tonga,* Nuku'alofa: 'Atenisi University.

Ve'ehala and T. P. Fanua (1977) 'Oral Traditions and Prehistory' in N. Rutherford (ed) *The Friendly Islands: A History of Tonga*, Melbourne: Oxford University Press.

Wood-Ellem, E. (1999) *Queen Sälote of Tonga,* Auckland: Auckland University Press.

Appendix 1

Tongan original of the *Lullaby of Manumataongo*

'Üpë 'o Manumataongo

Ke fakatulou mo e tauá
Ka u feia 'a e fakana'ana'á
'Üpë 'Otu Langi 'o Mu'á
Hivehiva 'a e vao kakalá
'E manuma'a pe'i ke na'á
Ka ta ö 'o 'eva 'i ho 'uhingá
Mamata ho paepae kakalá
Ko e tui 'a e fine Lapahá

Faka'otusia tu'u tauhoá
Mo e ve'eve'e Tatakamotongá
Ke va'inga 'i he nusipalatahá
Tävani e fakamatamoaná
Ko si'o faliki ko e alameá
Mo e fä 'o Langi Taetaeá
Tui 'a e Paepae-o-Tele'á
Mo 'Utulifuka kei ala leá

Puipui ange ki Mala'ekulá
Mo e kasa 'o e Uafu-ko-Vuná
Na'a taku ko ha fiematamu'á
Ke ke motokä mai 'i hoku tu'á
Ki he motu li'aki ko Niuá
Ko e no'opotu 'o Takalauá
'O hau 'i he funga fonuá
Mohenga he manu taufonuá

Tau:
Lëlea pea mo Veitatalo
Pe'i hua mai ha tau'a'alo
Lea-'a-e-tohi, fanga i Lifuka
'Ahoia mai mei taumu'a
Kae holo si'emau nofó
Ke me'ite 'a Manumataongó

Appendix 2

Tongan original of *The Queen's Tears at the Passing of Ha'amea*

Tutulu 'a 'Ene 'Afió 'i he Pekia 'a Ha'ameá

Ha'amea fai me'a fo'ou
Ho'o tali tokoto'i au
'I he loto fale 'o Finaú
Na'a te hü ai kae ngatü

'Ulukälala ke talanoa
Ki he anga ho'o folau holá
Ne ke fie'eiki 'apë 'alä
He finemotu'a Ha'a Haveá
Ne li'aki ai 'i Nu'usilá
Ka ke muimui ho makapuná
'Uluvalu mo Täufa
Siuilikutapu mo Fusipala
Mo e motu'a ko Ma'ulupekotofá

Ha'amea ë, te u lea
Ke ma'u ha 'ilo 'a e solá
Mo e to'utupu 'o e kuongá
He'eta fetaulaki he tapá
'Oku kau he läuleá
Ta 'i Olotele mo Lapaha
Ke ke tuitu'u ka u lavalava
Pea ta fetongi kakala hingoa
'I he tui 'a e Langi Kätoa
Pe'i ta 'ahia e Siangahú
Ke u sisi fakavainiaku
Kae kuta 'a e kau Lätü

Ta hake he Funga-faa'i-matá
Vakai e langi ko Siapuá
Na'a 'oku toe e *laufafá*
Ha melenga 'o e fala Tunguá
Ke ke ta'ovala Falealea
Tau afe hake 'i 'Uiha
Veimapu mo Faime'alava
Ke ke mu'omu'a ki he tou'á
Ka u muimui he olovahá

Te u nofo Ha'apai pë au
Ka ke fakaa'u atu e folau
'O hake 'i Ha'afuluhao
Pea mo e 'api ko Pouonó
Pea mo e fale piu 'o Moheofó
Loto Neiafu ne sïlongo
He tanunu 'a e pulukökö
Pea kuo hanu 'a Veitatalo
Si'i Veitatalo, si'i Veitatalo
Te 'ofa he 'api kuo mohé
Pea ko e mohe na 'e 'ä 'afë

He 'ikai te u lau Vava'u
'Oku 'ilo ia 'e ha'a maau
'A e 'ei 'a Ha'a Ngata Tupu
Ko Mele Siuilikutapu

Te u lea pë au 'i Tonga
He kuo li'aki 'a Lëlea
Ka ke lata pë he Likuteá
'I si'eta nofo Nuku'alofá
Si'i 'api ko Niukäsä
'Oku tu'u he talalo Siá
Pea mo e vai ko Fotu'afinemä
Na'e touliki ka kuo maha
'Ikai toenga ha tulutä

Tuku ai pë Taungapeká
Na'a 'ilo ai si'ota tu'á
Ko e fua'anga 'o e siná
'A e mätu'a le'o kavá

'Ofa he punou 'a Leafaá
Si'i 'öfefine 'o Tu'isilá
Tu'u 'o fafa ho'o tamá
Ke mo feholaki ki Ha'amoá
'O 'eva he mata 'Aleipatá
Talaki hotau käingá
Pea tala ki he Tu'i Manu'á
Kaufaki'i atu ki 'uta
He Vä-'o-Ofu-mo-Olosengá
Manono ë mo 'Apolima
To'o e kakapu 'o e mo'ungá
Fili mei ai hano ta'ovala

Kia Tungï mo Tu'ifaleua
Ko e fua 'o e kie hingoá

He fie tangata 'a Fïnaú
Ho'o 'omeia 'a Tu'ineaú
Ko e moimoi ho'o folaú
Kuo li'aki mai ka ke 'alú

Mokopuna 'o Matekitongá
He 'eiki 'o e ongo Niuá
'Ofa he foha 'o Mïsiní
He tehina 'o Mailefihí
He sino ni na'e toko taha pë
Te 'ofa he taha kae afé

Notes on Contributors

Tony Angelo is professor of law at Victoria University Wellington, specializing in Comparative and South Pacific Legal Studies. He has been a long-term adviser to many of the states and territories of the Pacific region, and constitutional and legal adviser to the Elders of Tokelau since 1983.
Department of Law, Victoria University of Wellington
Private Bag, Wellington, New Zealand
Phone: (64-4) 463-5626, Tony.angelo@vuw.ac.nz

Sabine Fenton is Director of the Centre for Translation and Interpreting Studies at the University of Auckland. She established the first programmes in Translation and Interpreting in New Zealand and has taught translation and interpreting in Laos, Thailand, and Vietnam. Her research publications cover the area of translation and interpreting pedagogy, ethics, and translation and interpreting in early New Zealand and their significance in shaping the country's history.
Centre for Translation and Interpreting Studies, The University of Auckland
Private Bag 92019, Auckland, New Zealand
Phone (64-9) 3737-599, s.fenton@auckland.ac.nz

Paul Geraghty is a linguist who is interested in all aspects of Fijian and Pacific languages, cultures and history, and his major works include *The History of the Fijian Languages* (Hawaii, 1984) and *Fijian Phrasebook* (Lonely Planet, 1994). After heading the Fiji government's Institute of Fijian Language and Culture for 14 years, he is currently Senior Lecturer in Linguistics at the University of the South Pacific.
School of Humanities, The University of the South Pacific
Suva, Fiji
Phone +67 9 321-2263, geraghty_p@usp.ac.fj

John O'Leary has recently completed his doctorate at Victoria University of Wellington. In 2003 he will be a visiting Fellow at the Australian National University's Humanities Research Centre, where he will study the work of the early new South Wales poet and ethnographer Eliza Hamilton Dunlop.
16 Newman Terrace, Thorndon
Wellington 6001, New Zealand
john.oleary@xtra.co.nz

Rachel Locker McKee is Programme Director of Deaf Studies in the School of Linguistics and Applied Language Studies at Victoria University of Wellington. Her professional experience as a sign language interpreter in New Zealand and USA led to her involvement in the establishment of training programmes for interpreters and for grassroots Deaf people as teachers of NZ Sign Language (NZSL). Her research publications have focused on analysis of sign language interpreting, description of the structure of NZSL, and the culture of the New Zealand Deaf community. McKee recently published a book, *People of the Eye: Stories from the Deaf World* which presents a collection of Deaf people's oral histories translated from NZSL.
School of Linguistics and Applied Language Studies,
Victoria University of Wellington
PO Box 600, Wellington, New Zealand
Phone: (64-4) 463-5626, rachel.mckee@vuw.ac.nz

Paul Moon is a Senior Lecturer at the Faculty of Maori Development – Te Ara Poutama – where he has taught since 1993. His specialist areas of research include the Treaty of Waitangi, the early period of Crown rule in New Zealand, and issues associated with economic development.

He graduated with a Bachelor of Arts degree in 1990, with a double major in History and Political Studies. This was followed by a Master of Philosophy degree in Development Studies, and a Doctor of Philosophy, also in Development Studies, focusing on economic history. He has, in addition, studied English literature, and economics, and has published over sixty academic articles on these and other topics.
Faculty of Maori Development, Auckland University of Technology
Private Bag, Auckland, New Zealand
Phone (64-9) 917-9999, Paul.Moon@AUT.ac.nz

Margaret Mutu is from the Ngati Kahu, Te Rarawa and Ngati Whatua tribal groupings of the Far North of New Zealand on her father's side and of the Robertson clan of Scotland on her mother's side. She is Professor and Head of the Department of Māori Studies at the University of Auckland. She has a BSc in mathematics, a PhD in linguistics and Māori Studies, and has taught Māori language and Treaty of Waitangi courses at the University of Auckland since 1986. Her research interests and publications extend over the areas of recording and translating oral traditions, Māori and Polynesian linguistics, translation studies, Māori resource management and conservation practices, Māori customary fisheries, the rating of Māori land and Māori resource claims against the Crown. She has published many articles on these areas and two books: one on Marquesan grammar and the other on the history and traditions of her own *hapū* (tribal subgroup).

Professor Mutu also has many responsibilities within the Māori community. These include being the chairperson of Ngāti Kahu's *rūnanga-ā-iwi* (tribal parliament), head negotiator for the settlement of the Ngāti Kahu claims against the Crown and a trustee on many Māori land and marae organizations. She has also represented Māori on many national bodies in New Zealand including the New Zealand Conservation Authority, the board of the National Institute of Water and Atmospheric Research (NIWA) Ltd, the Board of Enquiry into the New Zealand Coastal Policy Statement and was the convenor of Paepae/Taumata 2, the four mandated representatives of Māori who negotiated with the Crown over the Māori Customary Fisheries Regulations.
Department of Maori Studies, The University of Auckland
Private Bag 92019, New Zealand
Phone: (64-9) 3737-599, m.mutu@auckland.ac.nz

Raylene Ramsay is Professor of French at the University of Auckland. She has published on *French Women in Politics* (Berghahn, 2003), on French 'autofiction' (*The French New Autobiographies*, University Press of Florida 1996) and the French new novel (*Robbe-Grillet and Modernity*, 1992). Her translation of the poems of the Kanak woman writer and independence leader, Déwé Gorodé (*Dire le vrai/ To Tell the Truth*, Grain de sable, 2001) was the first step in an ongoing project to produce a cultural history of New Caledonia in English through a collection of translated and annotated texts. The present article on three major translators of Kanak texts is part of a wider reflection for a book on hybridity in the new literatures of Kanaky/New Caledonia.
Department of French, School of European Languages and Literatures,
The University of Auckland
Private Bag 92019, Auckland, New Zealand
Phone: (64-9) 3737-599, r.ramsay@auckland.ac.nz

Melenaite Taumoefolau is a senior lecturer at the Centre for Pacific Studies, University of Auckland. She has a wide background in language studies. Her first degree was in English and education; her MA was in

English as a second or foreign language; and her PhD was in linguistics and lexicography. She has a deep interest in the cultural component of language and how this may affect the teaching, linguistic description or translation of a language. This interest is reflected in the kinds of translation work that she does. Her translation of Queen Sälote's poetry from Tongan into English brings her into contact with issues of expressing in English many concepts that are uniquely Tongan. She currently teaches Tongan language and Pacific Studies to undergraduate and graduate students at the University of Auckland.
Centre for Pacific Studies, The University of Auckland
Private Bag 92019, Auckland, New Zealand
Phone: (64-9) 3737-599, m.taumoefolau@auckland.ac.nz

Tioni Vulu is a Translator and Interpreter of Tokelauan. He was formerly a member of the Tokelau Public Service and most recently Financial Management Advisor to the Government of Tokelau. He is a director of the Tokelau Telephone Authority, TELETOK
91 Victoria Street, Petone
Lower Hutt, New Zealand
Phone: (64-4) 569- 2212.

Author Index

A

Aldridge, N., 13, 18
Alice (in Wonderland), 13
Allen, A., 93
Alpers, A., 66
Amata, Monseigneur, 141
Appleby, A., 112
Awatere, D., 52
Awekotuku, N., 66

B

Bahan, B., 89
Barnett, R., 13
Barnstone, W., 80
Barraud, C., 84
Bassnett-McGuire, S., 70
Baudrillard, J., 161
Baxter, J. K., 64, 66
Baynton, D., 92
Benjamin, W., 38, 145
Bensa, A., 134, 135, 138, 148, 163
Benton, R., 13
Bergmann, A., 91, 115
Bhabha, H., 5, 9, 135, 136
Biggs, B., 12, 21, 42, 77
Bleek, W., 67
Bligh, W., 174
Boardman, D. W., 211
Bogliolo, F., 134
Bohan, E., 66
Bott Spillius, E., 243
Brain, J., 108
Bremer, R., 77
Bryan, J., 13
Bua, T., 187
Burns, R., 71
Busby, J., 14, 30, 41
Buzzard, D., 95

C

Cakau, T., 187
Cakobau, 185
Calder, A., 137
Calder, P., 108
Campbell, J., 149
Cargill, D., 175, 179, 198
Carroll, L., 13, 28
Casagrande, J. B., 244
Chatterton, T., 82
Cheyfitz, E., 26
Clark, H., 52
Clifford, J., 151
Collier, J., 65
Collins-Ahlgren, M., 93
Cook, Captain J., 173, 243
Cooper, G., 80
Cooper, G., 80
Corker, M., 105
Cox, L., 15
Cox, L., 15, 45
Croker, T., 71
Croskery, D., 110
Croskery, P., 89, 93, 121
Cross, W., 175
Curnow, A., 65

D

D'Entrecasteaux, A., 174
Daoumi, 142, 149
Davies, J., 176, 198
Davis, C., 81
De Gaulle, C., 136
De la Fontenelle, J., 139
De Ricci, J., 186
De Rochas, V., 141
Derrida, J., 38
Dickens, C., 76

Domett, A. 64, 83
Dousset-Leenhardt, R., 151
Dryden, J., 70
Duffy, J. T., 114
Dugdale, P., 96
Dunlop, E., 72, 273
Durie, M., 15
Durville, D., 2

E

Earle, A., 72
Edmond, R., 72
Edmond, R., 85
Elizabeth II, Queen of England, 243
Ellis, W., 72
Erijiyi, B., 152
Everitt, A., 120

F

Fanon, F., 144
Fant, L., 127
Fauré, M., 139
Faust, 5, 144, 146
Feillet, Governor, 137
Fenton, S., 42, 122, 129
Firth, R., 46
FitzGerald, E., 64, 75
Fitzroy, R., 46, 47
Fleras, A., 52
France, P., 192
Frishberg, N., 97

G

George V, King of England 49
Gillespie-Needham, D., 75
Girard, R., 149
Godin, P., 161
Gorodé, D., 149, 150, 156, 275
Grace, G., 244
Grey, Earl, 39

Grey, Sir G., 4, 63, 86, 87, 88
Guiart, J., 139, 153, 169

H

Hamilton, S., 89, 110
Hamlin, J., 72
Haudricourt, A. G., 139
Hazlewood, D., 180
Head, L., 54
Higgins, P., 116
Hika, H., 16, 17, 18, 22
Hinemoa, 63, 64, 66, 78, 79, 80, 81, 82, 83, 84, 85, 86
Hobson, W., 41, 44, 58, 60, 61
Hoffmeister, R., 89
Hollyman, J., 139
Holt, A., 89, 94
Horace, F., 70
Hugo, V., 144
Humpty Dumpty, 12, 13, 19, 21, 22, 23, 28
Hunt, J., 180

I

Ihage, W., 139
Isikeli, R., 187
Iti, T., 52

J

Jacquemond, R., 234
Jankowski, K., 91
Johnson, K., 122
Johnston, G., 98

K

Kálman, G., 81
Kawharu, H., 39
Keats, J., 82
Kelsey, J., 45
Kennedy, G., 98
Kerr, D., 68

Khayyam, Omar, 4, 64, 70, 75, 86
King, M., 49
Kirifi, H., 212, 240
Kurtovich, N., 156

L

La Pérouse, J. F., 174
Lane, H., 89, 92
Langham, Rev. F., 189
Le Père Gagnière, 140
Lee, Professor at Cambridge, 16
Lee, R., 117
Leenhardt, M., 6, 134, 135, 138, 139, 144, 150, 151, 152, 155, 156, 159, 169
Lefevere, A., 54, 244
Lesson, R. P., 64
Lévi-Strauss, C., 162
Levitt, D., 97, 101
Lévy-Bruhl, L., 162
Longfellow, H., 75

M

Ma'afu, Prince of Tonga, 185
Maaka, R., 55
Macmillan Brown, J., 66
Mailefihi, T., 244, 258, 259, 265, 266
Malaspina, A., 174
Malato, C., 142
Malinowski, B., 162
Manéo, T., 152
Manukau, M., 13
Manumataongo, Crown Prince of Tonga, 256
Marais, J., 39
Mariner, W., 177
Marsden, M., 13
Marsden, S., 40
Marsden, T., 13
Martin, Sir W., 48
Mary, Queen of England, 49
Matiu, M., 13, 28

Matiu, M., 15
Maui, 72, 73, 74, 75, 77, 85, 88
Maunsell, R., 20
Mauss, M., 162
McCormack, H., 102, 109
McCormack, H., 89
McDonnell, T., 15
McHugh, P., 46
McKee, D., 98
McKee, R., 92
McKenzie, J., 97
McRae, J., 13
McRae, J., 66
Mead, S. M., 66
Meek, A., 67
Mephistopheles, 147
Metzger, M., 122
Michel, L., 5, 134, 135, 138, 140, 141, 142, 143, 145, 146, 149, 150, 154, 162, 166, 168, 170
Milne, J., 65
Mokena, T., 13
Monaghan, L., 94
Moon, P., 42
Moore, T., 75
Moskovitz, D., 90
Mourelle, F. A., 174
Müller, F., 68
Murray, J., 76, 86, 87, 197
Mutu, M., 15

N

Nailatikau, E., 187
Napoleon III, 141
Naulivou, S., 187
Nida, E., 42
Nigoth, J., 151
Normanby, Lord, 41

O

Orange, C., 41
Orbell, M., 66

Ovid, P., 70
Owen, R., 68, 87
Ozanne-Rivierre, J-C. and F., 139
Ozolins, U., 122

P

Paddon, J., 137
Paerimu, E., 48
Parasnis, I., 108
Patelesio, M., 212
Pinney, C., 138
Polack, J., 72
Pope, A., 70
Prendergast, J., 39
Prichard, J., 68

Q

Quintillian, M., 70

R

Rafael, V., 26
Reed, M., 122
Reihana, H., 13
Rënata, R., 13
Richmond, C., 48
Robinson, D., 37, 135, 234
Robinson, Sir H., 186
Rogers, W., 42
Ross, J., 15
Ross, R., 18, 45
Rousseau, J. J., 138
Rutherford, J., 66

S

Salmond, A., 16
Sälote, Queen of Tonga, 242, 243
Satchell, W., 64, 84
Scarr, D., 187
Schein, J., 118
Schiller, F., 70, 87

Schirren, C., 64, 66
Schleiermacher, F., 70
Schoolcraft, H., 65, 72, 86
Schütz, A., 176
Scott, W., 82
Scott-Gibson, L., 91, 115
Segalen, V., 146
Shakespeare, W., 68
Sharp, A., 43
Shortland, E., 72
Siegel, J., 186
Simmons, D., 77
Sinclair, K., 41
Smith, E., 113
Snell-Hornby, M., 69
Spivak, G., 136
Spoonley, P., 52
Stocking, G., 67
Sullivan, R., 13

T

Tasman, A., 174
Tate, G., 124
Täufa'ähau Tupou IV, King of Tonga, 243
Tauroa, H., 49
Taurua, E., 13
Tawhiao, Maori King, 48
Taylor, C., 122
Taylor, R., 71, 72
Te Hemara, 48
Te Rata, King, 49
Thornton, A., 66
Tipa, W., 49
Tjibaou, J-M., 137, 158, 161
Tohu, M., 13
Townshend, S., 92, 113
Tu'i Ha'atakalaua dynasty, 257
Tu'i Kanokupolu dynasty, 257
Tu'i Tonga dynasty, 257
Turia, T., 52
Turner, G., 117, 122, 124
Tutanekai, 79

V

Venuti, L., 83
Victoria, Queen of England, 39, 186
Vogel, Sir J., 92

W

Waikato, Maori Chief, 16
Waite, J., 108
Walker, R. 18, 25, 44
Walker, R., 15, 43
Walton, T., 90
Ward, A., 46
Wattie, N., 67
Webster, J., 212
White, J., 71
Wilkinson, D., 186
Williams, D. V., 47
Williams, H., 12, 13, 17, 19, 22, 30, 33, 41, 54, 56, 57, 169
Williams, J., 179
Wilson, D., 13
Winston, E., 122
Wiri, R., 13
Wood, A. H., 189
Wood, A., 51
Woodard, H., 13
Wood-Ellem, E., 243

Y

Yate, W., 72

Subject Index

A

Aboriginal languages, 67
Aborigines Protection Society, 49
abuse, 40, 41, 120, 144
acculturation, 6, 104, 153, 163
allusion, 20, 69
ancient languages, 68
Anthropological Society of Paris, 64
anthropology, 1, 5, 37, 149, 166
archaicization, 82
assimilation, 40, 45, 46, 54, 92, 135, 158
assimilationist policies, 47
Auckland Deaf Club, 116
Auckland Institute of Technology, 98
Auckland Public Library, 68, 70, 80, 86, 88
Auckland University of Technology, 37, 104, 130, 274
Auslan, 98, 131
Australasian Signed English, 93, 101
Austronesian language family, 242

B

back translation, 159
Bible, 6, 22, 42, 152, 153, 154, 155, 156, 159, 160, 162, 170, 178, 179, 180, 182, 189, 190, 194, 195, 196, 213, 216
biblical translations, 6, 231
bilingualism, 104, 186
blackbirding, 186
British Crown, 37, 38, 40, 44
British Empire, 38
British Resident, 15, 16, 17, 19, 30, 41
BSL signs, 94

C

cannibalism, 84, 145, 146
Catholicism, 183, 184

Christianity, 7, 77, 137, 138, 153, 154, 158, 159, 177, 199, 232, 233
Church, 7, 28, 39, 40, 41, 198, 216, 223
Church Missionary Society, 40
Civil Rights movement, 97
CODAs, 121, 125
code switching, 104
colonial administration, 161
colonial history, 37
Colonial Land Commissions, 26
Colonial office, 15
colonialism, 1, 38, 136
colonization, 2, 26, 38, 52, 137, 158, 227
colonizers, 1, 4, 7, 39
colonizing moment, 234
colony, 47
Commonwealth, 192, 241
cross-cultural encounter, 3
Crown, 26, 27, 37, 40, 41, 44, 45, 47, 49, 50, 52, 54, 55, 200, 224, 237, 256, 274, 275
cultural differences, 242
cultural heritage, 8
cultural identity, 102
cultural ownership, 83
culture studies, 1
culture-specific items, 252

D

deaf adults, 96
Deaf Association of New Zealand, 89, 107, 130, 132
deaf children, 113
Deaf Community, 89, 96
deaf education, 90, 93, 97, 98, 113, 127
deaf parents, 96, 97, 104, 107, 113, 114, 121
deaf students, 106, 114
deaf volunteers, 101
Declaration of Human Rights, 230
Declaration of Independence, 3, 12, 13, 15, 17, 25, 28, 34, 57

decolonization, 7, 38, 39, 208, 209
decolonizing moment, 234
Deed of Cession, 7, 185, 186, 187, 188, 189, 199
domesticated, 168
Dublin University Magazine, 64, 84, 88
dynamic equivalence, 154

E

education and training, 7
empire, 37, 185
equivalent, 17, 18, 23, 42, 43, 158, 210, 214, 232, 249, 250
ethics, 124, 273
ethnocentrism, 191
ethnographer, 6, 71, 134, 135, 138, 152, 162, 163, 165, 273
ethnography, 1, 6, 37, 65, 154
eurocentric, 137, 138, 143, 151, 180
eurocentrism, 182
Exonorm, 6, 7, 172
exotic, 75

F

Fatal Impact, 2
feminism, 5, 149, 167
finger signs, 93
foreignized, 168
French [signing] system, 93

G

Gallaudet University, 127, 131, 132
German [oral] system, 93
Glasgow University, 190

H

He Whakaputanga, 12, 13, 14, 15, 16, 17, 18, 19, 21, 22, 23, 24, 25, 34
honorific language, 245
Humpty Dumpty principle, 12, 13,

19, 21, 22, 23, 28
hybrid, 2, 6, 7, 134, 138, 162, 163
hybridity, 5, 6, 135, 150, 163, 275

I

imitation, 69
imperialism, 44, 45
indigenous informants, 135
indigenous language, 5, 160
indigenous rights, 2
Institute of Fijian Language and Culture, 193
intercultural leaders, 107
International Congress on Education for the Deaf, 92
International Decade for the Eradication of Colonialism, 211
interpreter training course, 5, 102, 107
interpreters, 89, 90, 91, 96, 97, 98, 99, 100, 101, 102, 103, 104, 105, 106, 107, 108, 109, 110, 111, 112, 113, 114, 115, 116, 117, 118, 119, 120, 121, 122, 123, 124, 125, 126, 127, 128, 129, 172, 196, 274
interpreting profession, 129
interpreting services, 95

J

J. R. McKenzie Trust, 97

K

King Movement, 47
King of England, 12, 16, 18, 20, 25, 32, 33
kinship terms, 156
Kohimarama Conference, 48

L

Labour Party, 50
land deeds, 13, 14, 19, 20, 26
lingua franca, 6, 173, 179

linguist, 6, 163, 179, 180, 194, 273
linguistic borrowing, 82
linguistic de-colonization, 91
linguistic diversity, 172
linguistic oppression, 90
linguistics, 1, 143, 274, 276
lip-reading, 5, 90, 92, 94, 109
lip-speaking, 104
literacy, 14, 93, 94, 107, 124, 125, 172, 183, 193, 195, 196
literal translations, 70
literalism, 70
London Missionary Society, 150, 151

M

manualism, 92
Maori culture, 66, 77
Maori Graduates Association, 50
Maori Land Claims, 51
Maori Land Occupations, 52
Maori Language Commission, 106
Maori life, 47, 54, 76
Maori Parliaments, 48, 49
Maori protest movement, 46, 47, 54
Maori scholars, 66
Maori Songs, 67
Melanesia, 2, 6, 172, 242
metaphor, 20, 142, 143
metaphrase, 69
Methodists, 183, 184
Micronesia, 2, 242
miscommunication, 122
missionaries, 6, 7, 14, 16, 17, 40, 41, 42, 71, 72, 137, 139, 141, 149, 159, 160, 172, 175, 176, 177, 178, 179, 181, 182, 183, 184, 186, 190, 194, 232, 234
mistranslation, 12
mistranslations, 3, 14, 17, 26, 44
Modern House of Tokelau project, 219
multiculturalism, 135
Muriwhenua, 26, 28

N

National Library of South Africa, 68, 87
neo-colonialism, 232
New Caledonia, 133
New Testament, 151, 159, 230
New World, 65, 73
New Zealand Association of the Deaf, 97
New Zealand Company, 41
New Zealand Deaf Sports Association, 107
New Zealand Herald, 50, 51, 52, 53
New Zealand Quarterly Review, 64, 88
New Zealand Sign Language, 91, 93, 96, 97, 130, 131
New Zealand Society, 68, 87
NZSLTA Inc., 102

O

Old High Fijian, 7, 172, 179, 180, 182, 183, 184, 185, 189, 202
Old Testament, 153
omissions, 44
oral interpreting, 104
oral literature, 140
Oral Tradition Laboratory, 139
oral traditions, 15, 16, 18, 69, 139
oralism, 5, 94, 131
orthography, 175
Other, 134, 144, 145, 146, 150, 153, 155, 164, 167, 168

P

parents of deaf children, 97
Parliamentary Select Committee, 15
Pidgin English, 186
Pilgrim's Progress, 69
poetry, 8, 70, 79, 85, 144, 166, 242, 243, 244, 245, 247, 250, 251, 253, 254, 258, 265, 266, 276
Polynesia, 2, 4, 14, 88, 172, 197, 242, 243, 264
postcolonial, 1, 2, 5, 6, 37, 38, 52, 55, 134, 135, 136, 151, 154, 158, 159, 163
postcolonial studies, 158
postcolonial theory, 38, 151
postcolonial translation studies, 37
postcolonialism, 1
pre-colonial, 157
pre-missionary, 175
primitive languages, 68
pronominal system, 246
Protestantism, 159
Proto-Tongic, 242

Q

Queen of England, 4, 12, 21, 25, 26, 43, 58, 59, 60, 61
Queen Sälote, 8, 242, 243, 244, 267, 268, 276

R

Ranolf and Amohia, 64, 83, 86
Ratana movement, 50
reduplications, 251
resistance, 7, 37, 39, 44, 45, 46, 110, 143, 208, 234
reverse acculturation, 150
Robinson Crusoe, 69
romantic, 85
romantic philosophies, 71
romanticism, 66, 85
Royal Geographical Society of Vienna, 64
Rubaiyat of Omar Khayyam, 4, 64, 86

S

Scriptures, 6, 70, 172, 177, 180
sentimental, 76, 78, 79, 82, 84, 85, 160

settlers, 12, 27, 40, 41, 47, 137, 151, 153, 162
sign language, 4, 5, 89, 90, 92, 93, 95, 96, 97, 98, 99, 100, 101, 102, 103, 104, 105, 106, 112, 114, 115, 117, 122, 124, 125, 128, 129, 274
sign language interpreting, 125
simultaneous interpreting, 125
SLIANZ Inc., 99
source text, 55, 63, 66, 77, 78, 80, 81, 82, 168, 208, 220
South Pacific Commission, 139
sovereignty, 3, 12, 19, 20, 22, 23, 25, 26, 35, 37, 41, 42, 43, 44, 45, 50, 52, 53, 54, 185, 199, 200, 228, 238
Standard Fijian, 178, 193, 195
structural differences, 242
subaltern studies, 135
survival, 3, 37
Swadesh list, 173

T

Te Taura Whiri, 106
Te Tiriti o Waitangi, 12, 18, 19, 28, 35, 37, 42, 54, 57, 59, 60
The Evening Post, 53
The Greenstone Door, 64, 88
third space, 5, 6, 135, 149, 150, 162
Total Communication, 93, 94, 101
translated culture, 143
translation process, 151
translation strategy, 19, 22
Translation Studies, 1, 86, 88
translation theory, 78
translators, 5, 6, 7, 21, 134, 167, 168, 172, 196, 208, 211, 215, 221, 234, 275
transliterate, 105
Treaty of Tokehega, 217
Treaty of Waitangi, 3, 7, 12, 15, 18, 20, 21, 25, 27, 28, 35, 37, 38, 39, 42, 43, 44, 45, 46, 47, 48, 49, 50, 53, 54, 55, 56, 57, 58, 169, 274

U

United Nations Decolonization Committee, 7, 211
United Nations Visiting Mission, 219
United Tribes of New Zealand, 20, 22, 25, 30, 58
University of the South Pacific, 193
untranslatability, 6, 135, 163

V

Victorian, 64, 79, 81, 84, 85, 88, 92
Victorian readers, 85
Victorian readership, 81
vocational training, 111, 125

W

Waitangi Day, 52, 53
Waitangi Tribunal, 27, 28, 43, 45, 49, 50, 51, 52, 53, 57
Wesleyan Methodist Mission Society, 175
word for word translations, 167
World Federation for the Deaf, 91, 115

For Product Safety Concerns and Information please contact our EU
representative GPSR@taylorandfrancis.com
Taylor & Francis Verlag GmbH, Kaufingerstraße 24, 80331 München, Germany

www.ingramcontent.com/pod-product-compliance
Lightning Source LLC
Chambersburg PA
CBHW062004220426
43662CB00010B/1225